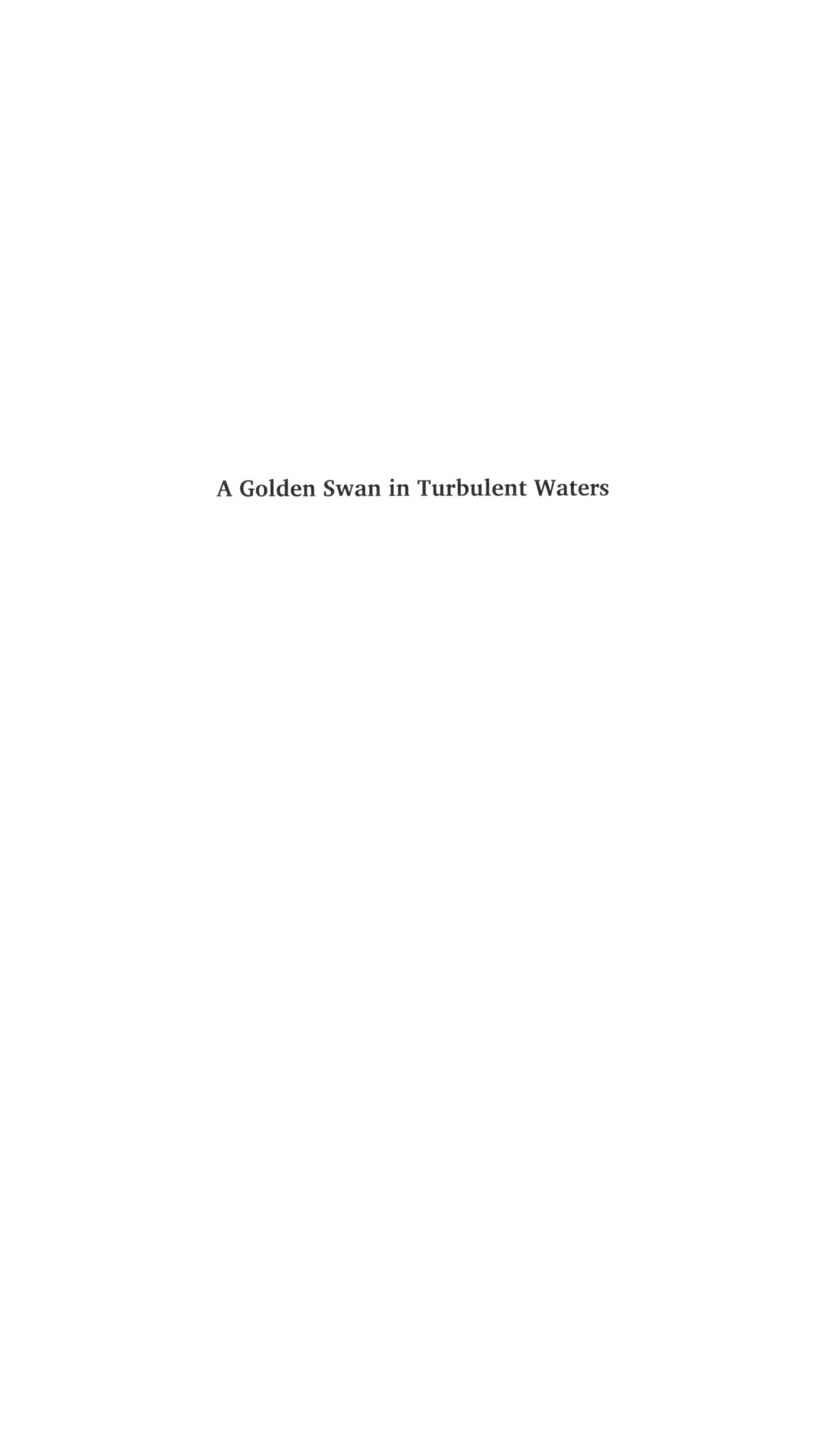

A Golden Swan in Turbulent Waters

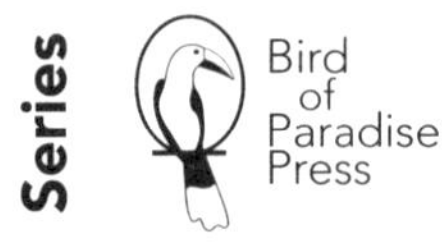

ABOUT BIRD OF PARADISE PRESS

Bird of Paradise Press is a non-profit book publisher based in the United States. The press specializes in Buddhist meditation and philosophy, as well as other topics from Buddhist perspectives including history, ethics, and governance. Its books are distributed worldwide and available in multiple languages. The bird mentioned in the company's name is said to be from a special place where beings can meet with favorable conditions to progress on their path to awakening.

Also by Shamar Rinpoche

BRINGING MIND TRAINING TO LIFE
An Exploration of the 5th Shamarpa's Concise Lojong Manual

THE PATH TO AWAKENING
How Buddhism's Seven Points of Mind Training Can Lead You to a Life of Enlightenment and Happiness

BOUNDLESS WISDOM
A Mahāmudrā Practice Manual

A GOLDEN SWAN IN TURBULENT WATERS
The Life and Times of the Tenth Karmapa Choying Dorje

THE KING OF PRAYERS
A Commentary on the Noble King of Prayers of Excellent Conduct

CREATING A TRANSPARENT DEMOCRACY
A New Model

BUDDHA NATURE
Our Potential for Wisdom, Compassion, and Happiness

A Golden Swan in Turbulent Waters

THE LIFE AND TIMES OF THE TENTH KARMAPA
CHOYING DORJE

Shamar Rinpoche

Bird of Paradise Press
Lexington, Virginia, USA
birdofparadisepress.org

Rabsel Publications
16, rue de Babylone
76430 La Remuée, France
www.rabsel.com
contact@rabsel.com

This project was supported by the DRAC and Normandy Region under the FADEL Normandie, France.

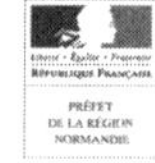

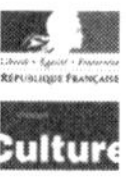

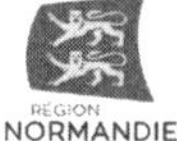

ISBN 978-2-36017-025-8

Table of Contents

Introduction

My early education studying Buddhist texts and learning about the history of the Karma Kagyu sect piqued my interest in 17th-century Tibetan history and the life of the Tenth Karmapa. How did a rather innocent bodhisattva cope with the turmoil of his day? How did this somewhat eccentric figure view the epochal changes and dramatic events of his lifetime – invasions by Mongol warlords, a nearly successful unification of Tibet under a secular ruler, the emergence of a powerful Dalai Lama (the Fifth) in whose hands political and religious powers were integrated after they had been separate for almost four centuries, and the widespread suppression of the Kama Kagyu sect?

Not until the past three years have I been able to explore closely the life of the Tenth Karmapa. With the exception of a Ph.D. thesis completed a few years ago,[1] I discovered that no book-length study about him has been published. Further, no one has written a major study of the Tenth Karmapa and his times for the benefit of a general audience and modern practitioners of Tibetan Buddhism.

My goal in writing this book is to enable readers to directly experience the Tenth Karmapa's life through his own writings as well as those of his contemporaries, notably the Fifth Dalai Lama, and

1 Mengele (2005). This work has not been available to me.

his 18th-century biographer. I also strive to explain for readers the complicated history of the Karmapa's times.

As the Fourteenth Shamarpa and a lineage holder in the Karma Kagyu sect of Tibetan Buddhism, I have received some of the main teachings and transmissions (those still extant) that the two primary figures in this book – the Tenth Karmapa and his guru the Sixth Shamarpa – received and in turn transmitted to other lineage holders several hundred years ago. I draw upon this special knowledge and experience to provide notes and comments on the many original texts I have translated. I trust this will make 17th- and 18th-century writings more accessible to 21st-century readers and will enrich their appreciation and understanding of the Tenth Karmapa.

This book is divided into three parts. The first surveys Tibetan history from the 13th through the 17th centuries. It provides the context for the biography of the Tenth Karmapa in the third section. My main sources for this first section are the English and especially the more detailed Tibetan version of Tsepon W. D. Shakabpa's *Tibet: A Political History.* Shakabpa was Tibet's Secretary of Finance from 1930 to 1950 and the current Dalai Lama's official in New Delhi until 1966. Even though an English translation of Shakabpa's Tibetan text became available in English in 2010 under the title *One Hundred Thousand Moons* (see bibliography at the end of this book), my quotes from Shakabpa are my own translation.

Part II gathers ten examples of the Tenth Karmapa's artworks – thangkas, sculptures, and carvings. Among the illustrations are some of Karmapa's artistic creations that are in my possession. They have never been published before.

My biography of the Tenth Karmapa found in Part III is not a traditional one in which the author researches all available resources and then creates a critical synthesis describing the subject's life. Rather, this "biography" is a compilation of translated passages from original sources stitched together in chronological order. In extensive annotations in footnotes and headnotes, I provide explanations and interpretations of the texts.

True to his multifaceted artistic talents, the Tenth Karmapa composed a number of texts and countless poems. Out of this legacy, three books survive as well as a few other scattered minor works. The books are filled with many poems and graced with very flowery language. The 17th-century woodblock edition of these works has been reprinted in a two-volume collection. (References can be found in the bibliography.) One of these books (*The Drum of Dharma: Autobiography of a Bodhisattva*) is Karmapa's life story, but it is not particularly useful as a historical record since it is packed with allegories, accounts of dreams, poems, and other literary reflections that are difficult to interpret. The same can be said for *The Story of My Trip, Song of a Bird of Paradise Along Its Journey,* another autobiography that was written at the request of his attendant-friend Kuntu Zangpo in 1651.

Karmapa does have some autobiographical writings that recount the first 25 years (1604–1630) of his life story. He buries these passages within a biography of his guru the Sixth Shamarpa (*The Bountiful Cow: Biography of a Bodhisattva*, identified in this book by the abbreviation KAC). An autobiography merged into a biography, only an eccentric like the Tenth Karmapa would conceive of such a literary device.

These autobiographical passages are the only source available to learn about what Karmapa himself did and thought. I have woven them all into my biography, with noted exceptions of many poems and long descriptive passages about nature and his surroundings.

The other primary source about the Tenth Karmapa's life is a biography written about 75 years after his death by Bey Lotsawa Tshewang Kunkhyab (Belo). He collaborated with the Eighth Situ (1700–1774) to write the biographies of the first twelve Karmapas and of other Karma Kagyu lineage holders (*The Garland of Omnipresent Wishfulfilling Crystal Gems.*) Situ is credited with the biographies of the first six Karmapas, while Belo wrote the remainder. Belo obviously drew upon the Tenth Karmapa's own writings, but judging by other information he included, he clearly had other written and/or orally transmitted sources available.

Two woodblock editions of *The Garland of Omnipresent Wishfulfilling Crystal Gems* – an original and a variant – exist today, as explained in the note at the conclusion of chapter 35. The sole difference between these editions is the biography of the Tenth Karmapa. For purposes of this book, I have used the biography appearing in the original edition because it is Belo's actual text, whereas the variant edition includes an abbreviated biography written in verse.

I have translated Belo's biography of the Tenth Karmapa almost in its entirety (identified in this book by the abbreviation BL). Although it is the foundation of my "biography," it does not appear here as a single, continuously running document. Rather, I have broken it into sections between which are interspersed relevant passages from the Karmapa's autobiography and other contemporary sources such as the Fifth Dalai Lama's autobiography (identified in this book by the abbreviation DL).

A relatively modern Tibetan biography of the Tenth Karmapa was written by Mendong Tshampa Rinpoche (born 1867). It draws extensively on Belo's work and is much shorter. Consequently, I have not utilized this text. Hugh Richardson has translated it into English. (See the bibliography for the reference.)

A word about my translations is in order. Rather than translating the Tibetan texts in a very strict fashion, I have tried to capture the spirit of the meaning in English while remaining faithful to the text.

A decision about how to transliterate Tibetan names and terms always poses a dilemma. I have consciously avoided using the Wylie system, which is found in many scholarly works, because it confuses general readers who cannot remember the peculiar spellings. Instead, I have used my own transliterations. And for Chinese names and terms, I have used the widely accepted *pin yin* system. An appendix to this book provides the Tibetan scripts and Wylie for my transliterations. A list of Chinese terms also is available in Chinese characters.

Finally, I am happy to call to readers' attention a forthcoming major exhibition of the Tenth Karmapa's art, the first ever, that the Rubin Museum of Art in New York will present. Prior to the exhibition opening (at the time of this book's publication, a date has not been announced), the museum has issued an extensive exhibition catalogue and monograph on the artist written by Karl Debreczeny – *The Black Hat Eccentric: Artistic Visions of the Tenth Karmapa* with contributions from several other scholars.

The simultaneous publication of the exhibition catalogue and my book is a fortuitous coincidence because Karmapa was not only a bodhisattva but also a seminal artist. My book does not explore the artistic dimensions of his life unless one of the translated texts mentions a specific thangka or piece of sculpture. Therefore, a reading of the exhibition catalogue and my book together will provide the fullest appreciation of the Tenth Karmapa.

Acknowledgments

Like many things in life, writing a book involves the cooperation and assistance of others. Production of A Golden Swan in Turbulent Waters is no exception. Many individuals have helped me nurture this project from the seed of an idea to its flowering as an actual publication. I gratefully acknowledge them here.

Several individuals and organizations have generously allowed me to reproduce illustrations of the Tenth Karmapa's artworks in their possession. Some images are drawn from the collection of the Rubin Museum of Art in New York City and reproduced here with its kind permission. Most of these appear in the museum's exhibition catalogue The Black Hat Eccentric: Artistic Visions of the Tenth Karmapa by Dr. Karl Debreczeny. He has freely shared his knowledge and contacts.

Alan Chen (陳慶隆), owner of Alan Chen's Fine Arts (有容古文物藝術) gallery in Taipei, Taiwan, most kindly has allowed the use of the image appearing on the front cover. This captivating statue of the Tenth Karmapa, believed to be created by him, reflects the power of his artistic abilities.

Three important collectors of Tibetan art in Switzerland – Alain Bordier in Guyeres and Heidi and Ulrich von Schroeder in Weesen – have permitted me to include images of three thangkas painted by the Tenth Karmapa. I thank them profusely.

In late 2010 Professor Lara Braitstein of McGill University and Shahin Parhami travelled to Lijiang and Shangri-la in Yunnan, China to search for and photo-document temples connected with the Tenth Karmapa. My thanks go to Mr. Parhami for permitting me to reproduce several of his photographs. In addition to reading and commenting on sections of the manuscript, Professor Braitstein assisted with the bibliographic citation and the Wiley transliteration of the Tibetan sources found in the bibliography.

Karma Trinlay Rinpoche in Paris undertook some bibliographic research that has enriched this book. He also reviewed early chapters in the book and made helpful suggestions.

Credit for the list of Tibetan terms appearing in the book belongs to Delphine Forget of Fleurac, Dordogne, France and Tina Draszczyk of Vienna, Austria. They converted my romanization of Tibetan terms into the Wylie system of transliteration that is commonly used in the academic world.

The talented graphic artist Carol Gerhardt has transformed my manuscript into the attractive book that readers see here. Michael Wong of Toronto, Canada created the maps that help readers locate the many place names found in the book. Neeraj Chettri has assisted with technical matters about publishing the book online and as an e-book.

Chris Fang and Marc Junkunc, together with Angela Byrne, have worked on promoting the book, including the creation of a website designed by Ms. Byrne.

Edmund Worthy edited the book through several versions and made invaluable suggestions for revising and restructuring my original manuscript. He has struggled to teach me the practices of Western historiography. Without his involvement this book could not have been completed and published.

Finally, an immense debt of gratitude is due to Sylvia Wong of Toronto, Canada who has collaborated with me on other books. Over many months she worked with me in person and via Skype to take down my dictation of the narrative in Part I of this book and my translations in Part III. She then polished my imperfect English and helped me draft the manuscript.

As important as the many contributions of the individuals acknowledged above are, I alone remain responsible for any errors that may be found in the book.

Shamar Rinpoche
July 2012

List of Historical Figures

(The following list is in alphabetical order. Lineage-incarnates appear in numerical order.)

Chagmo Goshri also known as (a.k.a) Chagmo Lama
Chagmo Lama was the Chieftain of Chagmo in the district of Golok in Kham. Through bribery, he gained control over the Tenth Karmapa as a child and his family. He then used Karmapa to fundraise for his own personal gain.

Dalai Lama (the Fourth) Yungten Gyatso (1589–1617)
The Dalai Lama is the spiritual head of the Gelug sect of Tibetan Buddhism, or the Yellow sect. The Fourth Dalai Lama tried to avoid fighting and war, but his attendant, Sonam Chopal, plotted with Kyisho Depa (see below) and the Mongol warlords to overthrow Tibet's government under the Tsang Desi.

Dalai Lama (the Fifth) Lozang Gyatso (1617–1682)
The Fifth Dalai Lama was made the ruler of Tibet in 1642 by the Mongolian warlord Gushri Khan. He is a pivotal figure in Tibetan political and religious history and the author of many scholarly works.

Gendun Yangri

A member of the Yangri family who collaborated with Chagmo Lama.

Gushri Khan (1582–1655)

The Mongolian warlord Gushri Khan invaded Tibet in 1639 and succeeded in defeating the Tibetan Tsang government. He then enthroned the Fifth Dalai Lama as the ruler of Tibet, and Sonam Chopal became Desi.

Gyaltsab (the Fifth) Dragpa Choyang (1618–1658)

The Gyaltsab incarnates were teachers in the Karma Kagyu sect. The Fifth Gyaltsab Rinpoche, a tactful diplomat, was able to protect some Kagyu monasteries from attack and takeover by the Gelug sect in the 17th century, after the Fifth Dalai Lama started to rule Tibet.

Gyaltsab (the Sixth) Norbu Zangpo (1659–1698)

The Tenth Karmapa acknowledged the Sixth Gyaltsab as his son and set up a separate administration for him. Beginning with the Seventh Gyaltsab and even until today, relations between the Gyaltsab line and the Karmapas have been strained.

Karmapa (the Tenth) Choying Dorje, a.k.a Jigten Wangchuk (1604–1674)

Karmapa is the spiritual head of the Karma Kagyu sect of Tibetan Buddhism. He is often referred to as the Karmapa Black Hat. In his writings, the Tenth Karmapa referred to himself as Jigten Wangchuk.

Kuntu Zangpo

A close disciple of the Tenth Karmapa, Kuntu Zangpo served him as an attendant. In the text, he is referred to as “ Rimdrowa” which means attendant.

Kyisho Depa Sonam Namgyal

A duke in central Tibet, Kyisho Depa Sonam Namgyal owned the land in and around Lhasa where the Sera, Drepung, and Gaden monasteries, affiliated with the Gelug sect, were built. He collaborated with Sonam Chopal and the Mongolians against the Tsang government.

Pawo Rinpoche (the Third) Tsuklak Gyatso, a.k.a. Bodhisattva Gawey Yang (1567–1633)

Pawo Rinpoche is a high-ranking teacher and lineage holder of the Karma Kagyu sect. The Third Pawo was a guru of the Tenth Karmapa.

Pema Sengey

Pema Sengey was the Chieftain of Mar, in the district of Golok, and the original landlord of the Tenth Karmapa and his family.

Shamarpa (the Sixth) Chokyi Wangchuk, a.k.a Garwang Thamchad Khyenpa (1584–1630)

Shamarpa, also known as the Karmapa Red Hat, is the second-ranking spiritual head of the Karma Kagyu sect of Tibetan Buddhism. He recognized and enthroned the Tenth Karmapa, became his guru and transmitted to him the entire *Karma Kagyu Golden Lineage* transmissions.

Shamarpa (the Seventh) Shiwa Drayang Kyi Gyalpo, a.k.a. Yeshe Nyingpo (1631–1694)

He was recognized by the Tenth Karmapa and received from him the entire *Karma Kagyu Golden Lineage* transmissions.

Situ (the Fifth) Chokyi Gyaltsen (1586–1657)

He was the abbot of Karma Gon, the "middle" seat monastery of the Karmapa. "Middle" refers to geographic location, not to the rank or size of the monastery.

Sonam Chopal (d. 1658)
Sonam Chopal was the ambitious attendant to the Fourth Dalai Lama and later the general and personal secretary to the Fifth Dalai Lama. He served as *Zhal Ngo*, or the chief of administration, for the Fifth Dalai Lama. He collaborated with Kyisho Depa and invited Gushri Khan to Tibet to overthrow the Tsang Desi. He became Desi of government in 1642.

The Tsang Desi Phuntsok Namgyal
Tsang was the name of an area in central Tibet. The late 16th- and 17th-century rulers of Tsang were known as the Tsang Desis (*Desi* means ruler). Desi Phuntsok Namgyal ruled from 1611–1621. He attempted to unite Tibet under one government.

The Tsang Desi Tenkyong Wangpo
The son of Phuntsok Namgyal, Tenkyong Wangpo was the last secular Desi of Tibet who ruled from 1621–1642. He continued his predecessor's efforts to unify Tibet and succeeded in extending Tsang rule throughout central Tibet.

Yangri Trungpa Shagrogpa
A member of the Yangri family who collaborated with Chagmo Lama.

Maps

Tibet and Surrounding Regions
Present-day boundaries
River / Lake
Mountain
DISTRICT
KINGDOM / REGION
Mongol controlled territory
Mongol controlled territory
L. Kokonor
Huanghe R.
(Yellow R.)
AMDO
LADAKH
Machu R.
TIBET
GOLOK
Drichu R.
Dzachu R.
Nyagchu R.
SI-
CHUAN
NGARI
NAGCHUKHA
KHAM
DERGE
Ngulchu R.
LITHANG
Ribo Gangchen
(Mt. Kailash)
Lake Mapam
(L. Manasarovar)
L. Namtso
TSANG
POWO
KONGPO
Tsangpo R.
Yalung R.
Yangtze R.
DHAGPO
YARLUNG
LHO DRAG
NEPAL
SIK-
KIM
BHUTAN
LIJIANG
Salween R.
Mekong R.
Brahmaputra R.
INDIA
ASSAM
YUNNAN

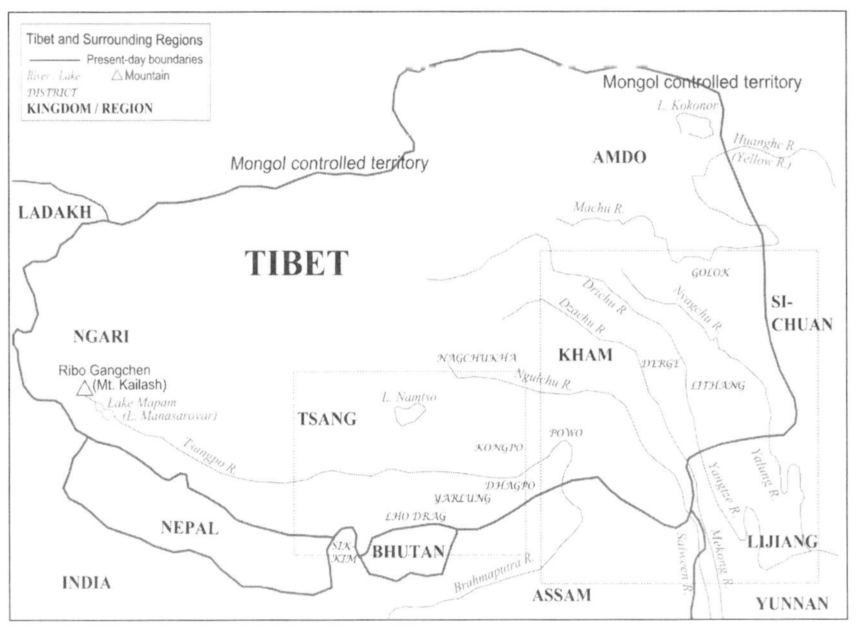

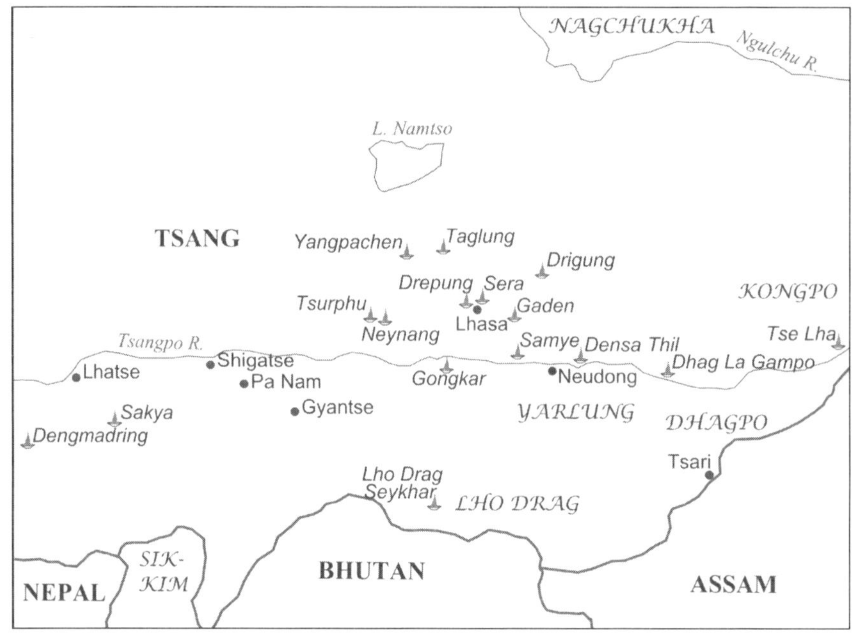

Central Tibet

Present-day boundaries
River / Lake △Mountain
●City / Town *Monastery*
DISTRICT
KINGDOM / REGION

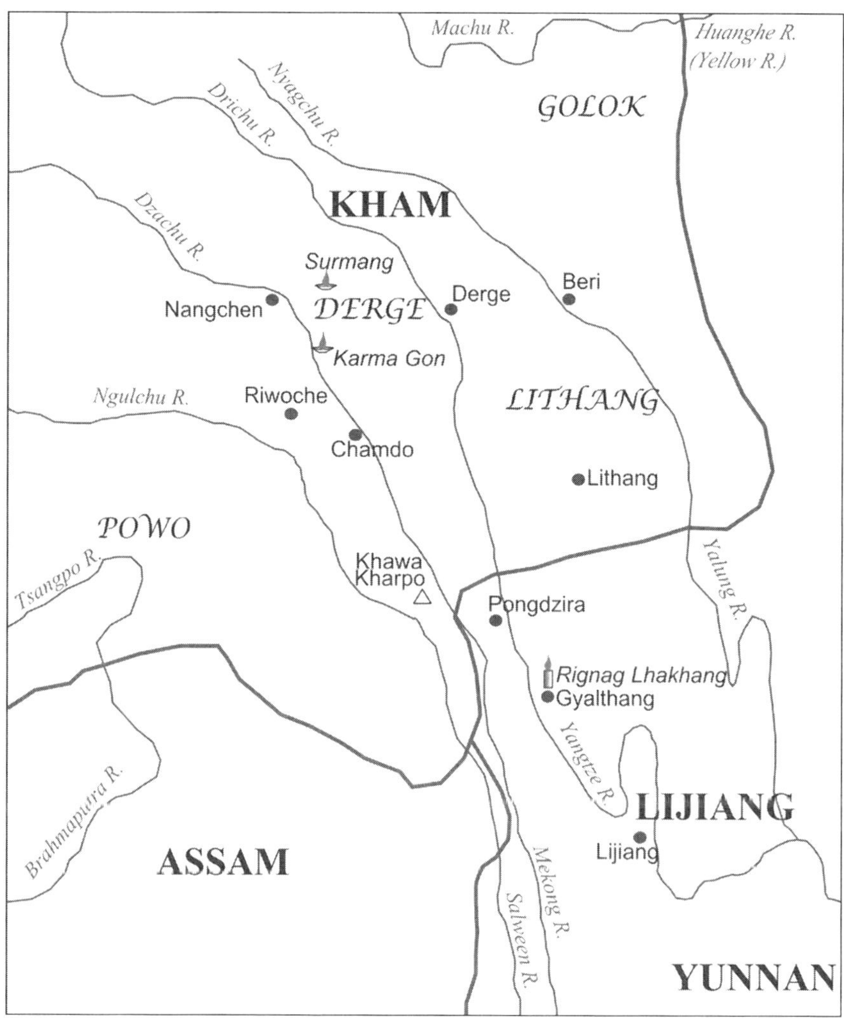

Eastern Tibet

——— Present-day boundaries
River / Lake △Mountain
●City / Town *Monastery*
DISTRICT
KINGDOM / REGION

Part I: Political Times of the Tenth Karmapa Choying Dorje

1. Tibet under the Sakya, Phagdru and Tsang Rule

The 13th through the 15th centuries were a period of relative political stability in Tibet, in spite of the pressure from Mongolian invaders. The thirteen generations of the Phagdru dynasty saw political reforms and a flowering of culture. Most notable was a separation of secular and religious power. Tensions among the Buddhist sects erupted occasionally, but by and large were kept in check, as the Karma Kagyu sect was preeminent.

Sakya Pandita and the Phagpa Rule

In the late 1100s and early 1200s, the great Mongol leader Genghis Khan emerged to lead his people on successful military campaigns across Central Asia, thereby consolidating Mongol supremacy over the region. Fearing invasion, the Tibetans sent a peace delegation to the Mongols in 1207, declaring their allegiance and submitting tribute that they paid for the next twenty years.

In 1240 Genghis Khan's grandson, Godan Khan, invaded and conquered Tibet. Having established his worldly power, Godan Khan turned his interest to Buddhism, which he thought would help him and his people. He became a disciple of the Sakya Pandita (1182–1251), one of the founders of the Sakya sect of Tibetan Buddhism.

Later, Kublai Khan, another grandson of Genghis Khan who founded the Yuan Dynasty in China, followed in Godan's footsteps and became a disciple of Chogyal Phagpa Rinpoche (1235–1280), the Sakya Pandita's nephew and head of the Sakya sect. Kublai offered the whole of Tibet to Phagpa and made him King of Tibet in 1254.

As the head of the Sakya sect and the political ruler of Tibet, Chogyal Phagpa was the first person in Tibetan history to hold both religious and secular authority over Tibet. He spent much of his time in Mongolia on the invitation of the Khan. The Sakyas controlled Tibet for almost a century, a period that came to be known as the Sakya Phagpa reign.

The Phagmo Dru or Phagdru Rule

Under the Sakya Phagpa ruling system, Tibet was divided into thirteen separate districts, each consisting of ten thousand households called a myriarchy. One myriarchy was governed by Dorje Gyalpo (1110–1170), a Kagyu monk from Kham who followed the teachings of Marpa and Milarepa. In 1156, he established his seat – the famous Densa Thil Monastery – in Neudong in central Tibet. His sect came to be known as the Phagdru Kagyu, "Phagdru" being an elision of Phagmo and Drupa.

In the early 1300s, Changchub Gyaltsen (1302–1364) became the head of the myriarchy of Phagmo Dru, or Phagdru Kagyu. The Mongolian Khan Toghan Temur (r. 1333–1368, the last emperor of the Yuan Dynasty) gave him the Chinese title "Tai Situ," an honorary title roughly equivalent in status to prime minister. He was then known as Tai Situ Changchub Gyaltsen. By the mid-1300s, the Sakya rule of Tibet had weakened considerably due to government corruption. Over the period 1354–1358, Tai Situ Changchub Gyaltsen successfully overthrew the government and its corrupt ministers and became head of the Tibetan government. During his rise to power, Changchub Gyaltsen did not align himself with any foreign military power.

Soon after taking power as the first ruler of the Phagmo Drupa or Phagdru Dynasty, Tai Situ Changchub Gyaltsen reformed and reorganized the government. He abolished the myriarchy system in which the majority of heads/patriarchs were Kagyupa lamas and replaced it with a secular *dzong* system rather like the fiefdoms of medieval Europe. Thirteen *dzongs* were established in all, each with a secular administration. Changchub Gyaltsen created agricultural farms and set up different animal husbandries. He also instituted a new tax system that was more favorable for the people and carried out many social reforms. He built the Phagdru dynasty palace at Thil or Densa Thil.

Under Tai Situ Changchub Gyaltsen, the Phagdru dynasty grew powerful. Tibet was autonomous – free from foreign interference – and internally, the government was free from the influences of monastic administrations of religious sects. Changchub Gyaltsen's reign is known in Tibetan history as a peaceful era when the arts and sciences flourished.

Shakabpa writes of Changchub Gyaltsen:[2]

> During his time, the country was so secure that it was said that an old woman carrying a sackful of gold could pass without fear from one end of Tibet to the other; thus, this period of internal security was known as the era of *Genmo Serkhor* ("Old Woman Carrying Gold").

After Changchub Gyaltsen, the Phagdru reign continued for twelve generations until the Tsang lineage came into power in the mid-16th century. It continued to keep the powers of state and religion separate. Thus, secular rule in Tibet lasted almost three centuries after Changchub Gyaltsen. It came to an end when the Mongolian warlord Gushri Khan invaded Tibet and won the war of 1639–1642. He established the Fifth Dalai Lama as the supreme authority over all of Tibet in 1642.

The Fifth Dalai Lama's rise to power occurred during the lifetime of the Tenth Karmapa Choying Dorje who was inadvertently caught up in the turbulence of the time. We will see in his biography (found in Part III of this book) how – in stark contrast to

2 *SH(ENG)*: 82

the ambitious politicians, religious administrators, and Mongolian warlords of his time – he abhorred power and politics and avoided them as much as he could. Before the war of 1639–1642, the Tenth Karmapa was respected as the highest spiritual master of Tibet, as were his two immediate predecessors, the Eighth and Ninth Karmapas.

During the rule of the Phagdru kings, the Karmapas, from the Fourth to the Tenth, were the spiritual teachers to the ruler, the dukes of the *dzongs*, and other government officials. Karmapa's religious influence and prestige elevated him to be regarded as Tibet's highest lama. The Karmapas, however, did not hold or exercise political power.

At the same time the Karmapas were spiritual gurus to Tibetan rulers, they played a similar role for several Chinese emperors of the Yuan and Ming dynasties. The Third Karmapa Rangjung Dorje (1284–1339) and the Fourth Karmapa Rolpe Dorje (1340–1383) were both the gurus of Mongol leaders who sat on the Chinese imperial throne during the Yuan Dynasty. The Fifth Karmapa Dezhin Shegpa (1384–1415) was the guru of Ming Dynasty emperor Yongle as well as the guru of Phagdru *Chen-nga*,[3] the ruler of Tibet. Thus began the emergence of the Karma Kagyu sect as the most revered Buddhist sect in Tibet, a status it maintained for almost three centuries until Gushri Khan's invasion of Tibet.

The Fourth Shamarpa and the Rinpung Rule

The Fourth Shamarpa Chokyi Dragpa (1453–1524) served as the Neudong *Chen-nga* for twelve years. In 1483 when the Phagdru King Kunga Legpa died, his son, crown prince Tashi Dragpa was too young to rule. Before the king passed away, he requested his guru, the Fourth Shamarpa, to assume the title of Neudong *Chen-nga* while he acted as the regent to the young prince.

---

3 The title *Chen-nga*, meaning "the one in the presence," originated from the time of Drigung Jigten Sumgon (1143–1217) when Drakpa Jungmo of the Lang clan served him for 16 years without ever leaving his presence. Later when the family ruled Tibet, the term became one of the forms of address for the sovereign of the Phagdru dynasty. Because Neudong was the capital during the Phagdru reign, Neudong *Chen-nga* refers to a Phagdru ruler.

As the Neudong *Chen-nga*, the Fourth Shamarpa did not become involved in the daily management matters. He made Rinpung Tsokyey Dorje prime minister (or Desi)[4] responsible for all administrative affairs of state. Shakabpa writes:[5]

> In the year of the Water Rabbit (1483), Gong-ma Kunga Legpa passed away. Before his death, he suffered greatly due to his attachment to his young son. *Chen-nga* Rinpoche Chokyi Dragpa (the Fourth Shamarpa) thus promised the dying king that he would assume the role of Phagdru king until the crown prince came of age. (After the king's death), the Fourth Shamarpa kept the Phagdru rule firmly.[6] He appointed Ringpung Tsokyey Dorje as the one who would handle government matters (in the role of a Desi).

The Fourth Shamarpa relegated all governmental affairs to the Desi Rinpung. In this way, he kept separate his role as a spiritual leader, and his role as a titular *Gong-ma*, a Tibetan term of respect reserved for outstanding rulers.

When Rinpung Tsokyey Dorje headed the government administration, he and his entire family were disciples of the Fourth Shamarpa. Early in the year of the Earth Sheep (1499), under the direction of the Fourth Shamarpa, all the *dzong* or district administrators gathered in a conference led by Desi Rinpung for the purpose of enthroning the twelve-year-old crown prince Ngawang Tashi Dragpa. Over the next seven years, the Fourth Shamarpa advised the young king in both spiritual and political affairs.

The king later married a daughter from the Rinpung family. From this point on, its political power and influence gradually increased, and the Phagdru kings, for all intents and purposes, became figureheads. During the latter part of the 1500's, the reins of political power finally switched from the Phagdru to the Rinpung family. In spite of their decline and weakness, the Phagmo Dru line of rulers remains one of the most respected in Tibetan history. They were deservedly addressed as *Gong-ma*.

---

4 Desi means ruler, prime minister, or head of government.

5 *SH(TIB)*: Volume 1, 348–349

6 "Firmly" here means "in a stable and dignified way."

Warnings of the Termas

The Nyingma sect, being the oldest Buddhist sect in Tibet, had long enjoyed broad influence among Tibetans. Even though the Nyingmas lacked a centralized organization, their impact was widespread because Nyingma lamas and temples extended throughout Tibet and the Himalayas.

Nyingma lamas believed that when the Indian yogi Guru Padmasambhava was in Tibet in the 8th century, he buried or hid under rocks or in caves sacred Buddhist texts or objects known as *termas*. Lamas who later discovered the *termas*[7] and revealed them to the people were known as *tertons*.[8]

Terma texts contained descriptions of rituals to eliminate evils and bad luck and were intended to be used in the future for the benefit of the people. A *terton* would teach students how to perform the rituals given in a *terma* text he had discovered and then give them the text. In this way, the *terton* would establish a new lineage for that ritual practice. Because Guru Padmasambhava's doctrine or teachings have been transmitted via the Nyingma sect, the *tertons* were often Nyingma lamas.

One section in a *terma* text called a *terlung* contains a prediction about an event, which might be positive or negative, in a given year. The *terlung* section also indicates the individuals who would be involved with the predicted event – the positive or negative spiritual masters, kings, or lords. Some predictions revealed civil wars and foreign invasions and sometimes specified the lunar calendar year in which they would occur.

In the 14th, 15th and 16th centuries, all the *terlung* sections found in the discovered *terma* texts contained the same prediction: one day the Yellow (Gelug) sect would invite the evil Mongolian armies into Tibet, destroy the genuine Dharma and ultimately bring about the downfall of Tibet. Some prophecies also suggested

7 *Termas* are treasures concealed by past masters, like Guru Rinpoche, meant to be discovered for the benefit of future generations. They could be in the form of Dharma texts, relics, or Dharma objects.

8 *Tertons*, usually from the Nyingma sect, discover hidden texts or *termas* containing revelations. They are the holders or keepers of these texts.

that the Sakyapas could prevent a future war with the Mongols by conducting *pujas* or prayer rites. Concerned that the Dharma in Tibet would be destroyed, all Sakya monasteries performed numerous *pujas* to ward off wars.

Rather than pay heed to the warnings, some Gelugpas were angry with the *terton* lamas and tried to discredit them. "*Tertons* are fakes. How can the Dharma come from rocks?" they declared. They felt that some *termas* intentionally criticized their sect.

Through a curious line of reasoning, the same Gelugpas also cast doubts on the legitimacy of the *termas*. The *tertons* had created an image of Guru Padmasambhava wearing a square hat with a peacock feather, which the Gelugpas argued an Indian yogi would not wear. Because this depiction of Guru Padmasambhava could not be true, the Gelugpas reasoned that the *termas* supposedly buried by him must be phony as well.

Whenever a *terton* discovered a new *terma*, tradition required a very high lama to confirm its authenticity. The *tertons* often asked the Karmapa to do this. Because the Gelugpas thought the predictions in the *termas* reflected badly on them, by extension, they considered the Karmapa an antagonist since he confirmed which *termas* were genuine.

The Jokhang Incident

Tsongkhapa (1357–1419) was the founder of the Yellow or Gelug sect of Tibetan Buddhism and a devotee of the Fourth Karmapa Rolpe Dorje. He also greatly respected the Fifth Karmapa Dezhin Shegpa. As a result, the Yellow sect based in Lhasa and the Karmapas enjoyed an excellent rapport until the time of the Seventh Karmapa Chodrag Gyatso (1454–1506).

For several centuries, the Jokhang Temple in Lhasa was regarded as Tibet's national temple. (It is still regarded as one of the most important temples of Tibet.) By the 1470's, many stores and homes of shopkeepers had sprouted up all around the temple walls.

As recorded in the Seventh Karmapa's biography:[9]

The Seventh Karmapa had the same dream three times, in which Maitreya Bodhisattava told him this:

The Jo Shakyamuni (statue) located in the area (of the Jokhang Temple) was surrounded by family houses. Due to this negative interdependent link, all the Buddhadharma in the world and especially in Tibet was declining, and (the Dharma community in Tibet was) full of contaminated monks (who did not keep *Vinaya*[10] – the vows and precepts of a monk).

If the residences of monks who observed perfect *Vinaya* could surround the Jokhang, then the genuine Buddhadharma would reflower.

The Jokhang area where the temple was located belonged to the Zhika Nelpa family who were the sponsors of the Karmapas. Therefore, the Seventh Karmapa asked them to do this (build the monks' quarters). But, due to the influence of others, Zhika Nelpa could not fulfill the request. Karmapa also could not build the residences for the monks (around the Jokhang Temple).

But he (the Seventh Karmapa) already owned a monk residence at Karma Dratshang near the Jokhang (area). He decided to expand those quarters to house *Vinaya*-observing monks in order not to ignore the prediction of Maitreya.

However, when the construction was underway, those people who wore monks' robes but actually intended to collect riches were overwhelmed by evil. They united with family-holders (lay supporters of Gelug). The genuine (or pure) monks of Sera and Drepung monasteries were powerless to stop them. Numbering about five hundred, the aggressors were armed and wore helmets. Those without helmets used their begging bowls for protection. They destroyed all the constructions.

9 *BL:* 559b–560a, 1972 edition re-printed by D. Gyaltsan and Kelsang Legshay in New Delhi.

10 One of three sections of the *Tripitaka* (Buddha's canon) that teaches ethics and discipline as the foundation for all Dharma practitioners.

> About two thousand of (the Seventh) Karmapa's followers were gathered there with weapons offered by the people.[11] They were enough to defend against the five hundred monks who launched the attack. They asked Karmapa for permission to fight back in self-defense. He said to them, "If we are genuine followers of the Buddha, then we will never commit such acts. If you are my genuine devotees, stop (don't do anything)."
>
> Later, the government under the Fourth Shamarpa (while the king was still a minor)[12] as well as many lords, such as Lord Jaba Thripon, all said they (the attacking monks) must be punished because they had destabilized the jurisdiction or area. The waging of war by monks was disgraceful. But Karmapa forcefully stopped them (the government officials and lords), and so they were very upset.

The Seventh Karmapa's expansion of the monks' residence near the Jokhang alarmed the administrations of both the Sera and Drepung monasteries of the Gelug sect. They perceived this action as a threat or intrusion into their territory. Contrary to their reaction, the Tibetan government and people believed that the Jokhang Temple belonged to all Tibetans. Thus, any sect or anyone could help to protect it. Nonetheless, the Sera and Drepung monks suspected the Seventh Karmapa of wishing to take over the temple. Quite to the contrary, Karmapa let the unruly monks go free without a trial or even a reprimand.

After the Jokhang incident, relations between the Sera and Drepung monks and Kagyupas were tense for several decades until the arrival of the Eighth Karmapa Mikyo Dorje (1507–1554). His knowledge of Dharma was unparalleled. He was a paragon bodhisattva revered by all sects. His prestige helped to heal the rift between the Gelug and the Karma Kagyu sects.

---

11 It is a tradition for hunters and laypeople to offer up their knives and weapons to the monasteries when they commit themselves not to kill living beings.

12 See earlier section "The Fourth Shamarpa and the Rinpung Rule" in this chapter.

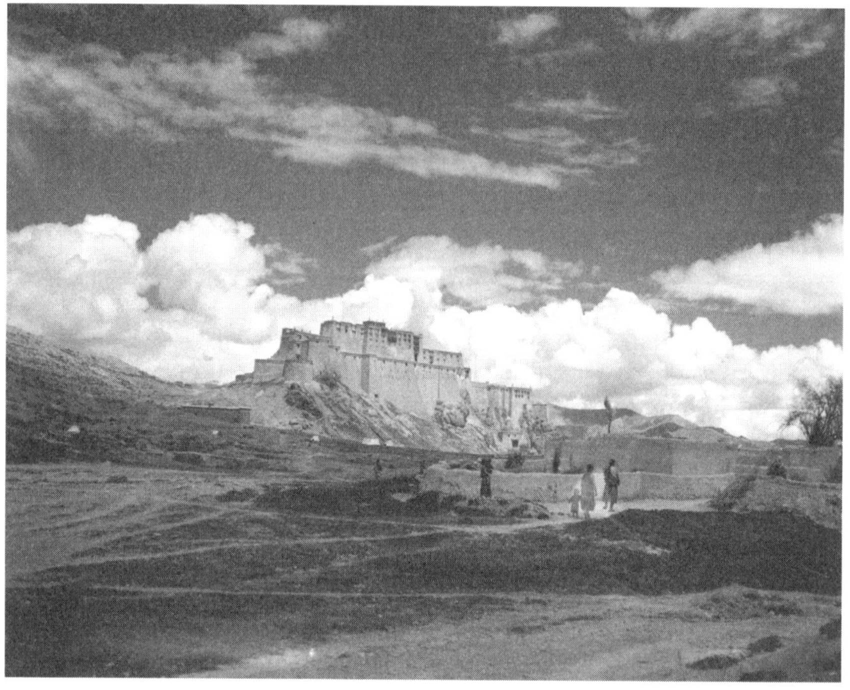

Shigatse dzong, 1935.
C. Suydam Cutting.
Gelatin silver print.
Gift of Mrs. C. Suydam Cutting, 1972.
Collection of the Newark Museum 73.1114.

The Sambdrub Tse Palace, built in Shigatse in the 16th century by the Tsang Desis, sits atop the hill depicted here. The Tenth Karmapa and Sixth Shamarpa both visited the palace in 1628.

The Tsang Ruling Government Established

During the life of the Ninth Karmapa Wangchuk Dorje (1556–1603), the leadership of the Tibetan government underwent another change. Control passed from the Rinpung to the Tsang family. The last Rinpung Desi was Ngagwang Jigdrag. His relative, Tsang Tseten Dorje who held a high post in the palace, started to rebel against the Rinpung rule around 1563.

In 1565, Tsang Tseten Dorje took control as the Tsang Desi.[13] He established his capital in Shigatse, and his palace was named Sambdrub Tse. He ruled until 1588.

When the Ninth Karmapa was twelve years old (1568), Tseten Dorje invited him to Sambdrub Tse, out of respect for him as the highest lama of Tibet. Afterwards, Karmapa went to the Rinpung estate of Ngagwang Jigdrag where he stayed for three months. At that time, Karmapa made peace between the families of Rinpung and Tsang and asked them not to take revenge on one another. As a result, there was no civil war in Tibet.

Because of the peace the Ninth Karmapa arranged, all the main and lesser lords of Tibet were grateful to him and looked upon him as the highest spiritual figure in Tibet. As well, they were prepared to defer to his authority even in governmental matters. However, the Ninth Karmapa was minimally involved in government affairs, choosing instead to concentrate on religious activities.

---

13 *SH(TIB)*: Volume 1, 358

2. Early Signs of a Rupture

After the prestige and popularity of the Eighth Karmapa mitigated the hard feelings caused by the Jokhang Temple episode, other incidents and misunderstandings happened between the administrations of several Gelug monasteries in central Tibet – Gaden, Sera and Drepung – and the Karma Kagyu. The falling-out happened in the first half of the 16th century and began to rupture what had been a cordial, mutually respectful relationship between the two religious groups. Not all Gelugpa masters and followers regarded the Karmapa and the Karma Kagyu in a negative light. The residents of two Gelug monasteries, Gaden Seykhar and Tashi Lhunpo, for example, did not bear grudges against the Karma Kagyu. Only the three Gelug administrations named above were involved in the feud.

Protocol Deemed an Insult

The Rinpung government followed the customary ranking of high lamas of various sects in a hierarchy. The sects themselves were also ranked, with the Karma Kagyu considered the highest. When high lamas would meet, they were expected to observe certain protocols. At Tsurphu Monastery for example, visitors, upon entering the main hall, would prostrate before the Karmapa Black Hat and the Karmapa Red Hat (Shamarpa).[14]

An incident took place during the lifetime of the Third Dalai Lama (1543–1588) that marked the first crack, as it were, between the administration of Drepung Monastery and the Karma Kagyu. The Third Dalai Lama was the abbot of Drepung Monastery; in addition, the monk of the Sera Monastery recognized him as their abbot.

At one point – the exact year is unknown – the Third Dalai Lama went to see the Ninth Karmapa and the Fifth Shamarpa at Tsurphu Monastery. The two Karma Kagyu masters followed customary protocol and received him according to his rank. The Ninth Karmapa remained seated on his throne, while the Fifth Shamarpa rose and stood on his throne. However, some of the Third Dalai Lama's administrators chose to interpret the fact that neither Karmapa nor Shamarpa came down from their thrones to receive the Dalai Lama as a great insult to their spiritual master. Those administrators used this to drive a wedge between the two sects.

In his autobiography, the Fifth Dalai Lama (1617–1682) alluded to this incident in the context of how to treat the Seventh Shamarpa (1631–1694) when he visited the Dalai Lama.[15]

> From Tsurphu, Shamar Chog Gi Tulku (the Seventh Shamarpa) came to Lhasa. My staff suggested that he was coming because we are now the powerful ones and he has no power. Therefore, we don't have to show him high courtesy.
>
> In the early time, when Thamchad Khyenpa Sonam Gyatso (the Third Dalai Lama) met the Ninth Karmapa Wangchuk Dorje and Fifth Shamarpa Konchog Yenlak, Karmapa did not stand on his throne. Just Shamarpa stood up. At that time, their eyes looked downward (i.e., a snobbish gesture).
>
> There is a proverb: whatever you do, the result will return to you. Actually, it's all right not to offer high courtesy because now we have power and they (of the Karma Kagyu sect) have none. If we

---

14 Shamarpa means "one with the red hat." In Tibetan historical records, Shamarpa is often referred to as the Karmapa Red Hat.

15 *DL*: Volume 2, 356

(now) put one of them on a young mule,[16] they have to accept it. How can they challenge us!

But, as he (Seventh Shamarpa) is a renowned high lama, if you don't respect him, it is exposing your own fault. Moreover, as I was born in the family of Chongyey Tagtse (a well-known aristocratic family), if I don't give respect, then I have no blood in my face (i.e., I am shameless). So I arranged to receive him with high courtesy.

Congratulatory Poem Answered with Anger

Another incident involving the Fourth Dalai Lama Yungten Gyatso (1589–1617) escalated the distrust between the Gaden Phobrang[17] and the Karma Kagyu. He was the great-grandson of Altan Khan and grew up in Mongolia. In 1601, the Iron Ox year, when he was twelve years old, he was invited to Gaden Monastery near Lhasa. Shakabpa writes of that occasion:[18]

At that time, the Sixth Shamar Thamchad Khyenpa Garwang Chokyi Wangchuk sent (the Fourth Dalai Lama) a very nicely written letter in poetic verse.[19] I myself have read it in a biography of the Fourth Dalai Lama.[20] The spirit of the message was congratulatory with an offering of auspicious wishes for the young Dalai Lama. The meaning of the words conveys wishes for the Dalai Lama to have a very good education in the Dharma and in all subjects of knowledge.

To this, a nice reply should have been written. Instead, in the history records, it is known that Tseganey Choje, who was the Third Dalai Lama's elder brother, and Zhukhang Rab Jampa, who was the Dalai Lama's secretary and whose actual name was Gelek Lhundrub, together wrote a rude reply. This was not warranted and showed their true character.

---

16 This means to treat them like nobodies.

17 Phobrang means monastery administration.

18 *SH(TIB)*: Volume 1, 386

19 Writing a letter in verse was the custom of the day, as it had been for many centuries in Tibetan culture.

20 The original footnote in Shakabpa's work states: The whole letter is found on page 29 of the Fourth Dalai Lama's biography, *Norbui Threngwa*.

* * *

Jamyang, the Sixth Shamarpa's secretary, said that the secretaries of Gaden Phobrang had no education.[21] This criticism enraged those Gelug administrators who in turn encouraged their Mongolian followers who were in Tibet on pilgrimage to loot the farms of the Tsurphu Monastery.

21 *SH(TIB)*: Volume 1, 391

3. A Potential Reconciliation Thwarted

In 1606 when the Fourth Dalai Lama was about seventeen years old, he visited southern Tibet and passed through the Gongkar area. Coincidentally, the Sixth Shamarpa was in the same general area. The two lamas could have met to repair the rift between the Fourth Dalai Lama's administration and the Karma Kagyu. However, some of the Dalai Lama's attendants and the Gaden Phobrang intervened to prevent such a meeting.[22] Shakabpa describes the situation as follows:[23]

> He (the Fourth Dalai Lama) arrived at Gongkar. At that time, the Sixth Shamar, Chokyi Wangchuk, was in the same area of Densa Thil. If only these two could have met, it would have proved beneficial to every aspect of life and society in Tibet. Moreover, both were willing to meet.
>
> The attendants of the (Fourth) Dalai Lama brought up an event from an earlier time – how they (the Ninth Karmapa, his administration and the Fifth Shamarpa) did not show proper courtesy (to

---

22 The English version of Shakabpa's Tibet, *A Political History*, page 98, states that the Karmapa's administrators also opposed this meeting. However, the fuller Tibetan version of Shakabpa's work does not mention this.

23 *SH(TIB)*: Volume 1, 389–390

> the Third Dalai Lama). They said, "(The Sixth) Shamarpa could still be as clever as before. If we were to tell him (the Fourth Dalai Lama) about it (what had happened to the Third Dalai Lama), and ask him not to meet (the Sixth Shamarpa), he would not listen. Therefore, if we were to go home, then the meeting would naturally not happen." They (the Fourth Dalai lama and his administrators) returned to Drepung.

The "event from an earlier time" refers to the incident one generation prior when the Third Dalai Lama went to meet the Ninth Karmapa and the Fifth Shamarpa at Tsurphu and felt he was not treated with respect. This event was described in the preceding chapter.

Shakabpa continues and identifies some Gelugpas who disagreed with the schemes of the Fourth Dalai Lama's administrators, thus indicating that opposition to the Karma Kagyu sect was confined to certain Gelugpa groups:

> Among the attendants, only two disagreed. Their names were Phulungpa and Drungtse Tsedzin. Unfortunately, they were in a small minority, and so they failed (to stop the scheming).
>
> During that period, whenever devotees / visitors came for an audience with the Dalai Lama, his attendants subjected them to a body search. All bags and papers were checked to make sure that no messages whatsoever would get through to the Dalai Lama from the Tsurphu side (i.e., the Karma Kagyu). To this end, the attendants harassed the visitors. Those who refused (to be searched) were beaten into compliance. Denpa Tshoched (the Dalai Lama's administrator) and Worpa Chozed conducted the body searches. They acted stupidly and caused disastrous consequences by their terrible actions.
>
> Gaden Thri Rinpoche Konchog Chophel (a contemporary of the Fourth Dalai Lama and chief abbot of Gaden Monastery) said they (the Fourth Dalai Lama's administrators) were small-minded attendants and he was disgusted with them.
>
> Another scholar, Kharnag Lotsa (a contemporary of the Fourth Dalai Lama) wrote in his biography of the Fourth Dalai Lama: "Then,

> he (the Fourth Dalai Lama) moved to Gongkar where he wanted to meet the king (the Tsang Desi), the crown prince, and Garwang Trulpe Ku (Sixth Shamarpa) to discuss how to restore peace for the whole welfare of Tibet. However, evil groups (people) disrupted it (the meeting)."

Shakabpa quotes the Fifth Dalai Lama's poem about what happened in the time of the Fourth Dalai Lama:[24]

> The lotus-holder removed his jeweled adornments,
> put on the orange robe,
> abandoned the peak of Mount Dru Zin,
> and humbly descended to the lap of the jewel-holder god,
> a highly admirable act.
> But those who are possessed with evil,
> who pretend to help,
> and exist in the inner and outer circles,
> ruined the auspicious happening.
> But who will say it is your fault,
> Like (the case of) Buddha and Legkar?

The term "lotus-holder" in general refers to Avalokiteshvara, the Bodhisattva of Compassion. In this context, it means the Fourth Dalai Lama, who was regarded as an emanation of Avalokiteshvara. The peak of Mount Dru Zin is the abode of Avalokiteshvara and here metaphorically alludes to the Gaden Monastery.

The Fifth Dalai Lama honors the Fourth Dalai Lama by referring to him as the lotus-holder. He is not speaking of himself here because Tibetans consider each reincarnation of a master as separate and distinct. The reincarnates are not regarded as one and the same person.

The poem states that the Fourth Dalai Lama humbled himself by removing his jeweled adornments, putting on a simple orange robe, and leaving Mount Dru Zin (the Gaden Monastery).

The descent to the lap of the jewel-holder refers to the Fourth Dalai Lama traveling to Tsang where the Sixth Shamarpa was at

---

24 *SH(TIB)*: Volume 1, 390

the time. The jewel-holder god refers to the Tsang Desi.

In the second verse, "those who are possessed with evil..." refers to the Gaden administrators who thwarted the meeting between the Fourth Dalai Lama and the Sixth Shamarpa. Therefore, the conflict remained unresolved. This is not the Fourth Dalai Lama's fault, just as it was not the Buddha's fault that the evil monk named Legkar caused him trouble and suffering. Due to his own egotistical problems, Legkar went around telling people that the Buddha was not a holy man.

In short, the harmful actions of the Fourth Dalai Lama's administrators, which hindered a potential reconciliation with the Karma Kagyu sect, were condemned by key figures of the time – the Fifth Dalai Lama and the chief abbot of the Gaden Monastery (Gaden Thri Rinpoche Konchog Chopel) and Kharnag Lotsa – as well as by the modern scholar Shakabpa.

The Sixth Shamarpa's Verses on a Scarf

Not long after the possible meeting with the Fourth Dalai Lama was thwarted by the schemes of his aides, the Sixth Shamarpa visited Lhasa. At the Jokhang Temple, he offered a white scarf to the Buddha, on which he had written predictions in a series of poems. Later, when the Fourth Dalai Lama's administrators found out about these poems, they selectively picked out just two verses as follows:[25]

> At the three cities of Zhag, Ti, Drag,
> where Je Choying was like a deer in the field
> why lock horns with him?
> Jowo Buddha, you know this should not happen.
> The earring of the ear,
> not as long as the measure of a half-finger,
> will one day extend to a length
> even Lord Shiva cannot reach.
> What to do then?

25 *SH(TIB)*: Volume 1, 391

Jowo Buddha, you know this should not happen.

These verses were composed when Je Choying, the Tenth Karmapa, was just a few years old. They foretold two future events.

The "three cities of Zhag, Ti, Drag" have not been satisfactorily identified to date. However, they may refer to three cities in Eastern Tibet where the Tenth Karmapa and his party camped. "A deer in the field" is a common metaphor found in Tibetan poems. It refers to one innocently and freely wandering in a field, in this case, the Tenth Karmapa Choying Dorje who would later travel to East Tibet. To lock horns with him means to attack him physically.

History demonstrates that the Sixth Shamarpa's prediction actually came true in 1644, more than 35 years after the verses on the scarf were written. At that time, the alliance formed by the Dalai Lama's administrators and the Mongolian warlord Gushri Khan fought and won a three-year war in Tibet which ended 1642.[26] Two years later, the scheming *Zhal Ngo*[27] Sonam Chopal, administrator of the Fourth and Fifth Dalai Lamas, ordered the Tenth Karmapa to be chased down and killed. The details of this are recorded in the many biographies of the Tenth Karmapa, and in chapter 30 of this book.

The second prediction in the second verse – a tiny earring less than the length of half-finger, stretching beyond the reach of even Lord Shiva – forewarned that an insignificant event could extend into an unavoidable catastrophe far in the future. In Hindu mythology, it is said that Shiva's stride or reach is so miraculously long that he can reach the earth from heaven in just three footsteps. Yet, the length of the earring stretched so that even Shiva with his incredible reach could not cover it.

We can reasonably surmise that the Sixth Shamarpa's reference to a "tiny earring" was an allusion to the minor misunderstanding that happened when the administrators of the Gaden and Drepung

26 More on this alliance is given in chapters 4–7.

27 *Zhal Ngo* is a Tibetan title for the chief administrator of a monastery. Sonam Chopal was the personal and general secretary to the Fifth Dalai Lama as well as head of Gaden administration, i.e., Gaden Phobrang.

monasteries mistakenly interpreted his congratulatory letter to Fourth Dalai Lama as an insult. This provoked some antagonism toward the Karma Kagyu that could have easily been resolved, if not for the later interference of the same administrators who prevented a meeting between the Sixth Shamarpa and Fourth Dalai Lama. Yet according to the Sixth Shamarpa's prediction, if an episode as small as an earring no longer than half a finger could not be resolved, then its aftereffect would extend endlessly and carry over many generations, as explained in the following paragraphs.

We now realize that because the meeting between the Sixth Shamarpa and the Fourth Dalai Lama was thwarted, the hostility toward the Karmapa and Karma Kagyu harbored by Sonam Chopal and other Gelug administrators aligned with him festered. Sonam Chopal eventually invited the Mongol Gushri Khan to invade Tibet in 1639. That war won by the Mongol warlord resulted in a Tibetan religious leader, namely the Fifth Dalai Lama, becoming the country's political ruler.[28] Tibet's religious and political powers were unified in the hands of one person after three centuries when they had been divided during the rule of Phagdru, Rinpung, and Tsang.

Regarding the Sixth Shamarpa's poem on a scarf, Shakabpa writes of the nonsensical interpretations by the Fourth Dalai Lama's administrators:[29]

> Then the administrators of the Dalai Lama made silly judgments about this poem. They interpreted "Zhag Ti Drag" to mean the Sera, Drepung, and Gaden monasteries.
>
> As to (the words) "lock horns," they made the Gelug sect the "yak" and the Kagyu sect the "lion," though there was no mention of a lion in the verse. They then concluded that the conflict alluded to the one between the Karma Kagyu and Gelugpa and that the conflict was small now but would expand so much that even Lord Shiva's reach could not grasp it.
>
> There was not one word that was insulting to the Gelug sect, but

28 The aftermath of the war of 1639–1642 is discussed in chapter 8.

29 *SH(TIB)*: Volume 1, 391–392

> they (the Dalai Lama's administrators) construed the poem as threatening to their sect. Although they were not intelligent, the administrators acted as if they were.
>
> They took revenge by requesting the Mongolians to loot the Karmapa's horse ranch.[30] This event is known to be the basis for the destruction of the well-being of Dharma and Tibetan society.

The Sixth Shamarpa's poem on a scarf was another small incident, but the Dalai Lama's administrators took offense and fueled hostility towards Karmapa and the Karma Kagyu. This eventually led to the Mongol invasion of Tibet, 1639–42.

After this war, the Fifth Dalai Lama went to China in 1652 and met the Qing Emperor Shunzhi, at the latter's invitation. For the first time since the end of the Yuan Dynasty in the 14th century, a Tibetan political leader travelled to the Chinese court and established a direct personal relationship with a Chinese emperor. A few religious leaders of different sects did visit the Ming court, but their relationships with the emperors were not political. To be sure, Tibetan heads of state during the Ming Dynasty sent tribute missions to China, but they did not appear in person. Ming emperors bestowed titles on Tibetan rulers and gave them seals (a sign of authority), which they could use to bolster their prestige and legitimacy. Nevertheless, unlike the situation in the Yuan Dynasty, Ming China did not exert control of Tibet. After Changchub Gyaltsen (1302–1364) came to power in Tibet (see chapter 1) until after the death of the Fifth Dalai Lama – which covered the period from the end of the Yuan Dynasty until the first decades of the Qing rule in China – the Chinese court did not interfere with an independent Tibet.

The meeting between the Fifth Dalai Lama and the Chinese emperor began a relationship between the Chinese imperial court and Tibet that would eventually lead to the Qing government's inter-

30 This second looting differs from the one mentioned at the end of chapter 2 when the angry Gelug administrators encouraged their Mongolian followers to loot the farms of Tsurphu Monastery after they had misinterpreted the congratulatory poem of Shamarpa as insulting.

ference in Tibetan political affairs and even in the religious affairs of the Gelugpa. Later in the 18th century, Tibet became subject to Qing's laws and edicts. China stationed troops in Lhasa, and a Chinese *amban*[31] exercised authority over the Tibetan government. The Qing rule of Tibet continued until the end of the Qing Dynasty in 1911 and today forms an important basis for China's claim on Tibet. This issue has no clear end in sight, which proves true the Sixth Sharmapa's prediction in his poem on a scarf.

---

31 Qing emperors appointed *ambans* (a term from the Manchu language of the Qing court) to function as their resident overlords of territories that recognized Chinese authority but still maintained many of their own political institutions.

4. The Alliance of Kyisho Depa and Gelug Administrators

In the early 17th century, the powerful duke Kyisho Depa Sonam Namgyal was the landlord of Lhasa – a bustling city and a popular pilgrimage destination due to the presence of the Jokhang Temple. The Sera, Drepung, and Gaden monasteries also were situated within Kyisho Depa's territory.

Kyisho Depa was wary of anyone or any power that might jeopardize his land, wealth, and title. He knew that the Tsang government planned to unite all the *dzongs* (districts) of Tibet into a unified state. So for him, the Tsang Desi and his government posed a serious threat to his comfortable position.

By himself Kyisho Depa had neither sufficient influence nor military clout to protect his land and properties against the Tsang Desi. Yet, he understood that the Gelugpas had both because the Mongol warlords who supported the Dalai Lama would go to battle for him.

Meanwhile, Sonam Chopal, the Fourth Dalai Lama's administrator who harbored private and personal ambitions as well as suspicions of the Tsang Desi, rallied other Gelugpas to gain more power for their own monasteries that provided lucrative streams of revenue. Further, they aspired to raise the prestige of their own sect over that of other sects. Wishing to expand their base, they knew they could rely on the Mongols for military support. For them, collaborating with their duke-landlord Kyisho Depa against the Tsang government served both his and their mutual interests.

Within the Gelug sect, the Fourth Dalai Lama, the genuine Gelug spiritual teachers under him, and many upright administrators refused to join the alliance with Kyisho Depa. They wanted no part of a conspiracy against their own government. Nevertheless, the Fourth Dalai Lama's crafty administrators gained the upper hand. To them, even though the Fourth Dalai Lama was their spiritual head, Kyisho Depa was their duke. Ultimately, they emerged as the powerful majority within the Gelugpas and formed an alliance with Kyisho Depa, thereby instigating a challenge to the Tsang ruling government.

Aftermath of the Looting of Karmapa's Horse Farm

We continue now to examine what happened after the looting of the Karmapa's horse farm around 1605 mentioned at the conclusion of the last chapter.

Fearing that the Tsang government would retaliate against the Mongols' looting, the insubordinate Gelug administrators and their landlord Kyisho Depa Sonam Namgyal (successor to his elder brother whose name was Sonam Apel) decided to strike first, contrary to the wishes of the Fourth Dalai Lama and others who wanted peace. In the following, Shakabpa describes the aftermath of the looting of Karmapa's horse farm:[32]

> However, the Fourth Dalai Lama and Shabdrung Yulgyal Norbu (nicknamed Apel, who was the elder brother of Kyisho Depa) both agreed that they would not launch an offensive at that time. They opted for a peaceful resolution to the situation.
>
> However, Kyisho Depa Sonam Namgyal, the Dalai Lama's administrator Denpa Tshoched, and their allies decided to attack first. They went ahead and summoned the Mongolian troops to prepare for battle.

32 *SH(TIB)*: Volume 1, 392

In Lhasa, Duke Kyisho Depa and his Mongolian troops attacked the Tsang armies. The Tsang ruling government along with their ally, Duke Yargyabpa, fought back in defense. The Kyisho alliance suffered a serious defeat, and the Mongolians were driven out of Tibet back to Mongolia. In 1605, the victorious Tsang government confiscated much of Kyisho Depa's territory. His co-conspirators, the Gelug administrators, however, escaped punishment.

Whatever the country, the act of inviting foreigners, in this case the Mongols, to attack one's own government amounts to treason. The Gelug administrators managed to escape this charge by casting themselves as victims. They accused the government of oppression and the Karma Kagyu of conspiring to take over their monasteries. They spread false charges of injustice and persecution. And to gain the sympathy and loyalty of their Mongolian supporters, they vociferously complained about the injustice of their plight.

Where there was no conflict, those Gelug administrators would create one. Where there was a conflict, they would exacerbate it and spin it to their advantage. By falsely charging that the Sixth Shamarpa's poem on the scarf was insulting and threatening to the Gelug sect, they made it a cause for the Mongolian pilgrims to loot Karmapa's horse ranch. When the Tsang government sent troops to repel the attackers, animosity naturally grew on both sides. Just as Shakabpa observed towards the end of the previous chapter, those Gelug administrators "destroyed the well-being of Dharma and society in Tibet."

5. The Tsang Unification and Reform Strategy

Emergence of the Tsang Unification and Reform Strategy

Reacting to Mongolian looting of Karmapa's horse farm in the early 17th century, the Tsang Desi realized that Tibetan farms were easy prey to the Mongol marauders. Local armies or militia were small and ineffective against the larger Mongol forces. The Desi recognized the need to centralize the different duke-landlords and their territories under one government and to develop a strong integrated army. This was the impetus for the Tsang Desi's plan to reform and unify Tibet.

The Tsang Desi Phuntsok Namgyal created a strategy and policy called *Cho Si Kar Jam Yug Chig*. The literal translation is as follows: *Cho Si* means religion and politics; *Kar* means white, implying positive; *Jam* means peaceful and smooth; *Yug* means whole; and *Chig* means one. A more fluid translation might read: a unified, positive system where religion and politics smoothly coexist and where the people enjoy the security needed to live in peace and harmony.

As discussed in the preceding chapter, the Tsang Desi's strategy seriously jeopardized Kyisho Depa. The government had already confiscated most of his land after the failed uprising in 1605. Kyisho Depa and the Gelug administrators understood that the Tsang

Desi's expansion of power must be stopped. They decided to go on the offensive. Together, they summoned their Mongolian allies and prepared to launch an outright war in Tibet.

Events Leading up to the War of 1618

The Tsang Desi family regarded the Eighth, Ninth, and Tenth Karmapas as well as the Fifth and Sixth Shamarpas as their personal gurus. Nevertheless, the Tsang Desi Phuntsok Namgyal was ecumenical in his treatment of all the sects. He venerated the teachers of the Karma Kagyu, Sakya, Nyingma, Gelug, Taglung Kagyu, and Jo Nang sects and supported them and their monasteries. Among the Gelug monasteries, he respected and supported the Gaden Seykhar Monastery, seat of the First Dalai Lama, located near the Desi's capital Shigatse.

To the Tsang Desi, Karmapa was the highest spiritual teacher of the land. In this respect, the Tsang Desi followed tradition. However, he did not elevate the Karma Kagyu sect to a superior position. At the same time, the Tsang Desi was aware that some administrators of the Gaden, Sera, and Drepung monasteries were aligned with Kyisho Depa. He also knew they had the backing of the Mongolian warlords.

The Tsang Desi's first step in implementing his unification and reform strategy was to bring under his rule those dukes who already sided with him. They would be easier to subdue than Kyisho Depa. Thus in 1610, the Tsang Desi successfully overpowered Duke Yargyabpa and the less powerful Duke Dhagpo Kurabpa.

Two years later, the Tsang Desi went to Lhasa for a *nyungney* retreat (a purification practice) at the Jokhang Temple. He had to take a vow for the retreat and requested an audience with the Fourth Dalai Lama, Yungten Gyatso, in whose presence he wanted to take his vow. He also wished to receive a long life empowerment from him. The Desi's request demonstrates that he trusted and respected the Fourth Dalai Lama.

The Dalai Lama's secretary Sonam Drakpa[33] forestalled the meeting. He informed the Dalai Lama that the Tsang Desi was the Gelugpa's enemy. He told the Tsang Desi that the Dalai Lama was in strict retreat and not available to meet. Therefore, just as the meeting between him and the Sixth Shamarpa several years before was thwarted, so too was an opportunity to develop a rapprochement between the Gelugpa sect and the Tsang government.

By early 1615, most of Kyisho Depa's territories had fallen under the control of the Tsang government. Two Mongolian warlords, the sons of warlord Kholoji, arrived in Lhasa with their armies. They were prepared to attack the Tsang government, but the Fourth Dalai Lama berated them and prevented their attack.

In roughly 1616 the Tsang Desi invited the young Tenth Karmapa to his capital. Shakabpa does not indicate which year, but Bey Lotsawa's biography of the Tenth Karmapa states that when Karmapa was twelve years old (1616), Desi Phuntsok Namgyal invited him and Pawo and Tehor Rinpoches. This was the first time the Tenth Karmapa travelled to central Tibet and visited Tsurphu Monastery; at the time he was still under the custody of Chagmo Lama. (This is discussed in the biography of the Tenth Karmapa in chapter 17 of this book.)

In 1616, the Tsang Desi asked Karmapa to initiate him as the ruler of Tibet, which was made official by a golden seal, crown, and a royal cloak. But the event was marred by a mistake the tailors made when they sewed decorative patterns upside down onto the Desi's cloak. Karmapa pointed out the mistake and said that it was inauspicious.

During the Karmapa's same visit to the Tsang Desi, the latter offered to build a *shedra* (Buddhist college) for Karmapa in Shigatse. Shakabpa describes what happened during the *shedra's* construction, which began after the Fourth Dalai Lama's death at the age of 27 in January 1617.[34] He had been instrumental in preventing

33 It is not clear whether this person is the same as Sonam Chopal, the Fourth Dalai Lama's chief administrator.

34 Some historical records allege that the Fourth Dalai Lama was poisoned. This claim is found in a modern publication: David L. Snellgrove and Hugh Richardson (2003), page 193. Hugh E. Richardson was a well-known British diplomat and Tibetologist.

the various conflicts, so his death meant the loss of an effective mediator. Shakabpa writes:[35]

> In the Fire Snake year (1617), on the 23rd day of the ninth month, the Fifth Dalai Lama was born the son of Hor Dudul Dorje. His family name was Chong Gyey Tagtse. Tsang Depa Phuntsok Namgyal was a disciple of Dhagpo Kagyupa. Moreover, he was committed to fully supporting the Karmapa. He started to develop a *shedra* for the Kagyu and Nyingma schools in an area between Shigatse city and the Tashi Lhunpo Monastery.[36]
>
> (During construction) when they (workers) were digging behind the Tashi Lhunpo Monastery, some rocks rolled down and hit the monks' kitchen in the monastery. Then, on a wall of the new building (*shedra*), there was written the words "Tashi Zilnon," which mean "Tashi the Subduer." These were the reasons[37] why many Mongolian pilgrims who came to central Tibet looted the Karmapa's farms in that year. As a result, in the seventh month of the Earth Horse year (1618), the allied forces of Tsangpa (the Tsang Desi) and (his ally, Duke) Kurabpa arrived in Lhasa.

War of 1618

In 1618, the Mongolian warlord Thumed Taigee with his two sons and their armies reached Lhasa. Kyisho Depa Sonam Namgyal offered him the statue of Jowo Lokeshvara, which was an Eleven-faced Avalokiteshvara that the first Buddhist king of Tibet, Tsontsen Gampo, used for his Dharma practice.

This Jowo Lokeshvara statue is considered a Tibetan national treasure. To offer it to a foreign warlord in exchange for his commitment to wage war against one's own government was unthinkable. The Gelug spiritual teachers were dismayed at this blatant be-

35 *SH(TIB)*: Volume 1, 397–398

36 This monastery is the seat of the Panchen Lama of the Gelug sect.

37 The rocks hitting the monks' kitchen at the Tashi Lhunpo Monastery and the words Tashi Zilnon that were interpreted to mean the Subduer of Tashi Lhunpo were the two reasons that provoked some Gelug administrators to instigate the attacks by the Mongolian pilgrims against the Kamarpa's farms. This was a different looting than the one Shakabpa cited which occurred around 1605 as a response to the poem of the Sixth Shamarpa. See chapter 3.

trayal. However, they could not stand up to the powerful alliance of Duke Kyisho and the majority of Gelug administrators from the Sera and Drepung monasteries. (The administrators of the Gaden Monastery did not join them at that time.) Shakabpa continues from the last excerpt:[38]

> They (the allied forces of Tsangpa and Kurabpa) fought and defeated the Mongolian alliance. The Mongolian alliance consisted of Mongolian warlords – Thumed Taigee, Sechen Tai Ming, and Khun Dul Lung Chokhu – and Kyisho Sonam Gyaltsen (also of the Kyisho Depa family). Some monks from the Sera and Drepung monasteries collaborated with them. The administration of Gaden Monastery of the Dalai Lama acted as mediator.[39]
>
> On the first day, the Tsang army was almost wiped out. But the next day, another huge Tsang army arrived. The Mongolians became frightened and withdrew. Kyisho Depa also ran away, and the ruling government confiscated everything of his. The Sera and Drepung monks and Kyisho Depa's men fled and scattered to Phenpo and north to Taglung. The Kurabpa and Tsangpa troops defeated all the monk armies.
>
> The head of Taglung (a Kagyu sect) arrived and acted as a mediator for the monks of Sera and Drepung. He asked that they be allowed to return to their respective Gelug monasteries. As a favor to the head of Taglung, the Tsang government granted his plea. In return, the Tsang government demanded 200 gold *zho* (a measurement of gold) from the Drepung Monastery. The Sera Monastery had to pay 100 gold *zho*. It was also stipulated that *Zhal Ngo* Sonam Chopal of Gaden should go to Tsang to present the gold to the government.
>
> The Sera and Drepung monasteries did not have anything to offer. Another Gelug monastery called Gyal had a treasure room belonging to the Dalai Lama. The government demanded the equivalent amount of gold *zho* be withdrawn from that treasury. Accompanied by government officials, Sonam Chopal went to the Gyal Monastery and somehow eventually managed to escape to Mongolia.

---

38 *SH(TIB)*: Volume 1, 398

39 Shakabpa is pointing out that unlike the Sera and Drepung administrators, the Gaden Monastery administrators did not take part in the aggression. Instead, they tried to mediate the situation but failed.

6. Tibet United

For the Sakya, Kagyu, and Nyingma sects, the war of 1618 revived fears of an invasion by the Mongols at the invitation of the Gelugpas and of the downfall of the Dharma. Many Nyingma *termas* of Guru Padmasambhava discovered during the preceding three centuries had predicted this. A future Mongolian invasion also concerned the Tsang government. So from its capital in Shigatse, it maintained close watch over Lhasa and the rebel Gelug monasteries.

When it came time to enthrone the Fifth Dalai Lama who was born in 1617, the Tsang Desi did not wish the enthronement to take place in the Gaden Monastery near Lhasa lest another invasion be plotted. Lhasa and central Tibet had proved to be a hotbed of conspirators. Allowing the Dalai Lama and, his administrators to remain in Lhasa might invite further instability and court disaster down the road.

The Tsang Desi decreed that the Fifth Dalai Lama should be enthroned in the Gaden Seykhar Monastery located near the Tsang capital. After the enthronement, the Fifth Dalai Lama should take up residency there. This monastery, the seat of the First Dalai Lama, posed less of a threat to the Desi since its administration had not been involved in any schemes with foreigners. Its monk community had conducted very proper religious practices all along and was not corrupted by politics. To sweeten this offer, the Tsang Desi proposed to underwrite and otherwise support the Fifth Dalai Lama's upbringing and education.

The chief of the Fourth and then the Fifth Dalai Lama's administrations, Sonam Chopal, flatly rejected the Tsang Desi's offer. He realized that proximity to the Tsang Desi would place him under close scrutiny.

The Dalai Lama was not enthroned, and his administrators once again manipulated the Tsang Desi's restrictions on the enthronement to their advantage. They continued to play the role of the oppressed or aggrieved party in order to rouse sympathy and support from the Mongols.

The Fifth Dalai Lama Enthroned after the Ambush of 1621

Unable to have the Fifth Dalai Lama enthroned, Sonam Chopal secretly went to Mongolia to seek military support from the warlords Hong Taigee and Lozang Tenzin. As a result, Mongolian troops again invaded Tibet. Shakabpa describes that day:[40]

> In 1621, two thousand Mongolian troops again arrived in Lhasa. They ambushed the Tsang army military camp. It was on the morning on the tenth day, seventh month of 1621. Many Tsang soldiers were killed.
>
> The Panchen Lama, Lozang Chokyi Gyaltsen, was in retreat at Drepung Monastery. The moment he learned of the fighting, he broke his retreat and left the monastery without a horse. He went to the battlefield and stopped the fighting.

As a consequence of this setback at the hands of the Mongols, over the next two years (1622–1623), the Tsang government returned everything it had taken from the Sera and Drepung monasteries after the war of 1618 as well as the territory of the Kyisho Depa family.

The Tsang Desi's indebtedness to the Panchen Lama for his

40 *SH(TIB)*: Volume 1, 401

timely intervention allowed Sonam Chopal to take advantage of the situation. He gained permission to enthrone the Fifth Dalai Lama at the Gaden Monastery in Lhasa.

Tibet Unified under Tsang

After his father the Tsang Desi Phuntsok Namgyal died of small pox in 1621, the crown prince Karma Tenkyong Wangpo succeeded as Desi.

In those days, Nagchukha Lake was the *de facto* northern border of the Tsang Desi's government. The Mongolian warlord Chogthu occupied the territory stretching north of the lake. Because he opposed other Mongolian warlords, the Tsang government forged an alliance with him. Chogthu's control of that key part of the Tibetan border prevented other Mongolians from using that route to enter Tibet.

In east Tibet, the three kingdoms of Derge, Nangchen (Gomde), and Beri were too distant from the center of Tsang power to pose any problem to the two Tsang Desis. However, in the late 1620's as the power of the Beri king grew and his territory began to expand eastward, the Tsang Desi Karma Tenkyong Wangpo entered into alliance with him, and he defended the Tsang's eastern flank against possible Mongol incursions.

The Tsang Desi's territory in terms of contemporary geography would roughly extend west to today's Ladakh, southwest to Nepal, south to Bhutan and up to Kongpo, southeast to Powo, east to the Dzachu River, northeast to Chamdo, north to Lake Nagchukha, and northwest to an area known as Jangthang which no group controlled.

During the late Ming Dynasty (1368–1644), China never posed a threat to Tsang rule. There were a few diplomatic exchanges between the Tsang Desi and Ming emperors. But China was unable to influence, and certainly not control, Tibetan affairs.

The unification and reform strategy devised by the Tsang Desi Phuntsok Namgyal and carried out by him and his son Karma Tenkyong Wangpo involved not only political unification of Tibet by military means but also social reforms which benefited the people.

The two Tsang Desis built schools for medicine, military affairs, and handicrafts. They established agricultural programs and also a Tibetan cultural center where literature was taught, promoted, and collected. Such programs and schools had not existed in Tibet since Kublai Khan's rule in the 13th century.

Considering the primitive, backward state of Tibetan society in the 16th and 17th centuries, it is quite remarkable that the Tsang Desis were so progressive. The Tsang Desi Karma Tenkyong Wangpo even allowed Christian missionaries to visit and stay in Tibet around 1627. Karma Kagyu lamas, however, objected to their presence, and the Jesuits were expelled.

Neither the Tenth Karmapa nor the Sixth Shamarpa was present in central Tibet at the time of these Christian missionaries. In 1624, they both left for Mount Kailash in the far west. From there, they travelled towards Nepal. Shamarpa even went as far as today's Kathmandu for a pilgrimage where he stayed for a while. They remained in a region called Nyanam, which is along the border of today's Nepal and Tibet. The Sixth Shamarpa died there in 1631, whereupon the Tenth Karmapa brought the body of his teacher back to the Tsurphu Monastery in Tibet. (Chapter 25 presents the details of the Sixth Shamarpa's death and the funeral rites conducted by the Tenth Karmapa.)

Tsang Karma Tenkyong Wangpo ruled Tibet from 1621 to 1642. He was able to subdue the different dukes and bring them under a unified Tibet. Through the Unification and Reform Strategy of the Tsang father and son, a major part of Tibet emerged as a unified country, and relatively enlightened social policies were established. For almost two decades Tsang Desi Tenkyong Wangpo was able to govern as an independent, secular ruler with little or no interference from religious leaders. However, he still needed to deal with Mongolian invasions, as did his father. Shakabpa writes of an attack in 1632:[41]

> In 1632, another Mongolian called Hal Hal attacked Amegeru. And so Tsangpa (Karma Tenkyong Wangpo) began to recruit an army

41 *SH(TIB)*: Volume 1, 406

from all over Tibet. Though he appeared powerful, he was insecure; thus he sent a messenger to Panchen Rinpoche and *Zhal Ngo* Sonam Chopal asking them to go to Hal Hal's Mongolian camp and mediate for peace. Both went together and managed to send the Mongolians back to their homeland. The Tsang government was very grateful, and Lhasa was given to Gaden Phobrang (main office of the Gelug administration).

Different Agendas

No Tibetan political or religious leaders in the first half of the 17th century shared the two Tsang Desis' vision and goal of creating a unified Tibet under a secular government, with a certain degree of separation between politics and religion. Nor, as has been mentioned earlier, did anyone else at the time have a similarly progressive reform agenda.

In contrast to the two Tsang Desis' agendas, the two leading religious sects of the time, the Gelugpas and the Kagyupas, had viewpoints as different from those of the Tsang Desis as from each other's. Sonam Chopal and the Sera and Drepung administrations pursued a strategy of aggrandizement for their sect, though they did not have the support of all Gelugpas, while the Tenth Karmapa and Sixth Shamarpa seemed unwilling to engage in politics and advocated against military conflict.

The objective of those Gelugpa administrators, especially Sonam Chopal of Gaden Phobrang, was to establish the supremacy of their sect and to gain political control in order to enrich their coffers. They sought to combine secular and religious power.

Sonam Chopal and his collaborators were so intent on achieving supremacy at any cost that they invited the Mongolians to invade their country. In 1616, for example, they became alarmed when the Tenth Karmapa was asked to initiate the Tsang Desi[42] since this would mean more power and influence to Karmapa and the Karma Kagyu. Feeling very insecure, Sonam Chopal traveled to meet Gushri Khan and urged him to attack the Tsang Desi.

42 See chapter 5.

For their parts, both the Tenth Karmapa and the Sixth Shamarpa viewed political leaders as greedy people who thought only of personal ambition and power. In their experience, chieftains, dukes, and rulers often controlled and used people with undue disregard and cruelty. The two bodhisattvas tried to stop abuse and mistreatment whenever they could.

For example, when the first Tsang Desi began a campaign to take over the territory of Duke Kurabpa around 1620, the Tenth Karmapa enlisted the Sixth Shamarpa to beseech the Tsang Desi to stop his military advances. In the words of the Tenth Karmapa:[43]

> Bodhisattva Chokyi Wangchuk (the Sixth Shamarpa) told the Tsang Desi, "You have enough (power) now. You are the big lord with a palace. There are many people under you already. Why do you still attack the smaller lords?"

In short, the Sixth Shamarpa and Tenth Karmapa always encouraged people to be content and to keep their desires in check. Their advice was spiritually sound but politically impractical.

---

43 See this excerpt from the Tenth Karmapa's writing in chapter 19.

7. The Mongol Invasion, 1639–1642

Prelude to the Mongol Invasion

During the first ten years of his rule, the Tsang Desi Karma Tenkyong Wangpo enjoyed relative peace from external threats. However, the attack of the Mongol Hal Hal in 1632 reminded him of his vulnerability and caused him to tighten his border security.

As mentioned in the previous chapter, one border defense was the Tsang Desi's alliance with Chogthu, the Mongolian warlord who held the territory northeast of central Tibet, which spanned the Kokonor region beyond Lake Nagchukha. Not only did Chogthu keep other Mongolian tribesmen from entering Tibet, but he also blocked Tibetans from passing through his territory into Mongolia. This posed a serious but not insurmountable problem for the Gaden Monastery's chief administrator, Sonam Chopal, and his colleagues in Lhasa who needed to remain in contact with their Mongol supporters. Chogthu's long border with Mongolia was simply too difficult to seal completely.

In the early 1630s, the Tsang Desi had formed an alliance against the Mongols with the ruler of the Beri kingdom in eastern Tibet (Kham), a practitioner of the Bon[44] religion. The Beri ruler at-

44 The indigenous religion of Tibet, which later embraced some Buddhist practices.

tacked some Gelug monasteries near his territory. Representatives from three of the besieged Gelug monasteries met to discuss their defense strategy. They decided to seek help from the Mongol warlord Gushri Khan who was encamped beyond Jangthang in northwest Tibet (near present-day Ladakh). He and his men were recent converts to Buddhism and became followers of the Gelug sect.

Sonam Chopal managed to join the delegation from the three besieged Gelug monasteries. They told Gushri Khan about the Tsang Desi's alliances with the Beri chieftain and Chogthu. They dramatized the precarious position of the Gelug sect in Tibet and urged Gushri Khan to attack Tibet. The Mongol Khan agreed but first decided to reconnoiter the situation in Tibet. He sent one messenger spy to west Tibet and another to east Tibet, instructing them to report back to him in Mongolia in a year's time.

The Tsang Desi caught word of Gushri Khan's plan and sought help from Chogthu. In 1635, Chogthu sent his son, Arsalang, with ten thousand troops to support the Tsang Desi in central Tibet. Somehow, Gushri Khan learned of this plan and immediately set out to intercept Arsalang. As Arsalang was proceeding towards Lhasa in the guise of a pilgrim, Gushri Khan met him in eastern Tibet. The two developed a friendship.

Along his way to Lhasa, Arsalang tried to meet the Tenth Karmapa. However, he considered Arsalang an evil man. (The Karmapa's biography in chapter 27 below indicates that the Tenth Karmapa refused Arsalang's request for an audience.)

Arsalang entered Lhasa, met the Fifth Dalai Lama, and became his devotee. Subsequently, he repudiated his father's alliance with the Tsang Desi and in 1636 attacked the Tsang army at Dam Zhung. During the military engagement, the Tsang government asked the Tenth Karmapa and the Taglung Shabdrung, head of Kagyu Taglung sect, along with other religious leaders to meet with Arsalang for the purpose of peacefully resolving the conflict. The religious leaders managed to halt the war, and peace was temporarily restored.

When Chogthu realized that his son had betrayed him, he dispatched troops to kill Arsalang. After Gushri Khan learned of Arsalang's death, he attacked Chogthu at Tso Ngon in a northern area taken over by Arsalang. Gushri Khan destroyed Chogthu's army and killed him in 1637.

In 1638, Gushri Khan went to central Tibet in the guise of a religious pilgrim. He met the Fifth Dalai Lama. In front of the Buddha statue in the Jokhang Temple, the Gelug administrators arranged to have Gushri Khan seated on a throne and gave him the title of *Tenzin Chokyi Gyalpo*, which means "The Religious King and Holder of the Buddhadharma." The Mongols, in turn, conferred Mongolian titles upon the Gelug administrators. Afterwards, Gushri Khan returned to the Kokonor region where he had decimated Chogthu's army a year before.

Then Gushri Khan's spies intercepted a letter to the Tsang Desi from the Chieftain of Beri who controlled the region of Kham. The letter revealed his scheme to attack the Gelugpas in response to the defeat of Chogthu.

Mongol Invasion 1639–1642

Gushri Khan quickly responded by sending a letter to the Fifth Dalai Lama, informing him of his intent and his readiness to attack first the Beri chieftain in Kham and then the Tsang Desi. The Fifth Dalai Lama's attendant Sonam Chopal went against his leader's wishes and on his own initiative asked Gushri Khan to destroy the Beri chieftain.

Gushri Khan thus launched an offensive against the Beri chieftain in Derge. So began the Mongol invasion of Tibet. Gushri Khan joined forces with the Derge King Lachen Jampa Phuntsok, and together they decimated the entire army of the Beri chieftain, also killing him in the winter of 1640.[45]

With this victory, Gushri Khan had conquered part of eastern Tibet and then set his sights on attacking Tsang in central Tibet. He sent a message to Sonam Chopal, asking him if he should march on to Lhasa.

In his autobiography, the Fifth Dalai Lama writes about the

45 *SH(ENG)*: 107

communications between Sonam Chopal and Gushri Khan:[46]

> At that time (likely in 1641), we received word that Gushri Khan would arrive (in Lhasa). However, some said that he would return to Mongolia. *Zhal Ngo* (i.e., Sonam Chopal who held title of *Zhal Ngo*, chief administrator) told me that he had sent a message in my name asking Gushri Khan to please attack the Tsangpa. He (*Zhal Ngo*) felt that the timing was right and it was our (the Gelugpas') opportunity to break free of the Tsang government. We would not get another chance otherwise.
>
> I said to *Zhal Ngo*, "Your writing that message without my knowledge was a big mistake. I told you the last time[47] that we should send the Mongolians back from Dam to Mongolia. That would have been good. At that time, you said I should do a *mo* (a divination)."
>
> I did a three-dice *mo* of the Mahakali. The divination gave an answer. I interpreted it according to the *mo* instruction book. Then I told *Zhal Ngo*, "The *mo* indicates that if we go to war against the Tsang government, we will succeed. However, the result is bad for the future."
>
> *Zhal Ngo* responded, "If we can succeed now, that is good enough. We don't care about the future. We will all be dead by then."

Sonam Chopal did not heed the prediction's warning. He was concerned only for his own power and ambition. The future of Tibet was not his concern. He and others in his administration acted against the teachings of the Buddha. They did not seek enlightenment for themselves or for others. Religion was to them a means to gain wealth, prestige, and power.

War in Tsang 1641–1642

When war finally broke out between the Tsang government and Gushri Khan in 1641, the Tenth Karmapa was in central Tibet. He beseeched the Tsang Desi not to fight but to surrender, even as Gushri Khan and his soldiers were attacking. The Tenth Karmapa's

---

46 *DL*: Volume 1, 201

47 This refers to the time around 1639 when Sonam Chopal, against the Dalai Lama's wishes, wrote to Gushri Khan asking him to attack the Beri chieftain.

only concern was the loss of lives, not political or military struggles.

The Tsang mounted a strong resistance. Sonam Chopal began to feel very uneasy and scared because he knew he could lose everything. He went to the Fifth Dalai Lama and asked him to pretend to mediate between the two competing armies. He was trying to cover his tracks in case his side lost. The Fifth Dalai Lama recorded how Sonam Chopal approached him that day in 1641:[48]

> That time, *Zhal Ngo* came to me looking scared. He said, "I thought the moment Gushri Khan (and his troops) arrived, the Tsangpa would not dare to retaliate. But as it turned out, it was not like that at all. We were overly confident about this war. Now I think you should go to the battlefield and pretend to be a mediator to stop the war."

In his autobiography the Fifth Dalai Lama recounted how he responded to his chief administrator:[49]

> Usually I don't dare to challenge *Zhal Ngo*. But that day, I felt so annoyed that I said to him, "I told you many times not to attack Tsangpa, but you never listened. The reason is the Tsangpa will never surrender unless he has lost everything. This is typical of one who is very strong. Now, even if we were to make peace, Tsangpa will never trust us again. Everybody knows we are the ones who invited the Khan to make this war. We shall feel the consequences after the Mongolians leave.
>
> "The decision I made when Gushri Khan arrived in Tsang is final – I will not make a two-step.[50] And it is the same decision now.
>
> "The war has started already. So now we must go ahead with it. If we win, we can achieve what we want, and if we lose, we will have to run to wherever possible."

48 *DL*: Volume 1, 203

49 *DL*: Volume 1, 204

50 This means he will not change his mind.

> I started to do the black magic of the wrathful Yamantaka.[51]

Gushri Khan and the Tsang Desi fought a very bloody war lasting about one year. In 1642 the war ended with the Mongol warlord victorious.

After the War

After Gushri Khan took over Tibet, he invited the Fifth Dalai Lama to Sambdrub Tse, the former Tsang palace in Shigatse, where he enthroned him as King of Tibet. About what he saw in Sambdrub Tse, the Fifth Dalai Lama wrote:[52]

> In this palace of Tsangpa were schools for literature, medicine, and Buddhist studies. They have done everything here. This Tsangpa was a good king. I was willing to meet him. But since I had already done so much black magic on him, I was afraid to do so.[53]

The Dalai Lama's comment strongly suggests that he had been brought up in the isolation of the upper monastery chambers surrounded by his attendants and Sonam Chopel who fed him misinformation. Even in today's era of high-tech telecommunications, people are misled by false information. How much easier was this to achieve in the Dalai Lama's day! It was next to impossible for the young Dalai Lama, who was then only in his mid-twenties, to begin to comprehend the extent of the political intrigues that enveloped him.

After standing in the middle of the Sambdrub Tse palace, the Dalai Lama knew he had been misled. His regret is evident from his own words quoted above.

The defeat of the Tsang government and rise of the Gelugpas as the religious and political heads of Tibet occurred during the very final years of the Ming Dynasty in China. Two years later in 1644, the Manchus won control of China and established the Qing Dy-

---

51 Yamantaka (Sanskrit): "Yama" is the name of the god of death, and "antaka" means "terminator of death."

52 *DL*: Volume 1, 217

53 Tibetans who believe in black magic think that if you meet the person you have cursed, the curse would backfire on you.

nasty. During the early years of this dynasty, Tibet's relationship with China began to change as will be discussed in the following chapter.

8. Aftermath of the War

Gushri Khan's victory in 1642 marked a turning point in Tibetan history in several respects. First, the Gelugpas became ascendant at the expense of the Kagyupas, and the Tenth Karmapa had to flee Tibet for his life. Second, a decade after the defeat of the Tsang government, the Gelug government of Tibet established a closer diplomatic relationship with China than had existed since the end of the Yuan Dynasty in the 14th century. Some years after the Fifth Dalai Lama's death in 1682, this relationship evolved to the point where Tibet became subservient to the Qing dynasty rulers. This eventually led to today's situation when China considers Tibet to be historically part of China.

A third outcome of the 1639–1642 war was the breakdown of the division between church and state that the Tsang rulers had instituted. Soon after winning the war, Gushri Khan in a grand ceremony installed the Fifth Dalai Lama as head of the secular government of Tibet. Thus, temporal power and spiritual authority were linked in the hands of one person for the first time in Tibet since the Yuan Dynasty. Although the Fifth Dalai Lama relied on his chief administrator Sonam Chopal to carry out many political duties, the ultimate authority rested in him. This unification of church and state existed in Tibet until 2011 when the Fourteenth Dalai Lama

Tenzin Gyatso formally relinquished his political position as head of the Tibetan government to an elected prime minister.

Karmapa's Escape and Exile

During the first few years after the Fifth Dalai Lama was established as leader of the Tibetan government, tensions ran high between the Gelug and the Kagyu, as well as some other sects. The former began forcibly to convert Kagyu monasteries. In an attempt to reach a reconciliation with the Fifth Dalai Lama, the Tenth Karmapa, who had always acted as a mediator for peace and never had taken part in the disputes between the Tsang Desi and the Gelug administrators and Mongol warlords, asked the Panchen Lama to intercede and to arrange a meeting between the two religious leaders. The Karmapa's biographer Bey Lotsawa recounts what the Panchen Lama told the Tenth Karmapa and the Fifth Dalai Lama:[54]

> "I, Panchen Lama, will vouch for you. I can attest for the fact that you, Gyalwa Wangpo Karmapa, are entirely blameless for any conflict between the Karma Kagyu sect and the Gelug sect."
>
> The Panchen Lama declared Karmapa's innocence to the Fifth Dalai Lama, "Karmapa is free of any blame. I bear witness to his being faultless and give you my personal guarantee on it. The Karma Kagyu administrators, on the other hand, have not dealt with the situation skillfully."

The Panchen Rinpoche went on to advise the Fifth Dalai Lama how to manage the situation. He also procured an order from the Fifth Dalai Lama to his followers not to act against the Karma Kagyu. When some troops from Kongpo in southeastern Tibet came to the aid of the remnants of the Tsang government, the Tenth Karmapa implored them not to fight and to return to where they came from. He told them he had surrendered to the Fifth Dalai Lama so that more lives would not be lost. The Kongpo fighters did not listen.[55] From the Karmapa's biographer Bey Lotsawa, we learn that some

54 *BL*: 175b. See chapter 29 below for more details about this incident.

55 See chapter 29 below for the details recorded in the biography written by Bey Lotsawa.

Karma Kagyu followers who advocated fighting "criticized Karmapa for abandoning the Tsang government and his responsibilities to the Karma Kagyu sect." However, Bey Lotsawa had this to say in the Karmapa's defense:[56]

> The Gyalwa Wangpo (Karmapa) always likened kingdoms to honey laced with poison. This was why he maintained a separation between the Karma Kagyu sect and the Tsang ruling government. Nevertheless, he still got all the blame.

In spite of the Fifth Dalai Lama's stated wish not to harm the Karma Kagyu, his chief administrator Sonam Chopal had other intentions in mind. Many Karma Kagyu monasteries were seized and converted into Gelug.

Further, Sonam Chopal and Gushri Khan did not abandon their attack on the Karmapa and his entourage. They gave chase to Karmapa's group while it was on route to Kham. Taglung Tashi Paldrub, the head of the Taglung sect, acted as a mediator to try and stop the attack. But Sonam Chopal twisted Karmapa's words in front of Gushri Khan and thus instigated the Mongol warlord to order Karmapa killed. Nevertheless, Karmapa and some of his followers escaped and proceeded to travel to Lijiang (in present-day Yunnan Province, China) where they stayed for a number of years.[57]

Contrasting Responses to Imperial Overtures

The Qing Dynasty formally came to power just two years after the Gelugpas and Mongols established control over Tibet in 1642. Even though the Qing rulers were nomadic people (Manchus) from outside the Great Wall, they were leery of the potentially troublesome Mongolians. Thus, they wanted to establish good relations with the Dalai Lama whom they believed had some influence over the Mongols. From 1648 to 1651, the young Manchu emperor dis-

56 *BL*: 175b

57 Sonam Chopal's schemes and attack on Karmapa and the latter's escape and exile in Lijiang are covered in detail in chapters 29–32 below.

patched envoys to Tibet inviting the Fifth Dalai Lama to Beijing.[58] The Dalai Lama accepted the third invitation and started his trip in 1652.

The Qing court also was aware of the Fifth Karmapa's famous visit to the Ming emperor Yongle in 1407. So a few years after the Dalai Lama's return from Beijing, it also courted the Tenth Karmapa, offering him gifts and a prestigious title. This occurred during the Karmapa's exile in Lijiang.

The Fifth Dalai Lama and the Tenth Karmapa reacted to the Qing overtures in starkly contrasting ways that point to their fundamentally different attitudes about religion and politics. The following accounts taken from the Dalai Lama's autobiography and the Karmapa's biography reveal this difference.

The Dalai Lama travelled nine months to China with an entourage befitting a major head of state. There was much discussion on the Chinese side about the appropriate protocol to follow with the Dalai Lama – whether or not the emperor should travel beyond the Great Wall to greet the Dalai Lama, what titles and gifts to bestow on him, and so forth. The Dalai Lama remained in the imperial capital only two months in late 1652 and early 1653. He describes his first meeting with the Emperor Shunzhi as follows:[59]

> The emperor came down from his throne and walked towards me. I was some distance away from him, about ten human arm-lengths. He came up to me, and my hand was held by him. His translator asked me, "How are you?"
>
> The emperor sat on his throne, about waist high, on which was a seat. About one human arm-length from his throne was a throne for me, a little lower than the emperor's. When tea was served, he asked me to drink first. I indicated that this was not proper. Then we drank tea at the same time…
>
> …I was hosted in a house specifically built for the holder of the title

58 *SH(ENG)*: 113–117 tells the story of the Fifth Dalai Lama's visit to the Qing capital in 1652–1653. For the relations between the Qing Dynasty and the Fifth Dalai Lama, also see Sperling (2003), Ahmad (1970), and Rockhill (1910).

59 *DL*: Volume 1, 393

"Dalai Lama."[60]

On his return trip to Tibet, the Fifth Dalai Lama received from the Qing emperor a document in gold conveying a title, which the Dalai Lama calls a *jasa*[61] (certificate of authorization), and a golden seal. He records this incident in his diary as follows:[62]

> I received from the Emperor a title on a long piece of folded paper in gold. Each fold measures the width of four half-thumbs[63] and the length of one out-stretched hand. There were fifteen folds in all.
>
> The title reads: "Heaven in the west, meritoriously and happily existing, all living beings as one under the sky of Buddhadharma."[64]
>
> The *jasa* and seal were written in three languages (Chinese, Mongolian and Tibetan) so that all people in the West may know about this (i.e., the *jasa* and seal). They were presented to me with great ceremony.
>
> What was written on the seal was translated (for me) by a Mongolian translator, but the translation was poor. What was written above was translated by a learned Chinese translator.
>
> When I received the seal and *jasa*, I wrote an auspicious prayer to Dod Kham Wang Chukmar (Mahakali) in gratitude to her, stamped the first (impression of the) seal (on the prayer) and offered it to her.

Near the end of his life, one act by the Dalai Lama indicates that the *jasa* had importance for him. Shortly before his death, he wrote a will transferring power to Sangye Gyatso, his prime minister or *desi*. This document he famously posted on a wall in the Potala palace together with his handprints and the *jasa* he received from the Qing court. He wanted to convey political legitimacy and prestige

60 *DL*: Volume 1, 394

61 Tibetans used the term *jasa* to refer to an edict or other document issued by a Chinese emperor stamped with an imperial seal.

62 *DL*: Volume 1, 415

63 Half-thumb is the length from the knuckle to the tip of the thumb.

64 Another more fluid way to translate the title is as follows: Vajradhara, Ocean Lama of all beings, as one under the sky of Buddhadharma who meritoriously and happily lives in the Western Heaven.

to Sangye Gyatso, and the *jasa* from the Qing court enhanced this.

Interpretations vary about the significance of the Dalai Lama's travel to the imperial court and his acceptance of the *jasa*.[65] Some, particularly recent Chinese historians, have said his trip showed deference to China and thus indicated Tibet was in China's orbit. Be this as it may, no records clearly indicate that Tibet was under the Qing's sway or control during the life of the Fifth Dalai Lama. After his death however, Sangye Gyatso concealed this event from the Qing court for fifteen years. When the Chinese discovered this deception, they sent their men to Lhasa and executed Sangye Gyatso. From this point on, China increasingly exerted its control over Tibet.

Seven years after the Fifth Dalai Lama returned from China, in 1660, the Iron Mouse year, the Tenth Karmapa received envoys from China bearing a letter in gold and many gifts. He politely thanked the Qing emperor who later offered a prestigious religious title that would have roughly put him on par with the Dalai Lama. He resolutely rejected the gifts and the title offered by the emperor as explained by Bey Lotsawa as follows:[66]

> A reply from Emperor Shunzhi in a gold letter came along with many offerings, including some from the empress and crown prince.
>
> In the letter, the emperor stated, "Now I will make you a new seal. I will also designate a permanent messenger between us. He will relay the correspondence between us every year."
>
> The emperor wanted to offer Karmapa the title "The Spiritual Leader of Tibet," the same title offered to the Fifth Karmapa by the Ming emperor (in 1407).
>
> Karmapa replied, "I have no interest in worldly titles. I don't need them."
>
> Situ Rinpoche (the Sixth), however, beseeched Karmapa, "You must accept!"

---

65 For some interpretations of the Dalai Lama's visit to China, see Ahmad (1970), Kamay (2003), Tuttle (2006), and van Shaik (2011).

66 *BL*: 186b. This episode is covered in chapter 35 of this book.

> "I don't need these things," Karmapa scolded him. "You people are after the Chinese silks and brocades. As for me, in my wisdom, I see the lakes in China filled with human blood."
>
> [*Bey Lotsawa comments*]: The Fifth Dalai Lama wrote in his autobiography, "Karmapa ran away. He went to China to bring Chinese soldiers." Now here, even this incident can prove whether Karmapa had such interests or not.[67]

Karmapa's Return to Tibet and Death

After about thirty years in exile, around 1669, Karmapa was invited back to his homeland by the Dalai Lama. The Karmapa started his journey to Tibet in 1672 when he was about sixty-eight years old and nearing the end of his life.

The timing of the invitation occurred after the war between the Chinese Qing military and the Mongolian warlord Khandro Lozang Tenkyong had concluded.[68] Bey Lotsawa credits Karmapa for helping to mediate an end to that war. The Fifth Dalai Lama apparently thought it inappropriate for the Karmapa to associate with Khandro, as he writes in his autobiography:[69]

> Lord Khandro's heart was possessed by evil, and he brought disaster to the area of Gyalthang. As a result, Karmapa's party could not remain there. Dalai Hung Taigee sent Mongolian troops led by Zhalpon Drophen and Dargye Tashi[70] to invite Karmapa to central Tibet.

The two religious leaders met face-to-face in 1672. Bey Lotsawa's biography of the Karmapa gives a short, simple account of this occasion, but the Dalai Lama's autobiography provides many

---

67 The autobiography of the Fifth Dalai Lama reveals that he thought or suspected that the Tenth Karmapa would ask the Qing court for military help. Yet, Bey Lotsawa's biography of the Tenth Karmapa reveals that Karmapa rejected the title. And so Bey Lotsawa's comments show that he disagreed with the Dalai Lama. Karmapa's scolding of Situ Rinpoche in this episode proves that Karmapa could not have intended to invite Chinese soldiers for help.

68 See chapter 37 for details about Karmapa's encounters with Khandro.

69 *DL*: Volume 2, 359, line 10

70 Zhalpon and Dargye are civilan government titles.

more details. (Both accounts are presented in chapter 37 below.) In their meeting, the Dalai Lama allowed Karmapa to return to his monastery at Tsurphu. After a year there, Karmapa, at the request of the Dalai Lama, went to perform special pujas at a retreat monastery about a day's travel from Lhasa. While there he fell ill and died in 1674 at the age of 70. The Dalai Lama's government commissioned the Karmapa's funeral services. Eight years later in 1682, the Dalai Lama died at the height of his political power.

The careers and actions of the Fifth Dalai Lama and Tenth Karmapa offer a study in contrasts. The Dalai Lama – a highly respected Buddhist scholar and a prolific author – was deeply involved in politics. By contrast, as will be seen in the following biography of the Karmapa's life drawn from his own writings and those of his esteemed 18th-century biographer Bey Lotsawa, the Karmapa disdained politics and concentrated on spreading the Dharma, doing good deeds, and creating religious works of poetry and art. He had many admirers including the Dalai Lama himself who said that the Karmapa "undoubtedly deserves our devotion."[71]

---

71 See chapter 37.

Part II: Examples of the Tenth Karmapa Choying Dorje's Artwork

The Tenth Karmapa was a prolific and talented artist. At an early age he started to paint and sculpt, and for the rest of his life he constantly created works of art that expressed his mission to spread the Dharma. His autobiographical writings and Bey Lotsawa's biography translated in Part III of this book contain numerous references to his artworks and creative activities.

Just as the Tenth Karmapa donated to the poor the offerings he received, he also regularly gave away his thangkas and sculptures to his disciples and others as aids for their Dharma practice. The beneficiaries of his artistic gifts were people from all walks of life—from the poor to the rich and royal, and from ordinary laymen to lamas and high rinpoches.

All his life, the Tenth Karmapa was particularly concerned about the welfare of animals. For example, as a youngster he was alarmed when he saw people shearing sheep. He feared the sheep might suffer. This compassion for animals is reflected in the sensitive way he often depicted them in thangkas.

Bey Lotsawa mentions that as a youth the Karmapa "liked to collect threads of different colors and practiced making the designs for embroidered cloth or brocade". This interest probably led to his subsequent innovation in creating *sithang* style thangkas described in chapters 23 and 28 below.

The Karmapa's painting style is original and incomparable. Although he absorbed Chinese influences during his exile in Lijiang, he created paintings uniquely his own. For example, many of the figures he painted show facial expressions and shapes quite different from the style of other traditional Tibetan painters.

This biography does not examine the Tenth Karmapa as an artist, but readers can gain a general appreciation of his immense and distinctive talents by viewing the illustrations that follow. Several of them depict art works never previously published. Many more illustrations can be found in the Rubin Museum of Art's catalogue (see Debreczeny (2012)), the first in-depth study of the Tenth Karmapa's art.

Buddha Sakyamuni attended by his disciples Sariputra and Maudgalyayana.
Attributed to the Tenth Karmapa Choying Dorje.
Pigment on silk.
68 x 44 cm.
Collection of Tibet Museum of the Alain Bordier Foundation, Gruyeres, Switzerland.

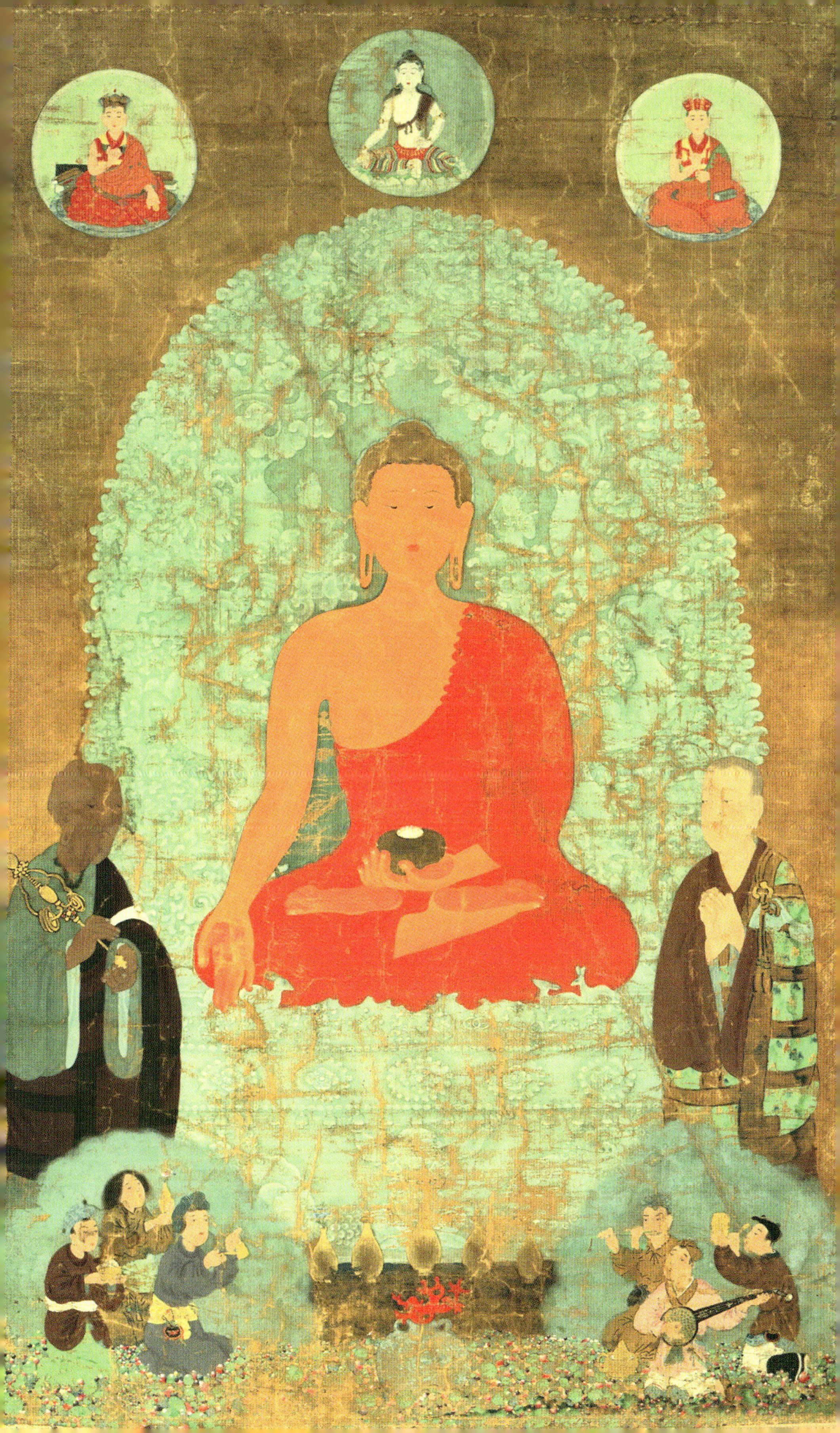

Figure 3. *Marpa receives Milarepa.*
Tenth Karmapa Choying Dorje.
Distemper on silk.
50.5 x 31 cm.
Collection of Heidi & Ulrich von Schroeder, Weesen, Switzerland

An inscription on the thangka (not by the Tenth Karmapa) states that he painted it and presented it to his close disciple and attendant Kunto Zangpo. The figure clad in brown with a blue shoulder bag likely is Milarepa who appears to be seeking teachings from Marpa. The figure dressed in green is Marpa's wife Dagmed Ma.

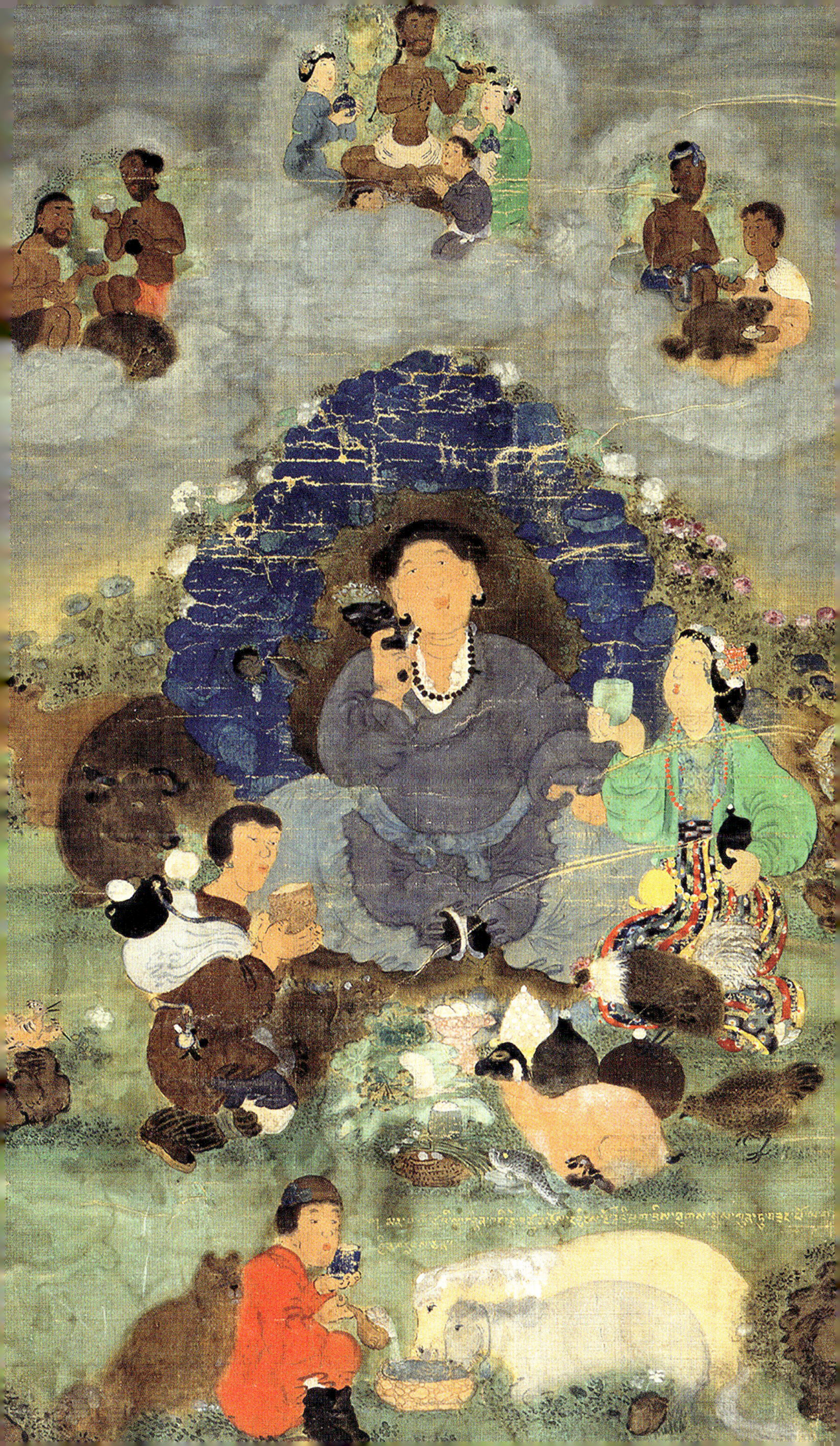

Milarepa (1040–1123) *seated outside a mountain cave.*

Attributed to the Tenth Karmapa.

Pigment on silk.

47.5 x 34.5 cm.

Collection of Tibet Museum of the Alain Bordier Foundation, Gruyeres, Switzerland.

In this thangka, Milarepa is shown converting a hunter after giving shelter to his prey – a deer chased by a hunting dog.

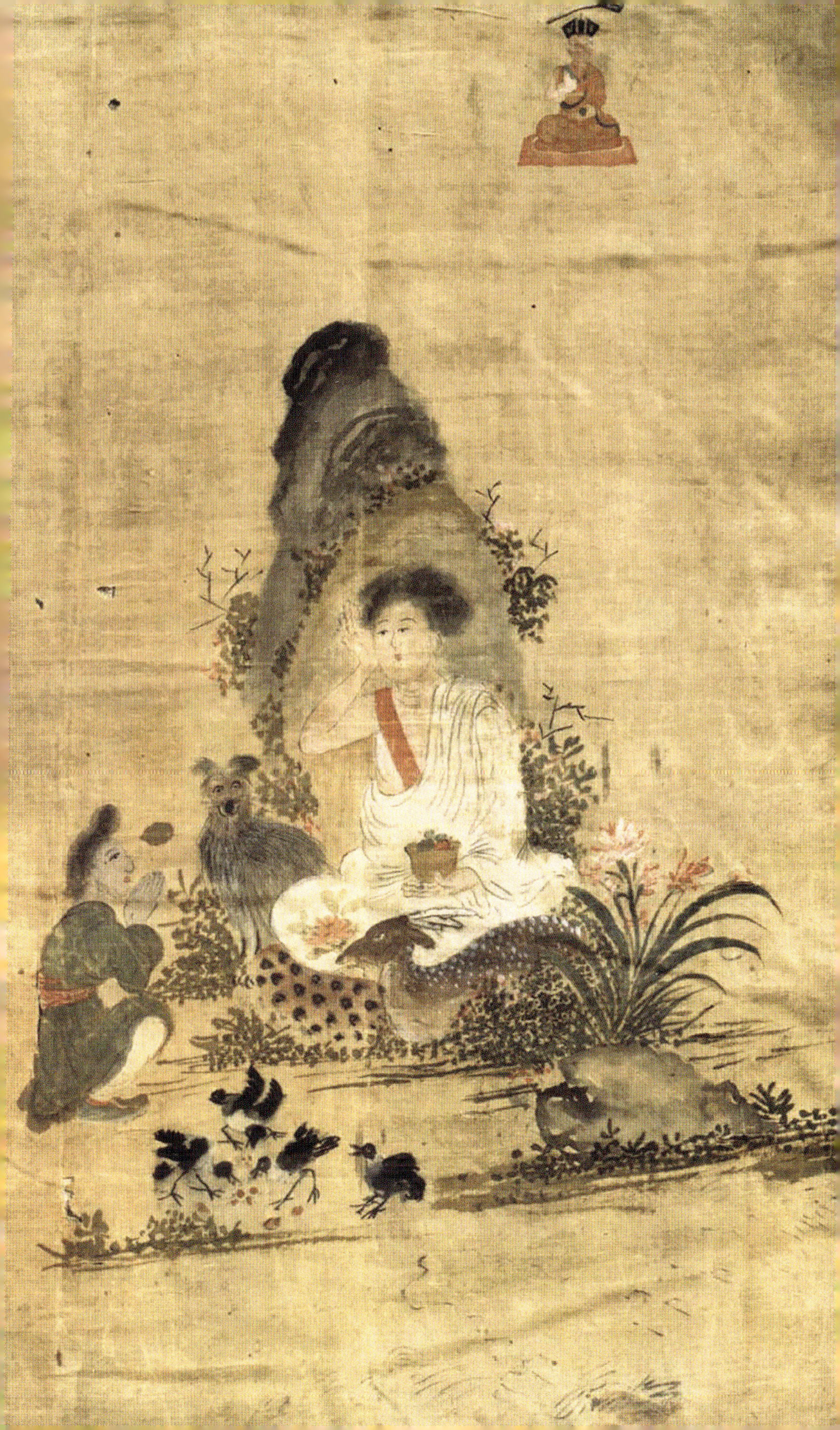

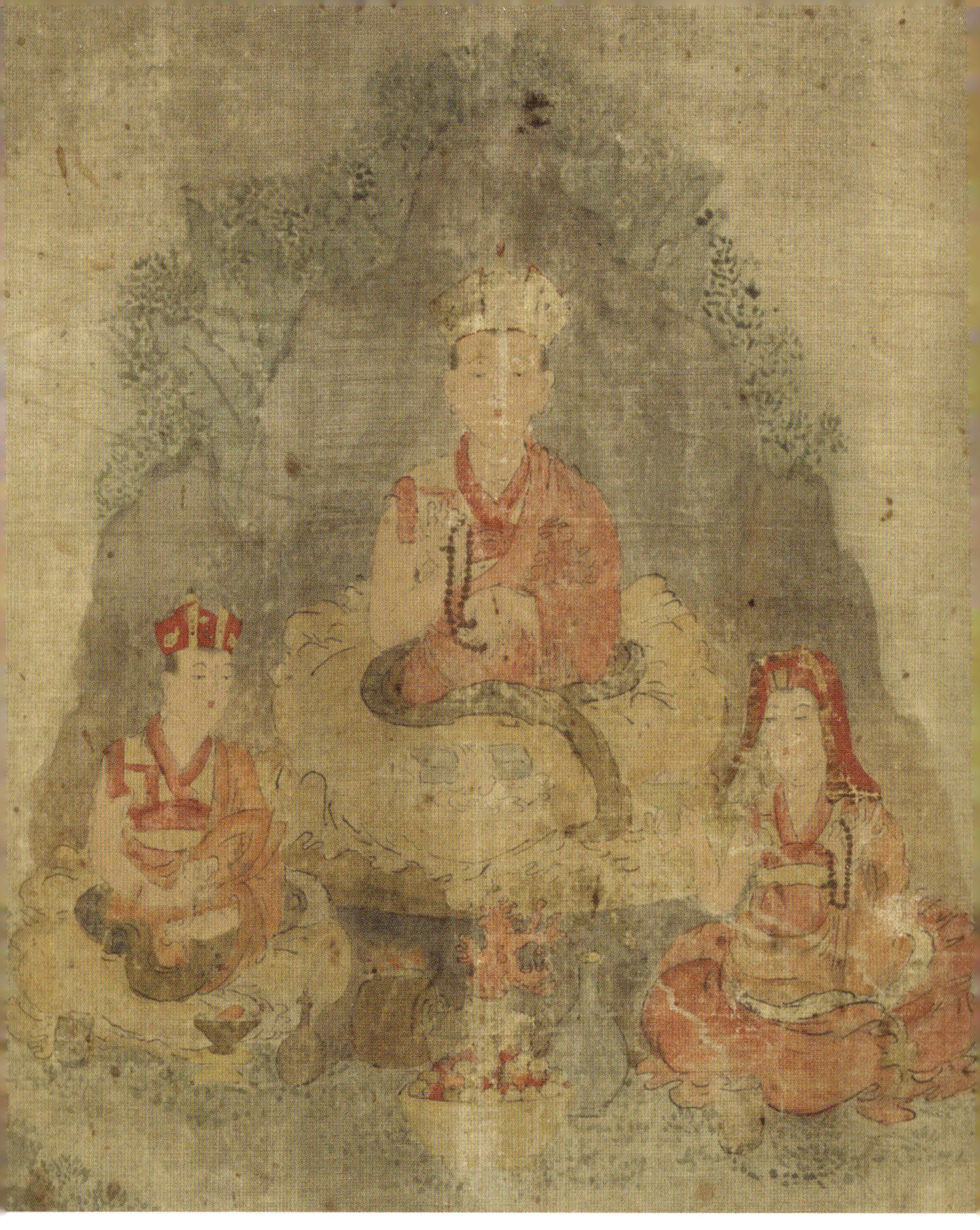

Karmapa in a Cave.

Attributed to Tenth Karmapa Choying Dorje.

Mineral pigment on silk.

15 3/4 x 10 5/8 in. (40 x 27 cm.).

Collection of Shamar Rinpoche.

Photo courtesy of the Rubin Museum of Art.

The Tenth Karmapa painted this thangka while living in exile in Lijiang and Gyalthang, 1648–1671. It is a self-portrait. The enlarged image of the thangka shows Kunto Zangpo (the Karmapa's faithful attendant for many years) at the Karmapa's right side, and on the left is the Sixth Gyaltsab Norbu Zangpo. Chenrezig is depicted at the top of the thangka.

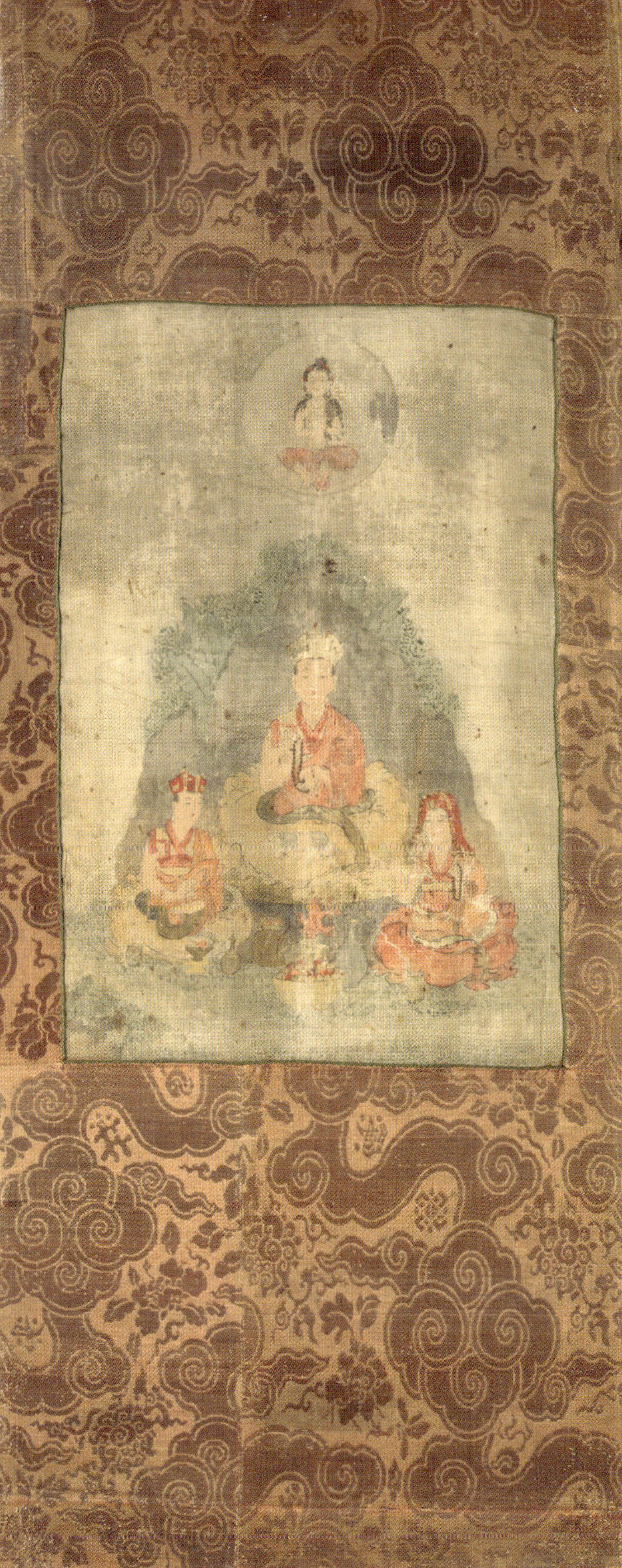

Sculpture of the Tenth Karmapa.
Probably by the Tenth Karmapa Choying Dorje.
Cast copper alloy.
Height: 5 7⁄8 in. (15 cm).
Collection of Alan Chen ((陳慶隆), Taipei, Taiwan.
Photograph courtesy of Rubin Museum of Art.

This sculpture is believed to be a self-portrait of the Tenth Karmapa. He likely made it in 1657. Bey Lotsawa's biography of the Tenth Karmapa states: "In that year Karmapa taught, sculpted, and painted as usual. He made an Avalokiteshvara statue and a statue of himself and gave them to the King (of Lijiang)."

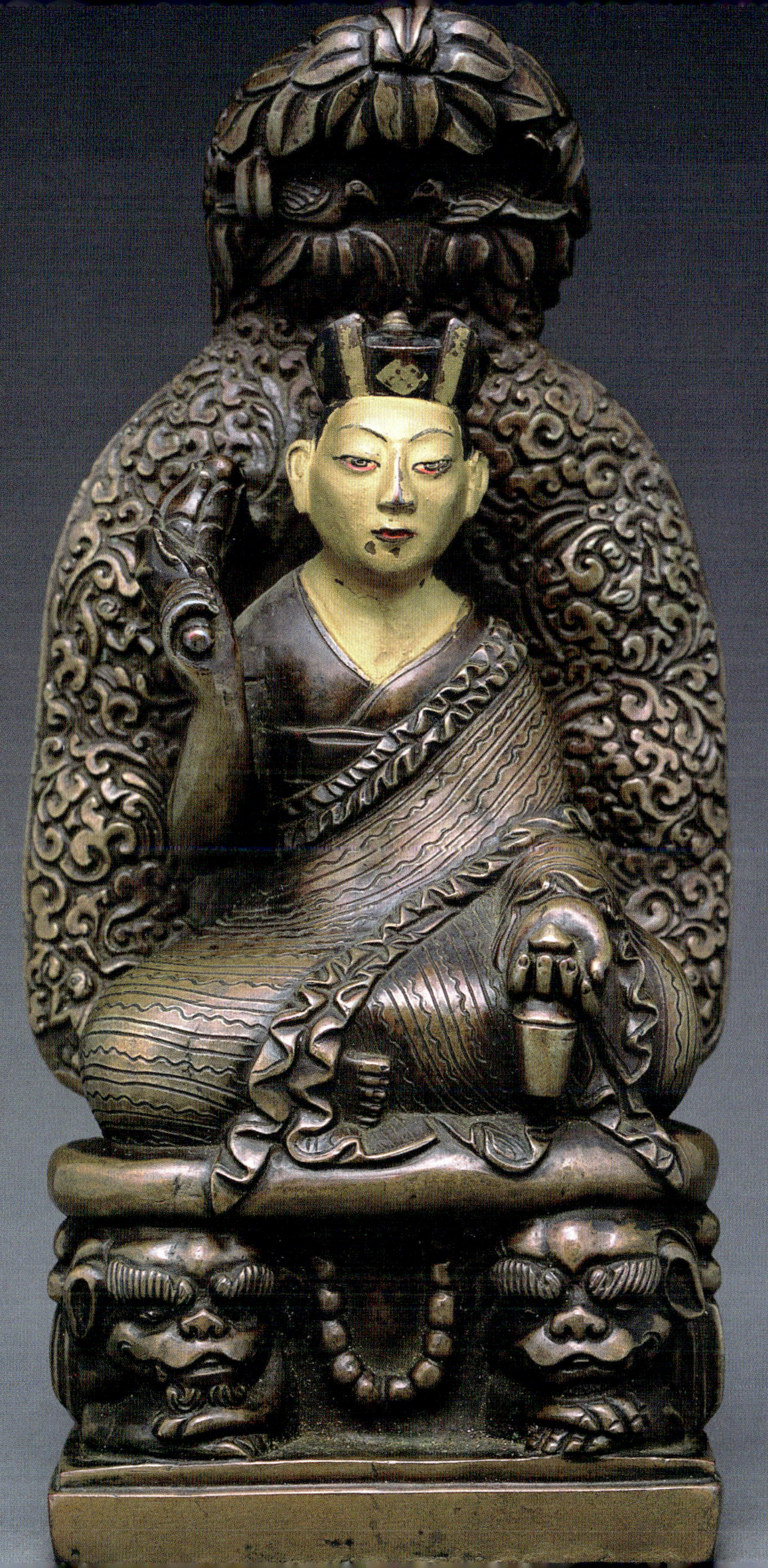

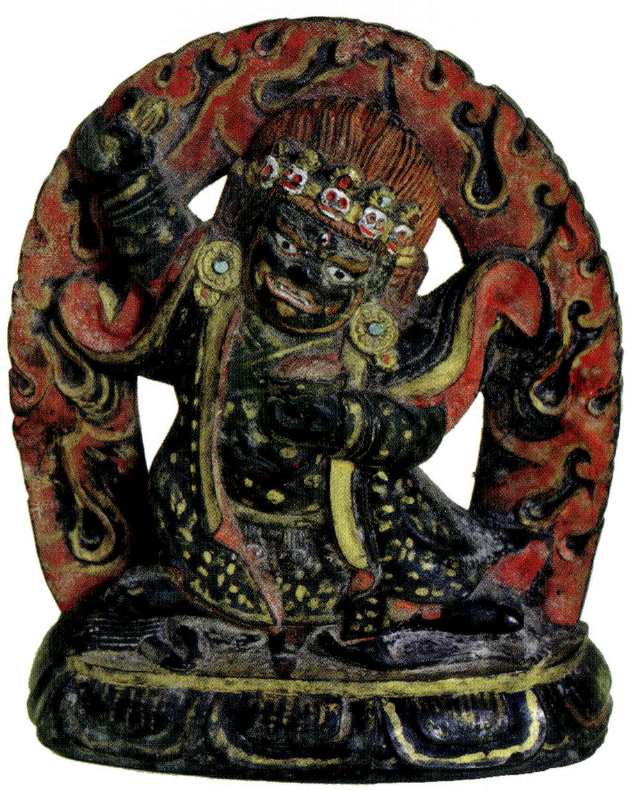

Two-armed Mahakala.
Believed to be carved by the Tenth Karmapa Choying Dorje.
Stone with pigment.
2¼ x 2 x ¾ in. (5.5 x 5 x 2 cm).
Collection of Shamar Rinpoche.
Photograph by Robert Peavy.

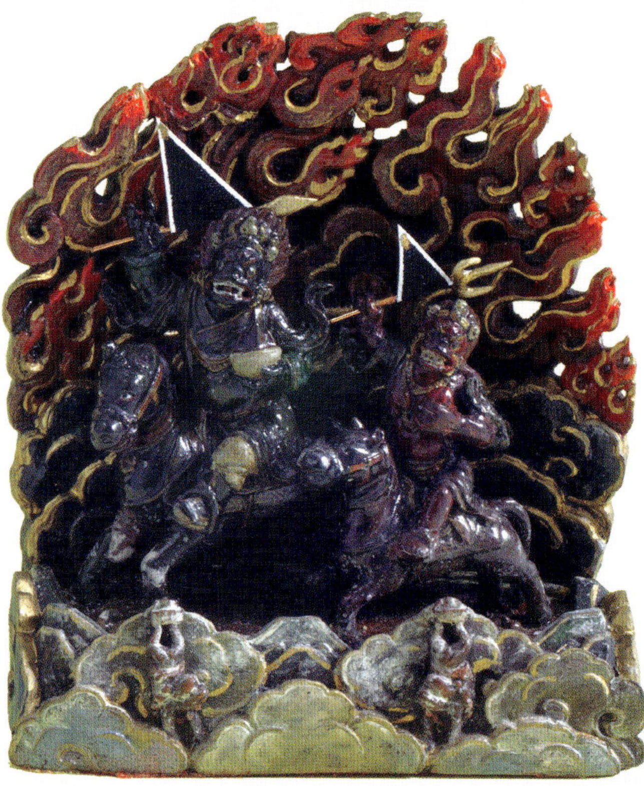

Shinjong.
Believed to be carved by the Tenth Karmapa Choying Dorje.
Stone and wood.
3 3/8 x 2 7/8 x 1 3/8 in. (8.75 x 7.25 x 3.5 cm).
Collection of Shamar Rinpoche.
Photograph by Robert Peavy.

This sculpture depicts Shinjong and his consort Dzakadza (to right in red). This sculpture and the two-armed Mahakala belonged to the Sixteenth Kamarpa who gave them to me (Shamar Rinpoche). They were brought from the Tsurphu Monastery.

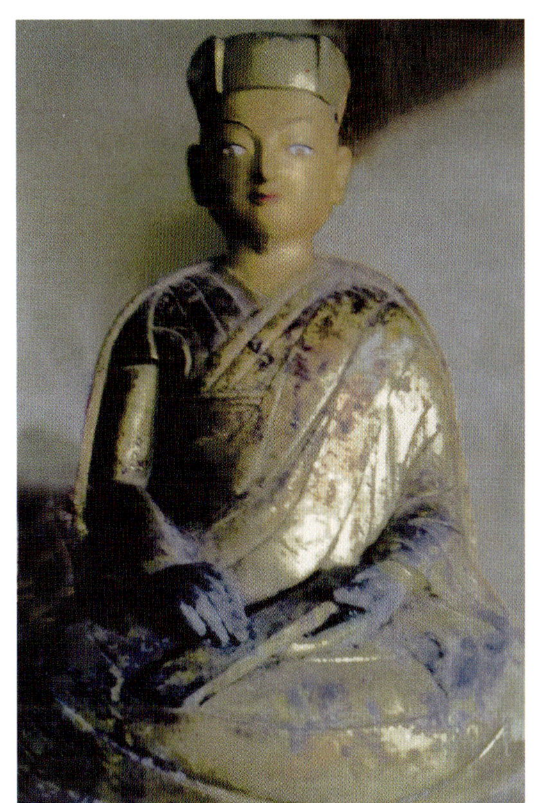

Sculpture of Tenth Karmapa.
Believed to be by the Tenth Karmapa Choying Dorje.
Bronze with pigments.
Dimensions unknown.

This statue of the Tenth Karmapa, reputedly by him, shows his long hair. In his autobiography, the Fifth Dalai Lama described the Tenth Karmapa and specifically mentioned this distinguishing feature of the Karmapa's appearance. In 2011 an antiquities dealer in Kathmandu, Nepal showed me (Shamar Rinpoche) this statue made out bronze and gave me the two pictures shown here. I believe that the sculpture may be from the Tsurphu Monastery in Tibet.

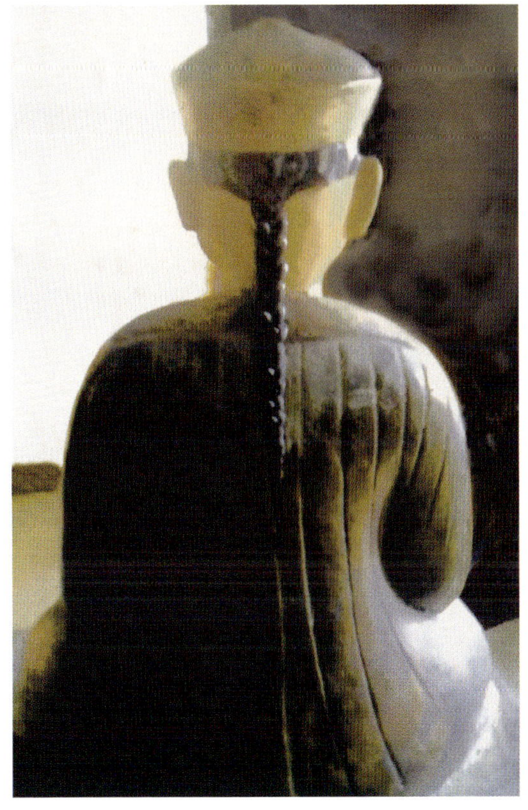

Green Tara.
Attributed to the Tenth Karmapa Choying Dorje.
Tibet; 17th century.
Brass with pigments.
7 7/8 in.
Rubin Museum of Art C2005.16.3 (HAR 65425).
Photograph courtesy of Rubin Museum.

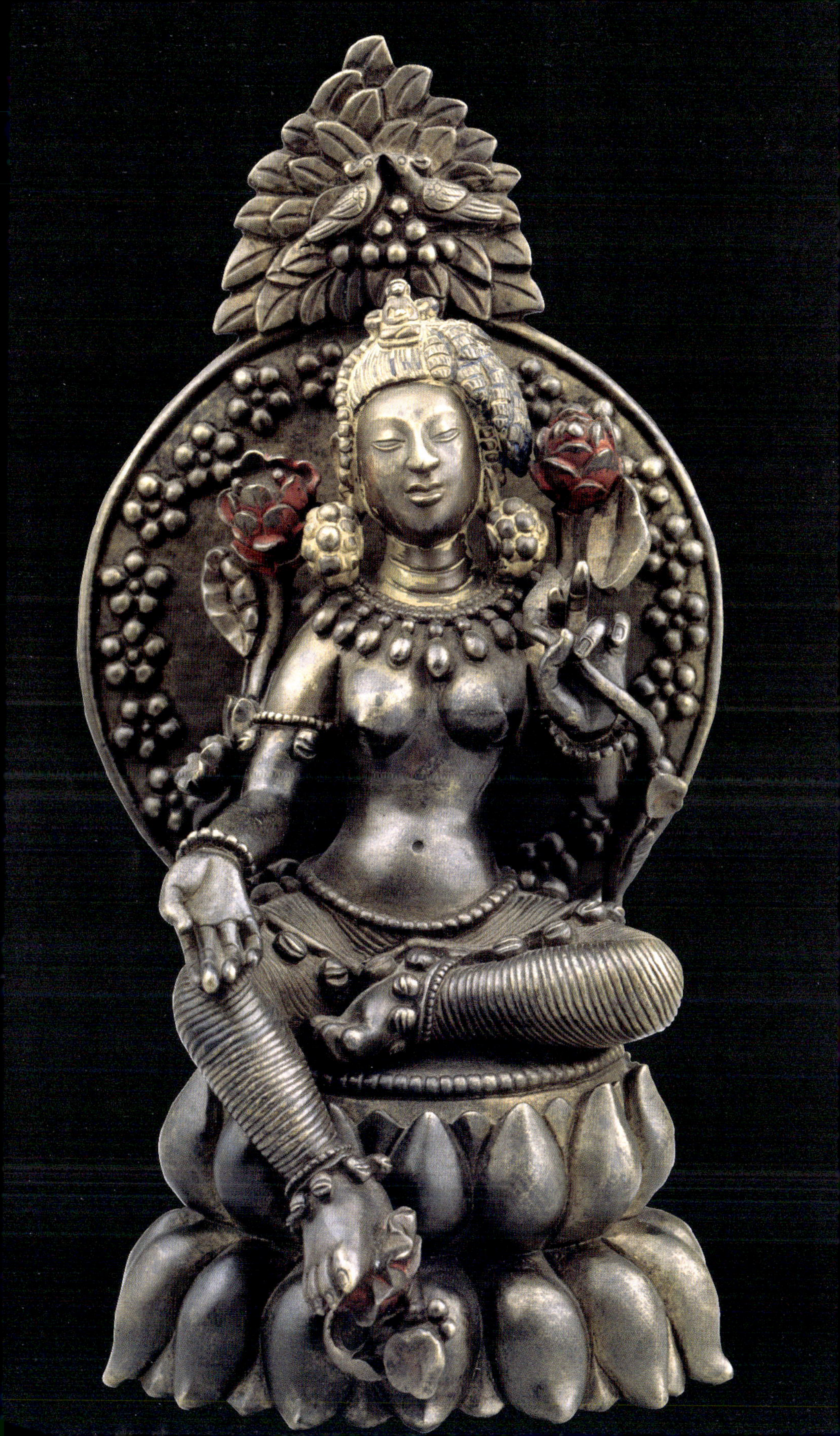

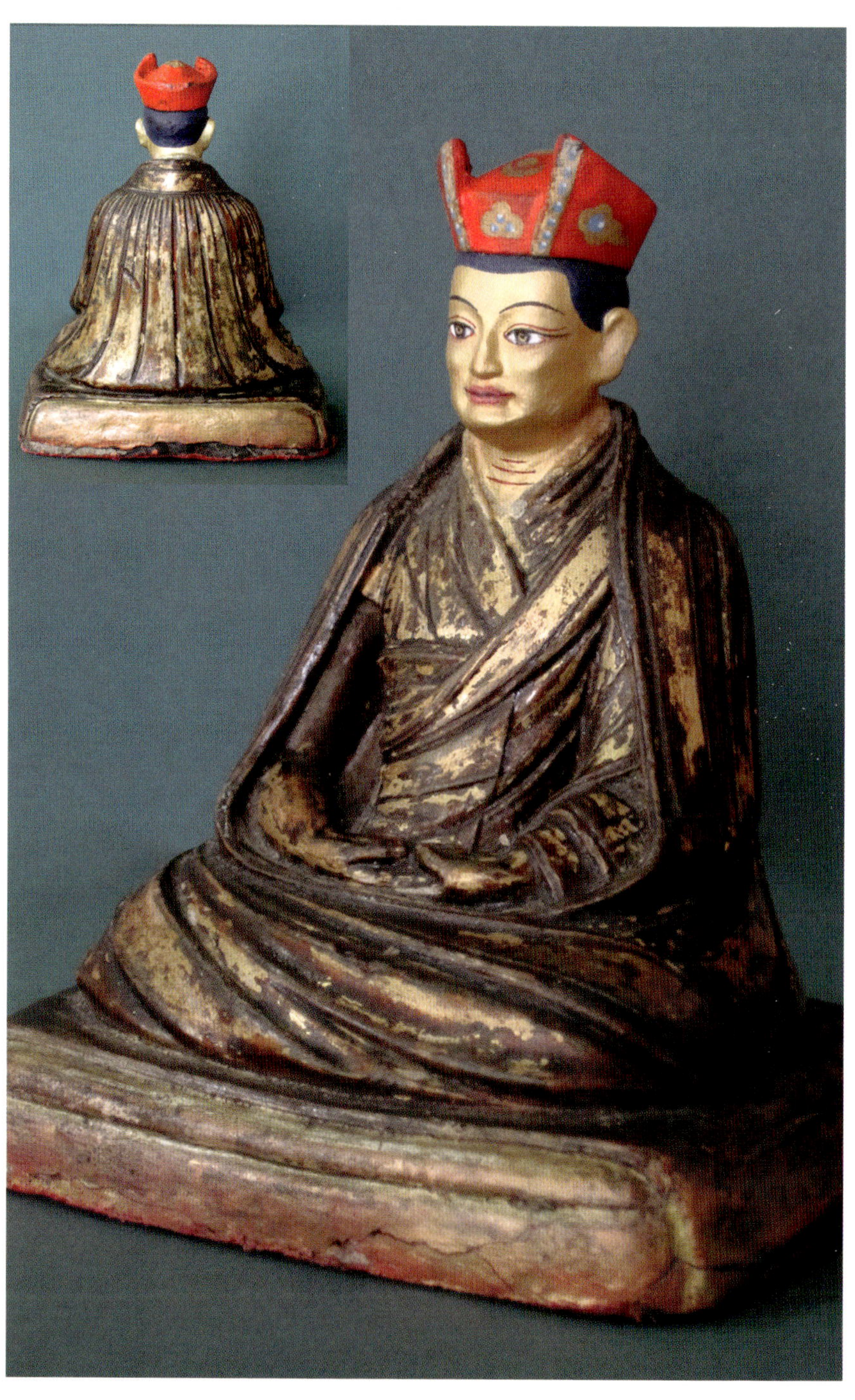

Sculpture of the Sixth Shamarpa.
Attributed to Tenth Karmapa Choying Dorje.
Wood with pigment.
4½ x 3¾ x 2¾ in. (11.5 x 9.5 x 7 cm).
Collection of Shamar Rinpoche.
Photographs by Carol Gerhardt.

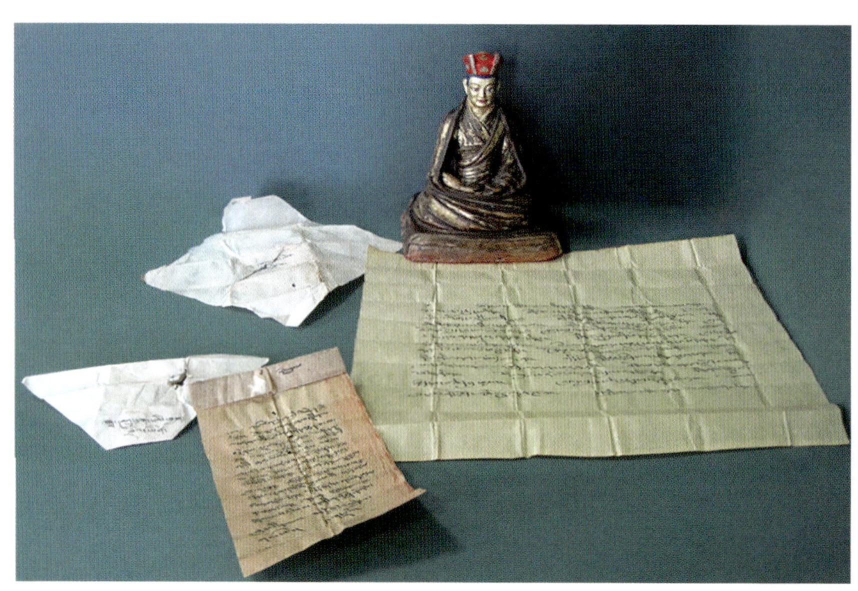

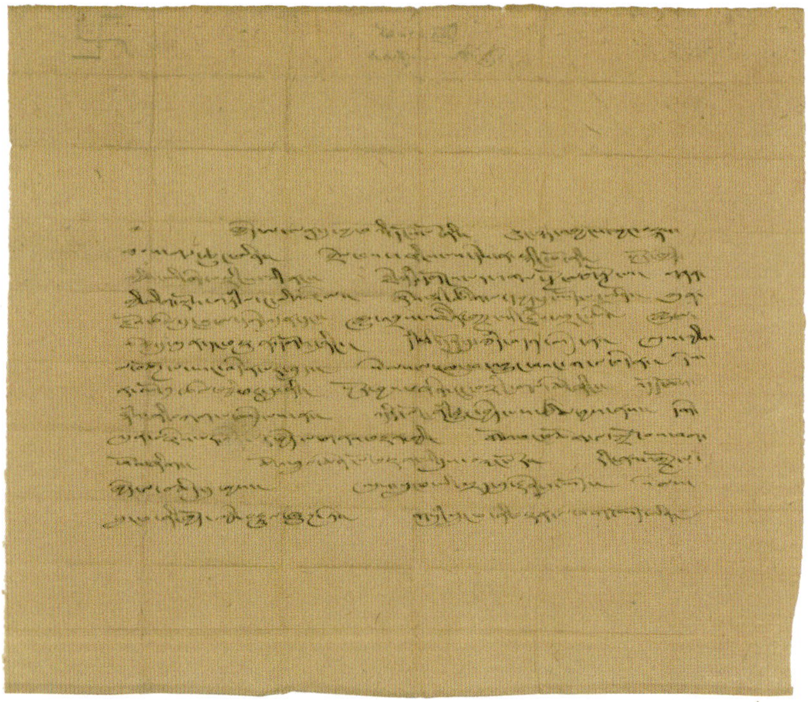

Approximately 35 years ago, the late Sabchu Rinpoche, whom the 16th Karmapa appointed as abbot of the Shree Karma Raj Mahavihar Temple situated in the northeast corner of the Swayambhu stupa complex in Kathmandu, Nepal, discovered this statue of the Sixth Shamarpa in a niche along a temple wall. In 1968, the Nepalese government turned the temple over to the Sixteenth Karmapa after he had demonstrated that it belonged to the Karma Kagyu sect based on the history of the Sixth Shamarpa.

When Sabchu Rinpoche removed the statue (Figure 11) from its centuries-old resting place, he examined its back and noticed a tiny slit at the base (see Figure 11.1). Upon examining the opening, he found two letters tightly folded into small rectangles. He returned the documents to the statue and sealed the opening with clay.

After the Sixteenth Karmapa asked me to oversee the temple in 1979, I took particular interest in the statue. It is practically an exact duplicate of a statue I saw in the Rumtek Monastery in Sikkim. The 16th Karmapa brought this carved statue to Rumtek with him from the Tsurphu Monastery in Tibet. It is slightly larger than the sculpture in the Shree Karma Raj Mahavihar Temple and is widely accepted as the Tenth Karmapa's creation. Therefore, I assume that the Tenth Karmapa also sculpted the statue of his guru found in the Shree Karma Raj Mahavihar Temple.

In early 2012, I opened the slit in the back of the statue and removed the two tightly folded letters with a pair of tweezers. Each letter was wrapped in a thin outer sheet that served as an envelope addressed to Karma Leg Drub, whom the Sixth Shamarpa had appointed as Rab Jampa (secretary) of the Shree Karma Raj Mahavihar Temple (for the contents of the statue, see Figure 11.2). Both envelopes had a note stating that the Sixth Shamarpa had written the letters in his hand. Neither letter gives the year when they were written. It is probable that Karma Leg Drug put the letters in the statue, which must have been his.

It is the practice to consecrate Buddhist statues by placing holy objects inside them. In addition to the letters, other objects were visible in the Sixth Shamarpa's statue, but I did not touch them. Because the letters belonged to Karma Leg Drug, I believe that the statue also was his and that he inserted the letters as a measure of devotion to the Sixth Shamarpa.

One letter concerns a routine business matter, but the other is more interesting (see Figure 11.3). In that letter composed in verse but translated below as prose, the Sixth Shamarpa tries to persuade the Rab Jampa not to resign.

> I am replying to you now. My delay in responding is not because I am ignoring you but because I have been busy.
>
> In the letter you wrote me last year, you mentioned that you cared only for my interests and that you did not mind what people say or think about you. But you should reconsider these points. In the absolute, everything is non-existent, but the logic of non-existence is not relevant when you work for society including lamas, monks and lay people. Therefore, don't ask to resign. Be patient and continue to work one more year.
>
> Worldly life has no meaning or end. Therefore, you do not need to reach any goal. Be satisfied with the passing of time. The real enjoyment in life is to achieve enlightenment.
>
> Looking after your health is important. Taking care of your mind requires practice. To protect "the three" (i.e., Buddha, Dharma, and Sangha) is necessary for Buddhism.
>
> I am writing to you as a long-time friend on the day of Buddha's demonstration of miracles (fourth day, sixth month of the lunar calendar).

Part III: Biography of the Tenth Karmapa Choying Dorje

Note to the Reader

This biography is a compilation of Tibetan sources translated into English and stitched together in chronological order. There are two major sources. The first is the Tenth Karmapa's biography of his guru, the Sixth Shamarpa, titled in English *The Bountiful Cow: Biography of a Bodhisattva*. Interwoven into the biography are extensive autobiographical passages that the Karmapa wrote about his own life up until the death of his guru in 1630, the point at which the book concludes.

At many points in *The Bountiful Cow*, the Karmapa includes his poetry and long flowery passages that do not convey factual information about the life of either the Shamarpa or the Karmapa. Consequently, these sections are not included in the present work.

In *The Bountiful Cow*, Karmapa refers to people by their full name and seldom uses pronouns. In some places he refers to himself in the first person and at other times by the name Jigten Wangchuk. With a few exceptions, this translation does not follow his practice but instead uses pronouns, which are more natural to readers of English. At various points, Karmapa also directly addresses someone as Rimdrowa. Literally meaning "attendant," Rimdrowa actually is Kuntu Zangpo, his disciple and attendant with whom he enjoyed a warm personal relationship.

The second source is the biography of the Tenth Karmapa written in the 18th century, less than one hundred years after the Karmapa's death, by the scholar Bey Lotsawa. This biography is part of the book *The Garland of Omnipresent Wishfulfilling Crystal Gems* co-authored with the Eighth Situ (1700–1774). Almost translated in its entirety (minor omissions are noted in the footnotes), Bey Lotsawa's biography is broken up into sequential parts.

A few other original sources are translated and incorporated into this biography. Most notable is the Fifth Dalai Lama's autobiography and diary.

For readers' convenience, the translations are organized into chapters, and some chapters are divided into subheadings. These do not appear in the original Tibetan sources.

To help the reader readily identify which of the two major sources is translated, a notation appears at the beginning of the passage. "10th Karmapa" indicates text from the Karmapa's *The Bountiful Cow,* while "BL" identifies text from Bey Lotsawa, and "DL" marks passages from the autobiography of the Fifth Dalai Lama. After chapter 26 that describes the death of the Sixth Shamarpa (the point when the Karmapa stopped writing *The Bountiful Cow*) and through the remainder of the book, all but a few passages are from BL. They are not identified; only translations from another source are marked.

In their works, the Karmapa and Bey Lotsawa occasionally interject their own observations or comments. These are clearly identified as such.

Each translated passage is explicitly referenced to the original Tibetan text. Footnotes giving page references appear at the beginning of a translation and usually each time a new page starts. When a section of a text is not translated, this is indicated in a footnote, and the general content of the omitted pages is explained.

Throughout the entire biography, readers will find copious notes to explain the texts. These occur in footnotes as well as within parenthetical remarks contained in the translation. Further, some passages are introduced with a comment or headnote that is set in italics so that readers can clearly identify it.

9. Birth

BL

Regarding[72] the Tenth Karmapa Choying Dorje, when the former Karmapa Wangchuk Dorje (the Ninth Karmapa) was ill, he was staying at Sung Rab Ling Monastery. He gave written instructions to Garwang Thamchad Khyenpa (the Sixth Shamarpa) with details about his next life – where he would be next born.

The birthplace would be one of the eighteen different provinces in Do Kham (a region in eastern Tibet) – Mar Rol (which is nowadays Golok). In that province, a family descended from the caste of Dhitsha lived in an area called Kamzi Thang.

The father's name was Khyikuthar. The mother's name was Atso. They had three sons. The eldest was Namkha. The middle was Abum. The youngest was the Tenth Karmapa.

The Tenth Karmapa was born on the twenty-eighth day of the third month in the year of the Wooden Dragon (1604). His mother gave birth to him peacefully at sunrise without pain.

When Atso was pregnant with Karmapa Choying Dorje, she

72 *BL*: 161a

dreamed that the effulgent body of Guru Padmasambhava[73] descended into her. On another night, she dreamed that a friend gave her a white conch shell, and she blew it like a horn. The sound was so loud that it reached everywhere. Atso thought to herself, "I am a woman. I should not be doing this. People will laugh at me." She immediately tucked the shell into the pocket of her garment. Later, she named the baby Ogyen Kyab (which means one who is protected by Guru Padmasambhava).

As[74] to the father, he dreamed that he donned a spotless white garment and crystal armor.

As soon as the Tenth Karmapa was born, the infant sat on his buttocks. He also tried to walk a few steps in each direction. Then he recited the *Six-syllable Avalokiteshvara* mantra[75] and the mantra of the *Diamond Sutra.*[76]

10th Karmapa

> *In answer to a request from his friend and attendant Kuntu Zangpo, the Tenth Karmapa recounts how the Sixth Shamarpa began to look for him and discover where he had been reborn. And so begins* The Bountiful Cow: Biography of a Bodhisattva *by the Tenth Karmapa. In the following passage, he refers to his teacher, the Sixth Shamarpa, as Bodhisattva Chokyi Wangchuk. Both the Ninth Karmapa and his disciple, the Sixth Shamarpa, have the same name "Chokyi Wangchuk."*

Bodhisattva[77] Chokyi Wangchuk (Sixth Shamarpa), who was enthroned by the sangha (community), succeeded as the regent of Bodhisattva Mipham Chokyi Wangchuk (Ninth Karmapa). He start-

73 Also known as Guru Rinpoche, the Lotus-born One from the Land of Ogyen. He was and still is revered as one of Tibet's greatest saints.

74 *BL*: 161b

75 A mantra is a set of sounds or syllables for recitation, which embodies the nature of a meditational deity. The six-syllable mantra of Avalokiteshvara (or Chenrezig), the deity of love and compassion, is: *om mani padme hung.*

76 The sutra's name in Tibetan is *rdo rje gchod pa*. The mantra in Sanskrit is *om gate gate paragate parasamgate bodhi svaha.*

77 *KAC*: 18

ed to think, "All right, a bodhisattva usually continues to help sentient beings rather than seek his own liberation. I should therefore find out if he is in a different world,[78] or whether he has been reborn in this world again. I have to check. However, this is not a suitable place[79] because it is filled with distractions. I must go to the same place that Bodhisattva Karmapa used for his retreat near Tsari Tso Kor (a lake in southeast Tibet)." Bodhisattva Chokyi Wangchuk thus went and stayed there.

While he was there, Bodhisattva Chokyi Wangchuk experienced two conditions that enabled him to achieve complete contemplation (or meditation). First, he was free from all regular noises that could distract a mind in contemplation. Second, he was free from the sight of any human, which could also be a distraction in either a good or bad way. Therefore, his mind was free from both speech and sight. Both these conditions served his contemplation well, and he experienced limitless joy of mind. He also composed many poems praising the optimal conditions for contemplation.[80]

At[81] the same time, Bodhisattva Chokyi Wangchuk could not stop thinking about Bodhisattva Mipham Chokyi Wangchuk (the Ninth Karmapa) who had passed away. From his devotion, tears streamed down his face uncontrollably.

In a dream of his luminous mind, Bodhisattva Chokyi Wangchuk suddenly saw that Bodhisattva Karmapa, who had died, had appeared again in this world – in a region to the east. At the same time, he saw an obstacle caused by karma. He saw that Bodhisattva Karmapa would have to travel in many tribal areas – like a boat carried by the waves and tossed here and there. Yet the boat would remain under the control of its navigator-captain.[82]

When Bodhisattva Chokyi Wangchuk woke from his luminous

78 This means a world different from ours, as in another planet or universe.

79 This means the place where Shamarpa was staying, which was not specified.

80 *KAC*: 19. Poems have not been translated.

81 *KAC*: 21

82 The reference to the captain's ability to maintain control of the boat meant that Karmapa would still be able to perform the activities of a bodhisattva despite the obstacles, which proved to be Chagmo Lama and the Yangris discussed in a later chapter.

dream,[83] he was exceptionally happy. He made the necessary preparations to go to the district of Mar (nowadays Golok) in the east, to pay respects to Bodhisattva Karmapa who had recently been born there. Some devotees of Bodhisattva Chokyi Wangchuk knew of his vision.

From among his close disciples, Bodhisattva Chokyi Wangchuk chose one who was devoted, intelligent, and trustworthy to be his messenger. His name was Ngonga. He bid Ngonga to go to the area secretly to meet the baby. He told him to prostrate to the baby and to say, "How are you? Are you doing well?" Ngonga should tell the family to take good care of the baby and to feed him well. He should also let the family know that the Sixth Shamarpa would come in the near future to see them.

Ngonga said he would do as instructed.

The messenger arrived at my house (here the Karmapa starts to write about himself in the first person). He told me that Bodhisattva Chokyi Wangchuk wanted to say to me, "How are you? I will come in the near future to see you." The moment I heard these words uttered from his mouth, I was overjoyed.

Though[84] I was just a baby, I talked and played with this messenger for many days. We passed the time very happily.

10th Karmapa

> On another occasion when Kuntu Zangpo asked Karmapa to tell of his own rebirth, the Tenth Karmapa writes:

When I, Jigten Wangchuk,[85] was staying and doing meditation in a remote forest near River Ngulchu, where white birds sang, my attendant Kuntu Zangpo made a request. He asked me to tell the

---

83 In Buddhist practice, someone who has a "luminous dream" is able to be aware of his dream while he is dreaming.

84 *KAC*: 22

85 The Tenth Karmapa refers to himself as Jigten Wangchuk in *KAC*. Jigten is one of the names of Chenrezig, the Bodhisattva of Love and Compassion.

details about my birth. Then[86] I told him.

In this *Dzambhudib*[87] continent, there are many different subcontinents divided by rivers such as River Ganga, River Yamuna, and River Narpat Singdhu, all flowing into India. River Tachog Cabab (Horse Mouth River) runs through central Tibet into India. The rivers Drichu, Machu, Dawai Chulung, and Gyalmo Ngulchu run through Dokham (east Tibet) into China.

In the district of Mar on one of the subcontinents divided by these rivers, in a highland, lived a rich householder whose name was Khyiku. He was very devoted to the Buddha, Dharma, and Sangha. He married the daughter of another family in the same caste. They had two sons and five daughters.[88]

Khyiku's wife was also very religious. She used to do the *Eight-branch Nyungney*[89] from time to time. One day, she had a dream. One of her girlfriends, Neudong, gave her a white conch shell. She took it and blew on it. The sound went everywhere. She thought, "The whole village can hear it!" She was scared and put the shell inside the pocket of her garment.

Later, she became pregnant (with the Tenth Karmapa). In a dream, she heard the recitation *"Om mani padme hung"* from her womb. From then on, she took good care of her health. One day close to the delivery, a big wind blew away all the branches and dust on the ground. The ground was completely swept clean. Then one morning when the sun had fully risen, the cows were milked and the milk-pots were full, my mother gave birth to me.

Immediately, I baby[90] sat up and smiled to the family. At that time, my father was not home. When he came home, he was so happy that he celebrated my birth. My parents started to think of a name for me. My mother named me Ogyen Khyab.

---

86 *KAC*: 23

87 *Dzambhudib* is a Sanskrit word that means "this world." Later, it came to represent the Asian continent, as is the case here.

88 Bey Lotsawa's account makes no mention of five daughters.

89 A Chenrezig practice.

90 "I baby" is a literal translation that means "I, who was a baby."

10. Early Childhood

BL

One[91] year after the baby Karmapa was born, his mother wished for them to take an empowerment[92] from a lama of the Jonang sect. The baby tulku[93] refused to take it. Another lama named Khyithul Garab Dorje was regarded as an emanation of Guru Padmasambhava. The baby said of him, "He is not Khyithul Garab Dorje. He is Rangjung Garab Dorje."[94] The baby tulku prostrated to the lama and agreed to receive empowerment from him.

In his early childhood, Karmapa spent time practicing the art of painting. He also liked to collect threads of different colors and practice making the designs for embroidered cloth or brocade.[95] Unlike his friend Tulku Phendhe who was quite an accomplished painter, the Ninth Karmapa was not very talented as a painter.

---

91 *BL*: 161b

92 Sanskrit: *abhisheka*; or English: initiation.

93 An incarnate lama.

94 Khyithul is a common name for a pet dog. The Tenth Karmapa likely thought it disrespectful to call a qualified lama by this name. Instead, he chose Rangjung which means spontaneous, denoting a high spiritual achievement. Garab Dorje means a happy *vajra*. Thus, Rangjung Garab Dorje means a spontaneously happy *vajra*. *Vajra* means diamond, which has an indestructible quality.

95 These fabrics are used to frame Tibetan paintings known as thangkas.

Once, when Phendhe made fun of the Ninth Karmapa's artwork, the latter retorted, "In the future, I shall make you ashamed."[96] Perhaps this was why the very young tenth incarnate took to practicing art so early in his life.

One day, the baby Karmapa's elder brother, Tashi,[97] carried him on his back. On that occasion, the baby handed some reeds[98] to his brother and said, "I am Karmapa. You should play the trumpets to properly receive me." Tashi took his baby brother to a ruin near their home called Chagri Ngonpo[99] which was regarded as a holy place – where a famous yogi, Domtsha Yeshe Drag, used to stay. People claimed that they could sometimes hear ceremonial music and smell perfume from there. The baby Karmapa circumambulated that place three times to pay respect.

In general, the very young Karmapa was very compassionate. For instance, one day, he saw people shearing sheep. "Don't give suffering to the animals!" he called out, wanting them to stop, but he was ignored. Crying, he spontaneously recited these words:

> One who has a kind mind towards animals
> is a noble person and a close friend to others.
> I am one who sees the animals in groups everywhere.
> They touch me deeply, and I love them.

10th Karmapa

Of this same incident, the Tenth Karmapa writes:

---

96 This means that in the future, Karmapa would become such a good painter that Phendhe would feel embarrassed in comparison.

97 His brother's full name is Namkha Tashi.

98 The Karmapa means his brother should blow the reeds like Tibetan trumpets called *rgya-ling*.

99 The name means "blue iron fence."

Another[100] day, when I was playing with other kids, I saw some people cutting the wool off of sheep. I baby said to them, "Please don't do that which harms. You should not make them naked. Don't you have any compassion for them?"

When they did not stop, I cried. Then, they stopped.

Whenever I went out and saw animals, I would say that they were my animals and that I have to take care of them always.

I was like that when I was a baby.

* * *

BL

On[101] another day, the baby Karmapa and his father were riding together on a horse. Sitting in front and secured in his father's arms, the baby cried, "Give me the reins and the whip!" The father did so. When the baby took them, he readily exclaimed in verse:

> The horse (on its own) moves wildly everywhere.
> If it is steered again and again by force (by will),
> one can change (its course) and lead it to town.
> As it is, I forcefully steer all sentient beings
> to the town of liberation.

Once while the baby bathed in a stream, he sang this jingle:

> The water here is to purify the body.
> But to purify the mind, the Dharma is the water.

Generally[102] at mealtimes, the baby Karmapa would hold a *mala* (prayer beads) and recite the *Six-syllable Avalokiteshvara* mantra.

One day, a monk called Thogmed who was the attendant of the previous Karmapa (the Ninth) came to visit the baby tulku. His nickname was Butsha Chatho. Thogmed was the name given to him when he became a monk. The baby immediately turned to his

100 *KAC*: 26
101 *BL*: 161b
102 *BL*: 162a

parents saying that the guest was Thogmed but also Chatho.[103]

Soon rumors about this amazing baby spread everywhere. Everyone thought that he was the new Karmapa reborn in Golok.

> [*Bey Lotsawa comments*]: Earlier, when the Fifth Shamarpa Konchok Yenlak was visiting the neighborhood of the Tenth Karmapa's mother who was much younger then, she stood in a line to pay her respects. When the Fifth Shamarpa came to her, instead of blessing her by touching her head with the ceremonial jar, he touched her head with both hands showing respect. He understood that this woman would become the mother of the future Karmapa. This incident became public knowledge. These early events in the life of the Tenth Karmapa, from his birth up until this point, are clearly recorded in his own autobiography.[104]

103 This means that the Karmapa recognized him.

104 By "autobiography," Bey Lotsawa means *The Bountiful Cow: Biography of a Bodhisattva* that contains autobiographical accounts of the Tenth Karmapa.

11. Custody Imposed

BL

> In the following passage, Bey Lotsawa describes a village chieftain in Chagmo known as Chagmo Lama who set out to bring the baby Tenth Karmapa under his control.

In[105] the area of Chagmo, the local chieftain, Chagmo Goshri, was called Chagmo Lama.[106] He and his nephew were greedy people. When they heard the news about the exceptional baby, they saw a lucrative opportunity in him. Immediately they plotted to gain control of him. The Chagmo family – the uncle and nephew – by their crafty and ambitious minds, sent a spy to (the district of) Golok (where the Tenth Karmapa's family lived). The feedback proved positive. The baby was, indeed, the true Karmapa reincarnation.

The Chagmo family bribed Pema Sengey, the local chief of Golok. They offered him a lot of wealth and asked him to give up

---

105 *BL*: 162a.

106 Chagmo Goshri was not a lama but a chieftain. People called him "lama" as a sign of respect.

the child Karmapa and his entire family to them (the Chagmos).[107] At the same time, ample gifts were also given to Karmapa's parents to win their favor. By these means, Chagmo Lama craftily procured release of the family from their chief. Later, the Chagmos would cajole them into joining their own family so that the two families appeared as one.[108] In essence, he had gained control of Karmapa and his family. From then on, he took them everywhere to solicit offerings, introducing the boy Karmapa to many people with one motive in mind – gathering wealth for himself.

> [*Bey Lotsawa comments*]: If you don't show the tail of the deer, you cannot sell donkey meat.[109]

The child Karmapa was taken to Yugur, a place of dual languages.[110] While he was there, he built a little stone house. The child was told that the stones belonged to Yugur Choyang who would get angry with Karmapa's parents if he found out that his stones were taken. The child replied, "He will not own these stones for long. Now I take over the earth and stones of Yugur Choyang." Not long after, Yugur Choyang passed away. The child Karmapa knew beforehand that the person was going to die.

When Karmapa was five, Chagmo Lama took him to the Machu River area. They stayed there for a while in order to collect offerings. The boy Karmapa received a lot of offerings from six Mongolian settlements there.[111] Among them, the Mongolian chief Thumed from Yong Shol Phu and his entourage went to pay their respects to Karmapa, bearing many offerings and gifts, and to receive his blessings. Magya Pomra, the mountain deity in that area,

---

107 In those days in Tibet, people were like serfs bound to the land. They lived in designated land-districts governed by chieftains and could not move between districts without permission. The Tenth Karmapa's family belonged to the chieftain of a village in Golok.

108 Chagmo Lama arranged for his family and Karmapa's family to live and travel together. Whenever they were on the road, they would camp together as one big encampment called a *garchen.*

109 Chagmo Lama was compared to donkey meat, which nobody wanted, while the Tenth Karmapa was the deer. This means that people would not give offerings to Chagmo Lama unless they could see the Tenth Karmapa.

110 The people in Yugur spoke Tibetan and Chinese.

111 *BL*: 162b. That area is very close to Inner Mongolia.

appeared as a white man riding a white horse and holding a white banner. Many gods and their attendants accompanied him. All of them appeared to receive Karmapa. The sky was filled with rainbows, and there were showers of flowers. Many wild deer also came out to follow Karmapa's party. These were a few of many wonderful signs.

Afterwards, they proceeded to Chagmo Lhunpotser (the residence of Chagmo Lama).

> [*Bey Lotsawa comments*]: In the autobiography of the Tenth Karmapa, he remarked, "My home was left behind like an abandoned bird's nest."

* * *

10th Karmapa

Here, the Tenth Karmapa describes in detail how Chagmo Lama and his cohorts schemed to acquire control of him and his family. In this passage, Karmapa uses the third person to narrate events prior to the time when Chagmo Lama's representative contacts his family, at which point he switches to the first person.

At[112] that time, the people in Moon River (poetic reference to Machu River) area caught news that a wonderful boy had been born to a family in Mar. In a meeting with his officials, the Chieftain (Chagmo Lama) said:

"In the past, a bodhisattva was born here in Moon River. We took charge of him at that time. It turned out quite profitable for us. Now this boy in Mar may or may not be a bodhisattva. But so long as people respect him as a special boy, and he belongs to us, then we can again make a big profit."

> [*The Tenth Karmapa comments*]: There is nothing humans won't do to collect wealth. To increase wealth, you must invest wealth, like the joining of streams over rocks into one river. Such was the thinking of this chieftain and his officials.

---

112 *KAC*: 28. Page 27 has been omitted, as the content is the same as described in *BL*. As well, poetic descriptions from pages 28–35 have been omitted.

"Does anyone have a good suggestion as to how to get the baby?" asked the Chieftain during the meeting.

"First, to get a boy of another region, you have to get permission from his lord. To get that permission, you have to give him gifts," said a crafty official.

[*The Tenth Karmapa comments*]: Irrespective of their language, customs, or habitat, all people reach for wealth as fish do for food in the water. In their love of wealth, they are all the same. There is not one human in samsara who would turn away from wealth.

"You are right, but we should give a small gift first. Then, we can give more depending on his readiness to cooperate with us," the Chieftain cautioned.

Then the cunning man, his eyes shifting to the side, said: "If we want to buy him, a small gift will bring the opposite result. He'll think it an insult, and we won't even stand a chance to talk to him. So we must give a big gift from the start. If you're worried about wasting your gifts and offerings, then don't bother. Just be satisfied with what you have now."

In the end, the man's craftiness got himself chosen as the Chieftain's envoy, and he went to Mar with a big gift.

In Mar, a shepherd pointed in the direction of Khyikuthar's (Karmapa's father) home, and the deceitful man came.

He would come to our house only from time to time.[113] He chatted comfortably with my father, but with me, he was always quiet, or he said very little. Whenever he was offered a drink (of alcohol), he would say, "I can't. I'm tired out from my journey, and I've got a headache."

He knew he had to be careful and to deflect attention away from his true motive for being there. To avert suspicion of him, he put up a false front. When he first arrived, he deliberately went to the home of another boy called Kigpa. He made it obvious to everyone that he respected that boy.

Then he went to the Chieftain of Mar called Pema Sengey. On

113 Karmapa switches to first person narration from this point on.

his first visit, he wanted to introduce himself and to find out what he was like.

The Chieftain (Pema Sengey) asked him, "Why have you come?"

"I'm just going here and there on business, and my business is profitable. My lord in Moon River has heard a lot about you, and he'd like to be your friend."

In this first meeting, much to the delight of his visitor, the Mar chieftain turned out to be a very vain man. The ever humble and grateful guest showered the host with compliments and was treated very well in return.

When the guest was about to leave, the Chieftain asked him, "When will you come again? You should come tomorrow."

"Oh, I'm just staying around here trying to make some deals. I'll try to come, but I cannot say for sure."

After five days, the man returned with horses loaded up with gifts. People in town were shocked at the overindulgence. They felt certain that the man was after one of their chief's daughters; or that his lord, the Chieftain of Moon River, must need help to fight his enemies.

An old man among Mar's residents was a disciple of the Fifth Shamarpa Konchog Ban. He guessed correctly the visitor's real motive. He told others, "I think he's here for the wonderful boy of the Khyiku family." Everyone thus became leery of the man from Golok.

One day, Lord Sengey of Mar (i.e., the chieftain) asked his friend-visitor, "I've received many gifts now, which I very much appreciate. What can I do for you in return?"

"These[114] gifts are just a token of my sincerity to be your friend. They are not much at all. It is the future of our friendship that is most important. Back home, we have good farmlands, but we are short of laborers. You have many people here; so if you could give us some of your people, we'd be grateful indeed."

"People in my province don't have to pay tax. They are not hardworking. They only know to enjoy what they have. They cannot

114 *KAC*: 35

be good for your lord, and they will not be happy there," said Lord Sengey.

"Whether or not they'd be happy, you'd know later. If not, they can always return here."

"What did your lord actually say? Do you have a letter from him?"

Pretending to search his pockets, the dishonest man explained, "Oh, I must have left it in my room, but I'll bring it tomorrow morning."

That night he wrote a fake letter, and went back the next day.

Chieftain Sengey read the letter, which said, "In my district, I have farms but no workers. You have many workers. If you could sell some of them to me, I shall be grateful. Please accept the gifts. My representative will tell you everything else verbally in person." The letter was marked "from Palace Lhunpotser."

Sengey then said, "Please enjoy your stay here for a few more days, and I shall let you know of my decision."

Lord Sengey of Mar then called together his officials to decide what to do. Their consensus was this: "Whenever we are approached by another district, they usually want something to benefit them. It is seldom for our good. You are our lord, but you should not act in haste. Please grant us some time to analyze the situation properly. We will think it over carefully and discuss it among ourselves. After three days, we shall give you our suggestion, seeing that you have asked us for our advice."

By then, the people of Mar all knew that Bodhisattva Chokyi Wangchuk (the Sixth Shamarpa) had sent a message that he would come to see me. They were happy that in the past Bodhisattva Konchog Ban (the Fifth Shamarpa) had set his lotus feet[115] upon their land. And now, Bodhisattva Chokyi Wangchuk would come again, so everyone thought the whole affair indeed auspicious.

However, the Mar people also knew that their lord had already accepted so many gifts. Something was bound to happen to me. They were worried because I would likely be sold. What would

115 This is a term of respect and honor, often used in reference to one's guru.

happen then? Everybody felt quite concerned.

In the next meeting, the Mar officials together presented their assessment of the situation. "Definitely, they want the Khyiku boy. We heard from an old disciple of Shamarpa that this baby is the reincarnation of the Ninth Karmapa. Therefore, Shamarpa will be here with hundreds of sangha members to enthrone this boy. We can give away another boy but certainly not this one."

"How then should we respond?" asked the lord.

Actually, he had already made up his mind. And his mind was stuck on the gifts, and he wanted more. So he said, "We should make it so that he (Chagmo Lama) will give us gifts continuously. We should say that if Shamarpa recognizes the baby to be Karmapa, then the baby should be returned to us. We will make him promise to return the child in that case. And if he refuses, then this will be our excuse to keep the boy."

Everyone was unhappy with this response but said nothing. Their lord then called the representative from Moon River and gave him that one condition.

Chagmo Lama of Moon River was very happy with the response. As advised by his representative, he sent a written reply in full compliance with the demand. It stated:

"Thank you. The boy and his family will be well taken care of here. If he should be recognized as Karmapa, then how could we keep him? A bodhisattva will be a bodhisattva. We cannot control him. Even if he is not recognized as one, we will still not control him. In other words, if and when the family should desire to return to you, they will be free to do so."

The written reply promised everything Lord of Mar had wanted, and the representative returned to Mar to deliver the letter.

Lord Sengey then contacted my family. At first, we were reluctant to leave, and my family begged him not to force us. He explained the whole thing to us, once again including the condition that we could return at any time. He asked us to move and stay there for some time.

Feeling that we had no choice, the family obeyed the order. We gave away everything – our house and farm – to our relatives.

My[116] parents packed up our things and with my brothers and me, set out for Moon River.

Along[117] the way, we spent one night on the bank of a big lake. Early in the morning, the singing of the ducks woke me, and I wrote this poem.

> Mother, why are we sleeping so late?
> Listen to the ducks like white lotuses in the lake,
> their sounds are like songs.
> The white ducks in the lake
> bloom like white lotuses.
> Their sounds are like the splashes
> made by heavenly maidens with their bracelets
> as they swim in the lake.[118]

Finally,[119] at the end of a long journey, we arrived at Lhunpotser, the palace of the Chieftain of Moon River.

116 *KAC*: 45. Poetic descriptions from KAC: 35–45 have not been translated.

117 *KAC*: 48

118 *KAC*: 49. Many poems were written during the trip to Moon River but have not been translated here.

119 *KAC*: 50

12. Life in Moon River

BL

At[120] Chagmo Lhunpotser, the Chagmos deliberately arranged for the child Karmapa to be by himself in a room on the top floor. Karmapa's parents and his two brothers were given rooms on the bottom floor. The Chagmos themselves occupied the middle level. As a result, they were able to intercept and control all visitors of the child Karmapa. They also kept the offerings without the parents' realization.

Desperate to spend some time with his son, Karmapa's father decided to confront Chagmo Lama about the separation. "How can you do such a thing? We are his parents!" Only then did the Chagmo Lama allow the young boy and his family to spend some time together.

Chagmo Lama was concerned that the Karmapa's family would run away. To entice them to stay, he offered the family some farmland, and a few cows. Karmapa's family was then able to make a new home and settle down in Chagmo.

---

120 *BL*: 162b

* * *

10th Karmapa

The Tenth Karmapa recounts how Chagmo Lama tried to separate him from his family.

"If[121] the baby were to stay with his family, then all the offerings would go to them," (said Chagmo Lama). The Chieftain thus positioned himself between my parents and the people who would come with offerings. He had a habit of lying and was expert at it. He[122] would mislead people and enjoyed it. Manipulative by nature, the Chieftain always managed to get the properties of others.

He said to my family, "It is very good that you have come. My district is known to be rich, but actually it is not.[123] What we have comes by skillful economizing and living within our means. So far, you have not kept your special boy in a particularly clean place. This is why I've decided to let him stay at the top of my palace. The rest of you should move to the village and live as villagers do."

Later,[124] he arranged a home for my parents elsewhere and split up my family.

In general, freedom is happiness.[125]
Certainly, a person who lives in the forest,
having abandoned the burden of samsara,
and survives by begging, is nonetheless happy.
Real unhappiness belongs to one controlled by another
– his freedom in another's hands.
Here I am, kidnapped by this vicious lord,
sleeping at the top of the house

---

121 *KAC*: 50

122 *KAC*: 51

123 Moon River at that time was, indeed, a relatively poor district.

124 *KAC*: 51

125 The very young Karmapa, having been separated from his family, felt sad one day. He wrote a long poem expressing the normal longings of a child his age. This excerpt from that poem can be found on *KAC*: 52–53.

where the wind is blowing.
How can I stay here happily?
Where is my mother now?
Where are my parents now?

During that period, my mother often cried, and my brothers felt sad.[126] In desperation, my father came to the palace and complained. He wanted to go back to Mar.

He said to the Chieftain, "Whatever promises were made by you and your representative, it appears that they are different, so I want to move back."

The Chieftain turned on a nice face and asked us to stay.

My father pressed on, "He is my son. My family has the right to be with him."

The[127] Chieftain relented and allowed my parents to visit me.

One day, the Chieftain said to my parents that they should not live where they were. Instead,[128] he would give my family some land where they should live and farm the land.

My family encountered many difficulties. They were given a farm, yet they had no farm tools like a plough, for instance. When they tried to borrow a plough from their neighbor, they were refused and ridiculed. They barely had any seeds for sowing, and so the crops were meager.

Once, when my parents came to see me, I saw them covered in dirt, having worked in the fields all day long. I was very sad.

I suggested to my family that they should drop the farming. Instead, they should buy some cows and use the butter, milk and yogurt for food. The family discussed this among themselves and agreed. My mother sold her jewelry. With the money, they bought some cows. The whole family then enjoyed having butter, yogurt and milk, and so did I.

I also told my family that they must make offering to the Buddha, Dharma, and Sangha. My advice was accepted. My mother

126 *KAC*: 54. Poems on pages 55–56 are not translated.

127 *KAC*: end of 57. Pages 58–61 (containing poems) are not translated.

128 *KAC*: 62

made butter lamps and offered them from time to time.

One[129] day a beggar came begging for food. My mother gave him some yogurt milk mixed with honey. At that time, I said to her, "Mother, all wealth and luck usually come from acts of generosity. You are now poor, but if you give to others, then the result will be greater. For example, a little seed can grow into a huge tree with thousands of leaves and fruits."

* * *

BL

Later, rumors ran rampant about the son of Phagmo Shalngo in Drigung possibly being the reincarnation of the Ninth Karmapa.[130] Chagmo Lama reacted by dismissing Karmapa's family. Chagmo Lama told the Karmapa's family that they could go anywhere they wanted. He himself left for central Tibet.

At that time, the boy Karmapa warned Chagmo Lama not to go, saying that he would not be able to reach Drigung. But Chagmo Lama ignored this advice. When the Chagmo party reached an area called Dzakhog, heavy snow blocked their road. They had no choice but to turn back. They endured much hardship before finally returning home.

129 *KAC*: 68. Karmapa gave his family many other similar pieces of advice about generosity (not translated here).

130 *BL*: 162b

13. Recognized and Enthroned

BL

In[131] the meantime, Shamar Thamchad Khyenpa (the Sixth Shamarpa) was in retreat near Tsari Tso Kor[132] (in southeast Tibet). He sent his attendant Zimpon Ngonga[133] to quietly visit the Tenth Karmapa with a small group of lamas.

Ngonga was to give the child a piece of paper with the name Choying Dorje written on it. Guru Padmasambhava had used this name in one of his predictions about Karmapa. The messenger was also to offer Karmapa a long life wishing prayer with this name composed and handwritten by the Sixth Shamarpa. In addition, special relics and white cushions decorated with double *dorjes*[134] were to be offered.

While the Chagmos were away en route to Drigung, Zimpon Ngonga and his group arrived and met with the child Karmapa. As a result, people everywhere respected the child as the Tenth Kar-

---

131 *BL*: 162b

132 Tsari was a hidden place situated today in a disputed territory between China and India, on China's side. "Tso Kar" means "White Lake."

133 Zimpon Ngonga was the same messenger who met Karmapa when he was still a baby.

134 A handheld metal implement used in prayer ceremonies.

mapa since the Sixth Shamarpa had recognized him. At the same time, the King of Lijiang also led a delegation to pay respects to Karmapa with many offerings.

> [*Bey Lotsawa comments*]: The Tenth Karmapa wrote poems in his autobiography such as, "If one is abandoned in an unknown place, he is not left there forever," etc.[135]

* * *

10th Karmapa

> The Tenth Karmapa writes of how having been recognized by the Sixth Shamarpa, conditions began to improve for his family.

One day,[136] Bodhisattva Chokyi Wangchuk (the Sixth Shamarpa) sent a messenger, Ngonga, from Tsari Tso Kor with a message for me along with many gifts. I was confirmed as Karmapa Bodhisattva Jigten Wangchuk. I became famous, and the fame spread everywhere.

My parents and brothers were then respected. Moreover, they knew that Bodhisattva Chokyi Wangchuk would soon arrive with the sangha.

People who were unkind to them previously and those who had refused to help them or loan them anything turned very friendly. They were bad people – flattering the rich and powerful, and abusing the lowly in status. On one occasion, my brothers, dressed in fine attire, were together in a gathering with such people.

I said quite sarcastically to my brothers so everyone could hear, "We've been here for a long time now. All of a sudden, here you are dressed in such fine clothes. Tell me, does it all come from the lord who promised us everything?"

My brother retorted, "Oh yes, this lord gave us everything, only in words. Reality was but a tiny plot of land!"

---

135 *BL*: 163a

136 *KAC*: 69

> [*The Tenth Karmapa comments*]: Standing[137] on a table to steal fruit, or asking a thief to keep your money, or relying on a bad lord, are causes of regret, and so forth.

Then later, Chagmo Lama sent a messenger to my parents with this request, "You have a lot of jewels now. Chagmo Lama would like some, too. He'd repay you later."

I told my father to give him some small items. He was, after all, a chieftain and would not need help from us. I[138] also told my father not to accept any payment in return.

137 *KAC*: 73

138 *KAC*: 74–101 not translated.

14. Enthronement and Afterward

BL

When[139] Karmapa was age seven[140] in the year of the Male Iron Dog (1610), in the month of *Go-dha*,[141] Gendun Yangri from central Tibet went to see him.[142] He arranged a big tent to be set up and invited Karmapa. There was also a greedy and pretentious monk, Yangri Trungpa Shagrogpa, who put on a show of elaborate offerings for Karmapa in his tent.

On the fourteenth day of the month of *Gyal-dha* (twelfth month called victory),[143] the Male Iron Dog year, the *garchen*[144] of Gyalwa Sixth Shamarpa and his party of three thousand monks from Nyinched Ling (a famous college established by the Sixth Shamarpa in Zatham in central Tibet) and the Zurchok Monastery arrived

---

139 *BL*: 162b

140 The Tibetan way of calculating age differs from the Western practice. In Tibetan and some other Asian cultures, a baby is considered one year old at birth.

141 *Go-dha* is the eleventh month. The Tibetan lunar months in order are: 1. *Chu-dha* 2. *O-dha* 3. *Nag-dha* or *Nagpa Dawa* 4. *Saga Dawa* 5. *Non-dha* 6. *Chutod Dhawa* 7. *Drozhin Dhawa* 8. *Thrum-dha* 9. *Yug-dha* 10.*Min-dha* 11. *Go-dha* 12. *Gyal-dha.*

142 *BL*: 163a

143 Since *Gyal-dha* is the final month of the Tibetan calendar, the year according to the Western calendar is 1611.

144 A big encampment

in Chagmo. The entire party set up camp. On the fifteenth day (a Thursday of that month), the Sixth Shamarpa and the Tenth Karmapa met.

The following month was the first month of the Iron Pig year (1611). On the twenty-third day, the Sixth Shamarpa himself bearing incense led a formal procession in accordance with tradition and invited the young Karmapa to his camp and to ascend the throne prepared for him. There, in a huge tent set up for the occasion, the Sixth Shamarpa conducted the enthronement ceremony for the Tenth Karmapa. He offered Karmapa the black and gold crown. In attendance were representatives from all Buddhist schools in Tibet, as well as kings, dignitaries, and devotees from everywhere.

After the enthronement, Shamar Garwang Thamchad Khyenpa requested the parents of Karmapa to allow their child to remain with him. He clearly stated that the child must stay with him to study the Dharma. Although the parents were willing, they explained that their son was fully under the control of the Chagmo Lama. Shamarpa then met with Chagmo Lama and repeated exactly what he had said to the parents.

Chagmo Lama and Yangri Trungpa Shagrogpa put up a united front. They thought that if they released Karmapa, they would lose authority over him. They then decided that Karmapa should stay with their group permanently.

Under the circumstances, the Sixth Shamarpa and the Tenth Karmapa together visited the birthplace of the Fourth Shamarpa where a rock bore the Fourth Shamarpa's footprint. In that same area, the Tenth Karmapa also left his own footprint on a rock. The Sixth Shamarpa could only give Karmapa one hundred recitations of "The Long Life Initiation of the Three Roots Combined."[145] That was all.[146] He could not give any other teachings. Therefore, Chagmo Lama's obstruction was the cause of the future decline of the Karma Kagyu.

---

145 This is an initiation specifically composed for Karmapa. It originated in the *Nying Thik* tradition of the Nyingma sect.

146 *BL*: 163b

10th Karmapa

> In the following passage, the Tenth Karmapa describes what happened after he was enthroned – how the Chagmo Lama took him away.

One[147] day Bodhisattva Chokyi Wangchuk gave this message to my family: "You have taken good care of your son. It is now time for him to learn the responsibilities of a bodhisattva. His life is not meant to be that of a layperson. Your son should stay with me, and I will look after him. He will receive a proper education due a bodhisattva. Further, I will support your family and give you the necessary provisions."

My family was very happy with this proposal. They discussed it among themselves and gave this reply, "We are prepared to do everything as you have asked. However, because our family has been given to the lord here, you will have to apply to him."

Bodhisattva Chokyi Wangchuk invited Chagmo Lama to his camp and appealed to him in this way, "As happened before, your great grandparents offered the best assistance possible to the Fifth Shamarpa Konchog Ban by presenting the Ninth Karmapa to him. It is now your turn to do as your ancestors did. You should present the child Karmapa to me. His duty is to work for sentient beings. In return, I will give you whatever wealth it takes to satisfy you."

All the while, the Chieftain's eyes were downcast, looking at the ground. When Bodhisattva Chokyi Wangchuk had finished speaking, Chagmo Lama replied neither yes nor no. He simply turned around and left for home.

> A pearl merchant mixes quasi-pearls148 with genuine ones and places them on the scale.
>
> From beginning to end, gullible people will always make the wrong choice.
>
> And so he (Chagmo Lama) calls on friends with the same nature as his for advice.

---

147 *KAC*: 101

148 Fake pearls.

But the so-called friends are not friends of the heart,
and they advise him thus:
"People usually have to give their own wealth
in order to get the wealth of others.
What you have makes people bring their wealth to you.
It is stupid to give away such assets."
Anything you do, whether it is good or bad,
will become clear in the end.
Between one who says the truth,
and one who lies to make the truth,
stupid people find it difficult to tell them apart.
If the color white is covered with charcoal,
wash it in water and it will be white again.
The conch, which is naturally white,
though painted black, will be white again.

Chagmo Lama followed his friends' advice.[149] He went back to Bodhisattva Chokyi Wangchuk and declared, "I purchased the boy a long time ago. He belongs totally to me. You want the boy for wealth, but his cost to me has yet to be recovered. I now offer you these gifts. If you need wealth, there are many places where you can go to get it. I cannot give you the boy now."

One who does not know how to differentiate between good and bad will not respect a supreme human.
One who talks ill brings downfall to himself later.
Who would like a person who hangs like a bat?[150]
A person like that is not respected.

Bodhisattva[151] Chokyi Wangchuk realized that some karmic effect was happening.[152] He also knew that things would be right when the karma was over. Therefore, he decided not to pursue in this

149 *KAC*: 109. (Poetic descriptions on pages 106–108 not translated.)

150 This alludes to someone who misrepresents the truth.

151 *KAC*: 110. (Poetic descriptions on pages 111–112 not translated.)

152 Buddha Shakyamuni also experienced such effects.

direction and to try again later.

During[153] that period (after the Sixth Shamarpa left), I wrote many poems. As well, Bodhisattva Chokyi Wangchuk gave me teachings only through signs, and I understood everything.

A person who intends to cross the ocean of samsara understands that the selflessness (nature) of phenomena is the ship that can cross the ocean.

Bodhisattva Chokyi Wangchuk's presence was to me a sign that made me realize that I had to depend on a ship. I understood that my lack of power during that time was due to some effect of my karma. Moreover, I recognized that my ship would need the support of a suitable wind to set sail. Though I would have to face many obstacles such as big waves and sharks on my journey, nevertheless, I could overcome them with the support of concentration and contemplation. Bodhisattva Chokyi Wangchuk's presence clearly showed me that in order to conquer evil emotions, I would need a lama, a guide. And Bodhisattva Chokyi Wangchuk was that guide.

I got all these points from signs, which I understood.

153 *KAC*: 113.

15. Early Travels

BL

Karmapa[154] remained in the custody of the Chagmos. One day, the young Karmapa was near a stream. He pointed to a rock as big as a human head. He picked it up and threw it to the ground shattering it. Out came many green worms. "These are living beings from hell. "*Om mani padme hung*!"[155] cried the young boy. For a while Karmapa held his eyes in a still gaze as in meditation. All the worms died instantly – Karmapa had liberated them.

At the age of eight, Karmapa was very artistic and creative.[156] Though still a child, he was able to make mechanical things that were described in the *Kalachakra* texts.

Situ Tulku Chokyi Gyaltsen arrived from the second seat mon-

---

154 Translation of *BL*: 163b continues here.

155 The six-syllable mantra of the "Bodhisattva of Loving Kindness and Compassion" known as Bodhisattva Chenrezig.

156 The child Karmapa grew up to be a very good artist. Some of the beautiful statues he sculpted and paintings he created of the Buddha and bodhisattvas are still extant. A number of images appear in Part II of this book. For many more examples, see the Rubin Museum exhibition catalogue *The Black Hat Eccentric: Artistic Visions of the Tenth Karmapa* written by Debreczeny (2012).

astery of Karmapa[157] with grand offerings. However, Chagmo Lama and Yangri Trungpa did not allow him to meet Karmapa.

The (Mongol) warlord Thumed Kholoji and his large party arrived.[158] In addition, the *Chöje* (head) Lama of Baram Kagyu[159] arrived. On the first day, the Red Hat (Shamarpa) and the Black Hat (Karmapa) together met all of them.

On the second day, the Mongolian warlord was barred from an audience with Karmapa. Yangri and Chagmo Lama lied and made their exit. They claimed that a prediction from a protector deity revealed that a Mongolian king and the Shamarpa's party would band together and take away Karmapa. Therefore, they had no choice but to take the child and flee. They escaped to a Bon monastery where they hid.

Since that day, and for a long time to come, the self-serving Chagmo and his group thwarted any possibility of the Karmapa travelling together with Shamarpa, or with Situ Rinpoche.

Meanwhile, Thumed Kholoji invited the Garwang Thamchad Khyenpa (the Sixth Shamarpa) and all his monks from Zurchok along with Je Situpa (Tai Situ) to his homeland.

The Ming Emperor of China, Wan Li, sent a messenger to Karmapa bearing many offerings and a request for prayers for him and his country. The offerings included fifty sacks of white sandalwood, black sandalwood, fifty sacks of tea, porcelain tea sets, and china. Among many other items, there were one hundred rolls each of light and heavy silk brocade suitable for making indoor and outdoor clothing. Chagmo Lama and Yangri kept all the gifts.

The Chieftain of Amdo whose name was Karma Tsering offered

---

157 Karma Gon was the second seat monastery established by the First Karmapa Dusum Khyenpa. Situ Rinpoche was in charge of it in those days. The first Karmapa Dusum Khyenpa consecrated three seat monasteries in all. He named them after the enlightened form, speech, and mind of Chakrasamvara. He named the monastery in Tsurphu Ogmin Kacho Thug Gi Densa, the enlightened mind of Chakrasamvara. To the monastery in Karma Gon he gave the name Ogmin Sachod Sung Gi Densa, the enlightened speech of Chakrasamvara. And he named the monastery in Kampo Neynang, Ogmin Sala Kuyi Densa, the enlightened form of Chakrasamvara.

158 Kholoji's region of control in Mongolia is in present-day Inner Mongolia. In those days, Mongolia was divided into areas ruled by warlords, like Kholoji (whose title was Dai Ching), who called themselves "kings."

159 Baram Kagyu is a subsect within the Kagyu sect.

Karmapa a very beautiful incense burner.[160] The moment it was offered, Karmapa recollected a time during the Yuan Dynasty, in one of his previous incarnations[161] when he was invited to the (imperial) palace in Zhong To.[162] He remembered the many details of the palace.

> [*Bey Lotsawa comments*]: The Tenth Karmapa recorded the detailed description of the palace from memory in his autobiography.

The King of Lijiang also sent a messenger with an invitation to the Tenth Karmapa. The King of Lijiang (in the northwestern part of today's Yunnan Province in China), Karma Lhundrub, whose title was Pungri Nangso, sent a messenger to deliver an invitation to Karmapa. During the messenger's stay, on one occasion, Chagmo Lama and Yangri whispered to him in passing, "Look, there is Karmapa who is always with the *manaho* (a red gemstone) *mala* (prayer beads) in hand. It is from Je Garwang Thamchad Khyenpa (the Sixth Shamarpa). He is reciting the Long Life Prayer composed and handwritten for him by Shamarpa and praying that he'll see him soon."

Karmapa received numerous letters from high lamas and chieftains of Ü and Tsang (large districts in central Tibet). He studied the letters, learning the words and how to write them. Because he practiced by copying the letters, his handwriting became very good.

While Karmapa was traveling in Bum Nyak (in east Tibet), he left a clear footprint in a rock. He visited many places in that area. There was a place called Mendalthang where he camped. Many devotees including the chiefs of Riwoche and Chamdo districts went to pay their respects. Riwoche and Chamdo were two warring provinces at the time. The young Karmapa acted as a mediator and resolved the conflicts, restoring peace to the area. He then visited

---

160 *BL*: 164a

161 It was the Third Karmapa who was invited by the Yuan Dynasty emperor Wenzong, also known as Tugh Temur (r. 1328–1332).

162 Zhong To is the Tibetan version of the Chinese term *Zhongdu*, which literally means central capital and refers to today's Beijing.

Upper Washul, Lower Washul, and Nyag Rong.

Karmapa then arrived at Lhunpotser.[163] He had a vision of the First Karmapa in a thangka, so he painted it as seen in his vision. He also had a vision of Milarepa in the form of a rainbow, and he painted that scene.

One day, messengers came with an invitation from the Chechen Dai Ching (warlord) in Mongolia. Karmapa and his entourage accepted and went there. He met with the Dai Ching and his people and made them promise not to kill again. Again, Chagmo Lama and Yangri obstructed the auspicious meeting of Shamarpa[164] and Karmapa while they were both in the same area.

Once, a fire burned on a hill called Laku in Dza Laku.[165] Karmapa threw barley everywhere, and the fire was extinguished.

* * *

10th Karmapa

Addressing Kuntu Zangpo as "Rimdrowa" (or my attendant), Karmapa recounts how the Sixth Shamarpa asked the Third Pawo Tsuklak Gyatso to teach and guide him. Pawo Rinpoche is a high-ranking Karma Kagyu teacher whom Karmapa addresses as "Bodhisattva Gawey Yang."[166]

Rimdrowa,[167] Bodhisattva Chokyi Wangchuk (the Sixth Shamarpa) knew when it would be the right time, what to do at the right time, and who would be the right person to help me – Bodhisattva Jigten Wangchuk – who was helpless (in getting free from the evil Chagmo Lama). Seeing that the time was not right for him to guide me, he tried to think who else would be suitable to guide me bodhisat-

---

163 *BL*: 164b. Lhunpotser was the residence of Chagmo Lama.

164 Karmapa's fame had spread everywhere even in Mongolia. The Mongol warlords wanted to receive his blessings. The Sixth Shamarapa was also in Mongolia at the time as a guest of Dai Ching Thumed Kholoji as previously noted.

165 Somewhere in Mongolia

166 Gawey Yang means "joyful voice."

167 *KAC*: 114

tva.[168] Then he understood. In the south of Tibet, Gawey Yang was a suitable guide, and he wrote to him:

"The reincarnation of my Lama (Ninth Karmapa) is now a teenager like a flower in bloom. I am here to guide him, yet some leftover karma is obstructing my assistance to him. Therefore, in the same way that your teacher (Ninth Karmapa) treated you in the past, you must now guide him as a spiritual teacher and a parent would. Please give him the vows and open the boundless (Dharma) door to him. If you do that, all sentient beings will be helped at the same time. Please come here to Moon River and help him."

The Sixth Shamarpa sent the message to Bodhisattva Gawey Yang who was (at that time) living in the valley with a medicine forest[169] in the south. Bodhisattva Gawey Yang replied that he would. He[170] came and became my guide. Bodhisattva Chokyi Wangchuk continued to travel to serve sentient beings.

168 This means "me, who is a bodhisattva."

169 In this forest many medicinal plants grow.

170 *KAC*: 115

16. Travels in Central Tibet

BL

When[171] Karmapa was eleven, he started to travel to central Tibet on the fourteenth day of the month *Chuda* (first month) in the Wood Tiger year (1614).[172] On the way, in Rotung, he left two footprints in a rock.

Trungpa and Garwang, head and chief abbot of the Surmang[173] Monastery respectively, invited Karmapa. At Surmang, they performed a Chakrasamvara[174] puja, and Karmapa attended. At that time, Yangri and Chagmo Lama were again suspicious of their hosts. They knew that the residents of Surmang were followers of the Sixth Shamarpa. They thought that Karmapa might be taken from them, so they kept watch day and night.[175]

In the valley of Pam Zhung, a hunter and his dog were chasing a wild mule. The distressed animal approached Karmapa seeking

171 Translation continues on *BL*: 164b

172 Karmapa made numerous stops along the way. Those details have not been fully translated.

173 Surmang is the seat monastery of Trungpa Rinpoche.

174 An important empowerment belonging to the *Anuttarayoga Tantra*.

175 *BL*: 164b

protection, and Karmapa blessed it. It then remained by his side.

Soon the hunter and his dog caught up. Karmapa struck a deal with the hunter – cash in exchange for the freedom of both the donkey and the dog. Moreover, the hunter agreed to give up hunting altogether. It was said that the two animals became friends and stayed together from then on.

Karmapa then arrived in the province called Powo in Southern Tibet,[176] (having travelled from the north reaching eastern Tibet in the south) – one of the eighteen provinces. People in that area were his followers. It was there that Karmapa started his recitation of the mantra of Avalokiteshvara more than one billion times.

Karmapa continued his journey to central Tibet. He arrived at a place with a rock called Baram Drag where there was a temple of Gampopa. In that temple was a very famous thangka of Gampopa commissioned by Gampopa's nephew-disciple, Gomtshul. When Karmapa rolled out this thangka, pieces of relics appeared and fell out of the scroll, and everyone present was surprised.

A delegation from the ruling Tsangpa Desi (Phuntsok Namgyal) arrived and delivered an invitation for Karmapa. Karmapa continued his journey.[177] Along the way, many lords and people came out to pay their respects and to receive his blessing. Just before reaching Yangpachen,[178] a boy in white suddenly appeared to welcome him. He wore a high turban on his head, which had five knots. In his hands, he held a glass incense bowl as a gesture of welcome. Many people also witnessed this wondrous boy who disappeared after a short while. Later it was verified that he was Nyen Chen Thang Lha, a great deity of Tibet. At that same time, many rainbows appeared over Karmapa's tent. There were also wonderful flower-like drizzles throughout the day.

When Karmapa arrived at Yangpachen, a huge procession of monks and lay people stood ready to welcome him. He was paid the highest honors, and he in turn gave everyone his blessing.

---

176 *BL*: 165a

177 *BL*:165b

178 Seat monastery of Shamarpa

From Yangpachen Karmapa proceeded to Tsurphu Monastery.[179] Upon his arrival, he mounted the lion throne at Tsurphu, and a formal enthronement ceremony took place. Numerous rainbows appeared in the sky during his stay just as during the Fifth Karmapa's stay at the Tai Tu Palace (in Nanjing, China).[180]

[*Bey Lotsawa comments*]: The Tenth Karmapa was then eleven years old, and one can refer to the words of the Tenth Karmapa as recorded in his autobiography.[181]

* * *

10th Karmapa

The Tenth Karmapa tells of his first trip to Tsurphu.

Rimdrowa[182] (my attendant), my travel to central Tibet started. Many people came to bid me farewell. There were also many who followed me on this journey. Everyone made preparations and saddled the horses and mules for travelling. As I had achieved my wishes for the devotees in the area where I was staying, I wanted to move on to help other sentient beings, so I proceeded towards central Tibet.

There were two possible routes to reach central Tibet – either by going south first or taking the northern route first. We headed north. It was autumn. The trees and fields were changing colors, and the leaves were falling, telling signs of the season. We could hear the songs of many waterfowl in the lakes.

The weather then deteriorated, and it felt unpleasant. Our route took us through many remote areas for a long time. When at last we reached a village, all of us were overjoyed to find relief and comfort. People in the village gave us ample food and drink. They

179 Seat monastery of Karmapa

180 This refers to the time in 1407 when the Fifth Karmapa visited the Ming emperor in his capital.

181 *BL*: 165b

182 *KAC*: 115

gave us many things including their horses. Again we journeyed on passing through remote areas. We encountered hunters who helped us. They gave us food and even some of their horses.

Gradually, more and more villagers met us. They came in large numbers to greet me. Apparently, news of my coming had spread quickly from village to village. Every village we reached was prepared to receive me with huge offerings.

Winter passed, and spring started. One day, we saw a snow-capped mountain from a distance. It looked just like a crystal house. We were all taken aback by the view. "What could it be?" we wondered. Then we understood it was the snowcap of Mount Kailash, which meant that we were approaching Lhasa and central Tibet.

At Yangpachen Monastery, the resident monks as well as the monks of Tsurphu received us. The abbot of Tsurphu, a relative of the Ninth Karmapa, led the delegation. He was very happy that I was near Tsurphu. Hundreds of monks holding incense and banners lined up to receive me. Thousands stood on the side of the road. I reached the top of the monastery.

The first thing I did was to go to the temple where the Fifth Shamarpa's body was enshrined in a silver stupa adorned by many precious gems. I prostrated in front of it and offered a long white scarf.[183] I spent a short time in Yangpachen and then headed for Tsurphu.

On the way, we made camp near a beautiful stream and spent three days there. Almost seven hundred monks and Tibetan, Chinese, and Mongolian delegations arrived there to receive me, to invite and accompany me to Tsurphu Monastery. At Tsurphu, ceremonies were conducted over many days.[184]

---

183 Scarves are exchanged as a form of respectful greeting.

184 *KAC*: beginning of 126; the rest of 126 to 128 is not translated.

17. Teachings at Tsurphu

BL

When[185] Karmapa was twelve and he was staying at Tsurphu, he received the full *Upasaka*[186] vows from the Third Pawo Rinpoche, Tsuklak Gyatso. The ceremony took place in the shrine room of Tsurphu, in front of the famous Buddha image. Karmapa was given a name by Pawo Rinpoche.[187]

Then Karmapa began to receive teachings from Pawo Rinpoche. First, he was given the White Tara *abhisheka*.[188] Over an extended period of many months, Karmapa received the instructions, oral transmissions, and the initiations of the Tantra teachings. He also received the *lung*[189] transmission of the collection of texts authored by the masters of the Kagyu lineage.

---

185 *BL*: 165b

186 An *Upasaka* is a lay follower of Gautama Buddha. The five *Upasaka* vows are: 1) not to take the life of a sentient being; 2) not to take what is not given; 3) to refrain from sexual misconduct; 4) to refrain from false speech; and 5) to refrain from drunkenness.

187 This name is not transliterated here.

188 *Abhisheka* means empowerment, and White Tara is generally revered as the Bodhisattva of Long Life, Merit, and Wisdom.

189 A *lung* is a reading transmission where a teacher reads aloud the text of a particular practice to the disciple(s).

* * *

10th Karmapa

The Tenth Karmapa writes about how he began to receive teachings and initiations from Pawo Rinpoche.

My[190] attendant, after I was in Tsurphu for two months, Bodhisattva Gawey Yang Tsuklak Gyatso arrived from Tseykar Monastery,[191] which is the source of the Kagyu lineage. Bodhisattva Gawey Yang then started to give me initiations starting with the refuge vows.[192] He also began to give me the oral transmission of the *Kanjur*.[193] Every day, I received teachings. Bodhisattva Gawey Yang told many stories about the Buddha and the bodhisattvas such as Marpa and Milarepa, and so forth. These stories taught me how to be a qualified bodhisattva.

* * *

BL

One[194] day, Karmapa asked Pawo Rinpoche, "How long will you live?"

"I don't have *ngon-she*,[195] so I don't know."

Karmapa immediately told him, "I can guarantee that you will live until age sixty three!"[196]

During his stay at Tsurphu, Karmapa recited an abridged version of the *Prajnaparamita*[197] *Sutra* every day.

---

190 *KAC*: 129

191 This monastery in Lho Drag was originally built by Milarepa – a forefather of the Kagyu lineage. Therefore, it is a historical location where the Kagyupa doctrine began.

192 To take refuge means to become a Buddhist by having faith in the Buddha, Dharma and Sangha, and following the teachings of the Buddha.

193 The *Kanjur* is the collection of the translated words and teachings of the Buddha in Tibetan.

194 *BL: 165b*

195 This term means the power to know the future.

196 *BL*: 166a

197 The sutra called *The Perfection of Transcendental Wisdom*.

One day, Karmapa received an invitation from the Desi of Tibet, Phuntsok Namgyal. He then traveled to the capital city at Samdrub Tse along with his entourage.

En route, Karmapa passed by Long Black Lake. He threw blessing pills into the lake. Instantly, everyone there heard beautiful melodic sounds and saw many rainbows in the sky.

At Zabphu[198] Lung, Karmapa saw a vision of Guru Padmasambhava surrounded by *siddhas*.

When Karmapa and his party arrived at Nam Ling Lu Dhing, a huge camp was already set up to welcome him (by the Tsangpa Desi's people). Huge lines of people were waiting to receive Karmapa. The most splendid offerings were presented to the very special guest of honor, whom the Tsang Desi Phuntsok Namgyal had invited.

It was at that time that the Desi offered Karmapa Lha Lung Monastery. Karmapa accepted and named it Karma Gung Gyal Ling.[199]

Karmapa also visited the Sung Rab Gyatso Ling Monastery.[200] It housed a big Buddha statue as well as a statue of the Ninth Karmapa. A painting by the Ninth Karmapa hung on a wall. Upon viewing it, Choying Dorje (the Tenth Karmapa) remarked, "This painting is not the work of a professional painter. However, it does have a wonderful and unique charm about it."

Karmapa together with his party[201] went to Drag Kar (or White Rock). There, Karmapa did a one-week retreat. Afterwards, he visited Lho Drag[202] Monastery. When he left, the Lho Drag *garpa*[203] joined his party.

Continuing on their journey, Karmapa, Pawo Rinpoche, and the *garpa* reached a river called Ruzhima. They hired boats to cross it.

---

198 *Zabphu* means valley.

199 This monastery is located in southern Tibet.

200 The Eighth Karmapa founded this monastery.

201 Pawo Rinpoche included.

202 Lho Drag is located in southeastern Tibet, in today's Shannan Prefecture, a region considered to be the birthplace of Tibetan civilization.

203 *Garpa* means encampment. In this instance, the term refers to the group of monks of Lho Drag, including the head lama, Nam Khay Nyingpowa. Yangri and Chagmo Lama were rude and insulting to these monks. As a result, Karmapa apologized to the monks and ordered Yangri and Chagmo Lama not to aggravate them.

During the crossing, two of the boats began to fall apart. Karmapa immediately entered into a meditative state until everyone safely reached shore.

During his travels, Karmapa continued to receive teachings and *lungs* from Pawo Rinpoche. Due to a request by the Tsang Desi, Karmapa went to the famous Sakya college – Dre Yul Skyed Tshal. Afterwards, he visited a temple in the vicinity called Ga Dong that housed a famous Maitreya statue and a Mahakali (the female form of Mahakala) statue called Gadong Lhamo. Karmapa received the collections of the Eighth Karmapa's written books as well as those of the Fifth Shamarpa.

18. Dharma Transmission in Pa Nam and Pilgrimage near Lho Drag

In the period roughly between 1616 and 1618, when the Karmapa was in his mid-teens, he was based mainly at Pa Nam (near Shigatse) in central Tibet where he received many teachings and initiations from Pawo Rinpoche. His studies were briefly interrupted when he accepted an invitation from the Tsang ruler to visit the Tsang capital for the first time. Elaborate ceremonies were held there. He had an opportunity to observe and form opinions about the Tsang political leaders. From Pa Nam, Karmapa and Pawo Rinpoche in about 1619 travelled to Lo Drag where Karmapa made a pilgrimage to the many holy sites there.

BL

Karmapa[204] and his party then arrived in Pa Nam where they stayed for some time.

One day, Karmapa saw a vision of a boy in turquoise color. The boy bowed to him several times. Later, Pawo Rinpoche explained that the special apparition was one of three *nagas*[205] who became

204 *BL*: 166a

205 *Nagas* are mythical serpent-like creatures, some of which can be Dharma protectors.

the protector of the Third Karmapa Rangjung Dorje.

It was also at Pa Nam that Karmapa started to receive the *lung* transmission of the *Kanjur* (an extensive collection of Buddhist doctrines) from Pawo Rinpoche.[206]

Karmapa received another invitation from the Tsang[207] Desi and accepted it.

Desi[208] Phuntsok Namgyal, his ministers and civilians in a very large procession received Karmapa. They accompanied him to the Samdrub Tse palace where the Tsang Desi formally presented him with many splendid offerings. Tehor Rinpoche[209] was among Karmapa's entourage.

* * *

10th Karmapa

The[210] Tsang Desi (Phuntsok Namgyal), and I went (to the Tsang capital).

Kuntu Zangpo one day requested me to recount the time I was in Moon River when the great bodhisattva (the Sixth Shamarpa) came to see me. He wanted me to tell him how we spent time together and how the obstacle created by bad people took away my opportunity to be with him. I then proceeded to tell him.

At one time, the Tsang Desi (Phuntsok Namgyal) decided that he should subdue the other lords so they would all come under his rule. The Tsang Desi first collaborated with Yarmo Lung (Duke Kurabpa), a ruler of a neighboring region. Together, they attacked the other lords who fell under the Desi's control. Many people were killed in the wars.

The Tsang Desi and Duke Yarmo Lung both respected Buddhism

206 *BL*: 166b

207 Tsang is the name of the dynastic rulers of central Tibet during that time.

208 The translation continues from *BL*: 166b, second line.

209 The Tsang ruling government established a ranking system of spiritual teachers with set protocols. Tehor Rinpoche was a Karma Kagyu spiritual teacher who ranked sixth and last according to the Tsang ranking.

210 *KAC*: 132

out of a desire to attain power, health and longevity. The people and animals suffered greatly from the unnecessary wars created by the ruling lords. Countless lives were lost from the fighting as well as from diseases that ran rampant under those conditions. In addition, the natural disasters, which happened from time to time, took great numbers of lives, as the people were helpless to cope. The rulers bullied and robbed others of their wealth. Punishments meted out under the legal system were excessively cruel and severe such as the cutting of noses, ears, and so forth, for small crimes committed.

* * *

BL

During[211] his stay (at Samdrub Tse Palace), the Tenth Karmapa conducted an empowerment especially to initiate the Desi and the (Tang) line of future rulers. (This was an initiation of the Tsang Desi as a ruler of Tibet.) He then conducted the actual ceremony wherein a golden seal, a crown, and a cloak were presented to the Desi. Unfortunately, the eight auspicious symbols were embroidered onto the cloak upside down. Nobody noticed the mistake except Karmapa, who pointed it out and warned that it was a bad omen for the future.

On all the walls of the ceremonial hall in the palace was hung the famous tapestry, *rigdhen yolwa*.[212] In this hall, the Karmapa *Yab Sey*[213] were seated on golden thrones. Karmapa sat in the center on the highest throne; Pawo sat to his lower right, and Tehor Rinpoche was to his lower left.

That day also marked the first meeting between Crown Prince Karma Tenkyong Wangpo and the Karmapa *Yab Sey*. A grand and

211 *BL*: 166b

212 The tapestry was a very precious brocade wall hanging, originally made during the Rinpung rule that preceded Tsang. *Yolwa* means tapestry, and *rig dhen* is the name of a dynasty of the mythical Shambhala kingdom.

213 *Yab Sey* is a term of protocol created by the Tsang Desi and applicable in a ceremonial setting. The Karma Kagyu *Yab Sey* consists of six high-ranking figures: Karmapa, Shamarpa, Gyaltsab, Situ, Pawo, and Tehor. When the term is used, it can mean all six rinpoches or just several of them. In this case the Karmapa *Yab Sey* refers to the Tenth Karmapa, Pawo and Tehor Rinpoches.

elaborate ceremony was conducted. It was also the first day of the season of short (winter) days. However, in the capital, daylight lasted for an unusually long time, astonishing the astrologers, one of whom remarked, "The day has extended almost another five hours!"

Karmapa[214] and his party returned to Pa Nam.

On New Year's Day of the Fire Snake year (1617), he performed a very long bodhisattva prayer ceremony. On the full moon day of the first month, Karmapa received the *Kalachakra* initiation from Pawo Rinpoche. On the 27th day of the same month, Pawo Rinpoche completed the *lung* transmission of the *Kanjur* to Karmapa.[215]

Afterwards, Karmapa received initiations continuously. He received the collection of two hundred and forty-four sub-initiations of Tantric deities. He received a set of one hundred Chenrezig practices in the tradition of *Siddha Mitra*; twenty-eight Tantric deity initiations called the *Vajra* Rosary in the tradition of *Shakya Hri Bhatra*; and another twelve Tantras. All these initiations Karmapa received while he was at Pa Nam.

During that time, Karmapa's father's drinking problem made him a target. Yangri and Chagmo Lama seized the opportunity to hurt the family. They complained to the Desi and managed to obtain an order to expel Karmapa's family. The parents and the two brothers were kicked out of Karmapa's camp (or Karmapa's entourage). That happened.

While still in Pa Nam, Karmapa met Dhagpo Rinpoche from the north, the *terton* of Poworakshi, Duke Kanam Depa of Powo, and many people from Kongpo and Riwoche. They paid their respects to Karmapa and presented him with many offerings. Karmapa and his party spent the whole year in Pa Nam.

The following year was the Earth Horse year (1618). Again, on Losar (Tibetan New Year), a grand prayer ceremony took place. Messengers of the Ming (dynasty) Emperor Wan Li arrived from China bearing imperial gold letters. In addition, there were forty rolls of exquisite brocades for indoor wear and forty rolls for out-

214 *BL*: 167a

215 This was the transmission that began in Tsurphu when Karmapa was twelve.

door wear, among many other wonderful gifts.

After their stay at Pa Nam, Karmapa and Pawo Rinpoche together left for Lho Drag (in southern Tibet, Shannan Prefecture today). To bid them farewell, the Tsang Desi personally made a trip from his capital Samdrub Tse. Karmapa gave him a long life initiation before his departure.

Lho Drag

Karmapa[216] and his party arrived in Lho Drag.[217] Pawo Rinpoche arranged a grand and splendid reception to welcome Karmapa and presented him with many wonderful offerings.

While he was in Lho Drag, Karmapa made a pilgrimage to the surrounding areas: the farm where Milarepa met Marpa for the first time, as predicted by Marpa's teacher, the Indian *Mahasiddha*[218] Naropa (1016–1100); Lho Drowo Lung, which was Marpa's seat monastery; and other holy places.

At that time in Lhasa, Kyisho Depa, a local duke, was conspiring with some Mongolian warlords to overthrow the Tsang ruling government. The warlords were also supporters of the Gelug or Yellow sect. Kyisho Depa invited their armies[219] into Tibet, and they joined forces. Together, they plotted an ambush and were set to attack the government troops.

As soon as Karmapa caught word of this treachery, he conducted a special prayer, and the rebels gave up their ambush. This happened in Marmephug during his visit in Lho Drag.

Karmapa then continued his pilgrimage. He arrived at Neudong Palace on the full moon (the thirteenth) day of the eleventh month, built during the Phagdru reign.[220] To honor him, the palace administration organized a huge reception with much pomp. Never-

216 *BL*: 167b

217 Lho Drag is where Milarepa (1052–1135) built a nine-storey temple by order of his guru, Marpa (1012–1097). It had since become Pawo Rinpoche's seat monastery called Lho Drag Seykhar.

218 *Mahasiddha* is a great "accomplished one" in meditation.

219 These were the Mongolian armies from what is now Outer Mongolia.

220 The Phagdru's rule in Tibet preceded Rinpung, which preceded Tsang.

theless, Karmapa stated that he could foresee from omens that the status of the Phagdru family would very soon decline. During his stay at the palace, Karmapa performed a special ceremony to bless a set of special thangkas of the Kagyu lineage, which the Phagdru family had commissioned.

The New Year (Earth Sheep or 1619) ceremonies began. Chinese monks arrived from Bird's Leg Mountain in China. The elderly Nyungney Reychen, a holy lama, also arrived, (physically) carried by his disciples who numbered in the hundreds.[221]

Karmapa, along with Pawo Rinpoche, Tehor Rinpoche and the Sakyong Thri Rinpoche of Phagdru together went to Thromsa Karma Lhakhang.[222] There, Pawo Rinpoche fell ill. Karmapa served him like an attendant. He also performed a long life puja for his teacher over a few days.

221 *BL*: 168a

222 Karma temple in Thromsa. Thromsa is the name of a place, and *Lhakhang* means temple.

19. Duke Kurabpa in Trouble

During Karmapa and Pawo Rinpoche's stay at Lhunpo Gang, a palace-residence of the Kurabpa family, Karmapa received many initiations and teachings from Pawo Rinpoche. He also received collections of actual Dharma books. While they were there, Duke Kurabpa was jailed because Chagmo Lama and his associates slandered him in front of the Tsang Desi. The Sixth Shamarpa tried to get a pardon for Duke Kurabpa. He also tried to stop the Tsang Desi from waging war with the Kurabpa family. However, the Tsang Desi did not take his advice.

BL

After[223] Pawo Rinpoche recovered from his illness, he accompanied Karmapa to Lhunpo Gang (in the area of Pa Nam). There, he transmitted very high teachings to Karmapa. They were: *The Six Yogas (of Naropa)*,[224] *The Seven Mandalas*[225] *of Ngok Tradition*, *The Mahakali Initiation*, *The Six Yidams* and *The Six Instructions of Siddha*

223 *BL*: 168a

224 A main system of practice of the Kagyu sect, *The Six Yogas of Naropa* are six inner yoga practices taught by the Indian *mahasiddha* Naropa.

225 *Mandala* literally means "the center with its surrounding." It is a poetic reference to the abode or place of worship of a deity. As an offering, it represents the entire universe.

Mitra Tradition. Karmapa also received the initiations of: *The Thirteen Yamantakas, The Five Deities of the Red Yamantaka, The Four Deities of Hayagriv,*[226] *The Nine Red Avalokiteshvaras, The Five Red Avalokiteshvaras, The Nine Long Life Buddhas, The Black Chakrasamvara,* and *The Hayagriva in the Kyergangpa Tradition.*

Further, Karmapa received the collection of books of Lama Shang,[227] the collection of books of Gampopa, the collection of books of Gotshangpa, the collection of books of Yang Gonpa, and the collection of books of Thogmed Zangpo. He also received the instructions for the *Wishfulfilling Jewel of Mind Training,* all the *Lojong* practices, and the practice of *Khandro Nyingthik.*

Pawo Rinpoche submitted a legal case to the (Tsang) government about how badly the Chagmo Lama and (his associates) the Yangris exploited the Tenth Karmapa. Accordingly, the government rendered the verdict that the entire Chagmo party should remove themselves from Karmapa's *garpa* and return to their homeland in Golok. Yangri Trungpa and Yangri Shagrogpa and their people were ordered to resign from Karmapa's administration, and to return home where they should do practice retreats.

After Losar of the Iron Monkey year (1620), Karmapa continued to receive teachings from Pawo Rinpoche. He received the complete Kadampa doctrines, all *Three Dohas*[228] *of Saraha, The Collection of Chenrezig Practices of Tsontsen Gampo,* as well as all the profound subjects of Buddhist philosophy.

During that time, Karmapa conferred the title *Goshri*[229] on Tehor Rinpoche Tenzin Tharghey along with the title-seal.

Karmapa made thangkas of the Buddha. He also made thangkas

---

226 Hayagriva is a Tantric meditational deity deemed as the wrathful manifestation of Avalokiteshvara.

227 Disciple of Gampopa and founder of Tsalpa Kagyu – one of the four major sects of Kagyupa – now almost extinct.

228 A *doha* is a form of poetry usually sung spontaneously by masters like Milarepa and Saraha.It expresses a profound view of mind, commonly referred to as "a song of realization."

229 *Goshri* is the Tibetan transliteration of the Chinese title *guoshi* or national master or teacher. A Ming emperor first bestowed this title on the Seventh Karmapa's (1454–1506) secretary Paljor Dhondrub. The emperor authorized the Karmapa to confer this title on other Tibetan lamas as he saw fit. Subsequent Karmapas continued the practice. When the Tenth Kamapa gave Tehor Rinpoche this title, Gyaltsab, a lineage holder of the Karma Kagyu sect, also held the same title.

of Manjusri, the Six-armed Mahakala, the Four-armed Mahakala, Nagarjuna, and the *Mahasiddha* Saraha. His thangkas were very beautiful, and he offered them to his guru Pawo Rinpoche. Karmapa also sculpted a Tara statue made from a very special bronze.

Also, it was during that time that Karmapa's parents were allowed to rejoin Karmapa's camp.

Because Yangri and Chagmo Lama slandered the Kurabpa family in front of the Tsang Desi (the head of government), Depa Pelmar Neydzangwa (a main member of the Kurabpa family) was jailed.

The Tenth Karmapa then went to see the Sixth Shamarpa. He asked him to talk to the Tsang Desi to release Duke Kurabpa (Depa Pelmar Neydzangwa). Together with Pawo Rinpoche, Tehor Rinpoche, and the Tenth Karmapa, Shamarpa went to see the Tsang Desi to seek the release of the duke. Shamarpa offered the Tsang Desi a highly valued riding saddle studded with precious stones. The Tenth Karmapa also joined Shamarpa in his appeal. They asked the Desi not to attack (the territory of the) Kurabpa family and to set Neydzangwa free. But the Tsang Desi did not cooperate and proceeded to attack the Kurabpa family. As a result, he seized all of Duke Kurabpa's land, properties, and palaces, including the palace called Yartod Lhunpo Gang.

Later, because of his wrongful actions, and his refusal to yield to the compassionate pleas of his spiritual teachers, the senior Desi Phuntsok Namgyal suddenly contracted small pox and died.[230] Such was the consequence of karma.

* * *

10th Karmapa

Karmapa writes about the ambitious Tsang Desi who wanted to expand his territory and began to subdue the smaller lords, and his eventual demise. Karmapa's comments offer further glimpses into the political times in which he lived.

230 *BL*: 169a

The[231] Tsang Desi's thinking was that since he was already very powerful, the Duke Yarmo Lung,[232] his neighbor, should also submit to him. He wanted to attack his ally.

At that time, Bodhisattva Gawey Yang (Pawo Rinpoche) and I were staying at the palace (i.e., Lhunpo Gang) of Duke Yarmo Lung. When Bodhisattva Chokyi Wangchuk heard that the Tsang Desi was planning to attack Yarmo Lung, he went to the Tsang Desi and insisted that he stop his aggression.

Bodhisattva Chokyi Wangchuk told the Tsang Desi, "You have enough now. You are the big lord with a palace. There are so many people under you already. Why do you still attack the smaller lords?"

The Tsang Desi refused to listen. He went ahead and attacked Duke Yarmo Lung and defeated him.

Bodhisattva Chokyi Wangchuk was very disappointed. He could not bear to see innocent people killed. He decided to travel to help Duke Yarmo Lung and his people. I heard that Bodhisattva Chokyi Wangchuk was coming to help. I was so happy and sent a message to him requesting him to please come quickly to help and explaining that I was waiting for him. Then Bodhisattva Chokyi Wangchuk arrived. I[233] along with many monks and Duke Yarmo Lung and his army formed a line to receive him. I started to prostrate to Bodhisattva Chokyi Wangchuk when he was at a distance. I held a gold-plated silver pot and welcomed him.

Bodhisattva Chokyi Wangchuk gave me a beautiful thangka of Avalokiteshvara. He said to me, "This is for you. He is the one you should follow." We had many conversations together, and he told me all about his travels in Lijiang (in China) and in the eastern regions of Tibet. After we spent many days together, Bodhisattva Chokyi Wangchuk left for the Tsang capital.

Duke Yarmo Lung was very sad after he lost the war. His palace was destroyed. I went to console him. I also sent a messenger to

---

231 *KAC*: 159. Poetic descriptions have not been translated in this abridged excerpt that starts from *KAC*: 159 and ends on *KAC*: 166.

232 The same as Duke Kurabpa

233 *KAC*: 159

Bodhisattva Chokyi Wangchuk and requested him to ask the Tsang Desi not to kill his former ally. Bodhisattva Chokyi Wangchuk asked the Tsang Desi to stop his attacks and to spare the life of the Duke. He reminded him that Bodhisattva Gawey Yang and I were there with the Duke. At first, the Tsang Desi did not want to listen. Bodhisattva Chokyi Wangchuk said, "In that case, I shall leave and not see you any more." The Tsang Desi softened his stance and decided to send Bodhisattva Gawey Yang and me gifts as penance.

Meanwhile, the Tsang Desi developed a relationship with a Mongolian warlord, who had suffered defeat under another warlord. While the Tsang Desi was away at one of his wars, his wife passed away. The Desi was sad and tried to return home. The journey would take about a month. On his way home, he came down with small pox. He made a stop at the palace of Yarmo Lung (Yartod Lhunpo Gang which had belonged to Duke Kurabpa). The palace and town were deserted and in ruins. They were empty of people and supplies. Everything had been destroyed by the Tsangpa's own armies. And so it was that the Tsang Desi died amidst the dire conditions he had created.[234]

* * *

BL

When[235] the royal family invited the Black Hat and Red Hat Karmapas (the Karmapa and Shamarpa) and Pawo Rinpoche to perform the death rites for the Desi, the three refused to go. Instead, they left together for Lho Drag. The members of the ruling government were so upset that they harshly and openly criticized the three spiritual masters.

Shamarpa and Karmapa, along with Pawo Rinpoche and Tehor Rinpoche, were together at Tromsa, south Tibet. The Sixth Shamarpa then offered Karmapa everything he had – all of his monasteries and monks, all his farms and people. He offered Karmapa everything including his seat monastery.

---

234 *KAC*: 166

235 *BL*: 169a

After Tromsa, the whole party proceeded to Seykhar Monastery in Lho Drag, where Karmapa recognized the reincarnation of the Fourth Gyaltsab Rinpoche, Dragpa Thondrub. Soon afterwards, the Tsang family invited the party to the royal estate called Panam Park. There they performed a puja for the deceased Desi Phuntsok Namgyal.

Shamarpa, Karmapa, Pawo, Gyaltsab and Situ Rinpoche then arrived at the Samdrub Tse Palace. They again performed a very big ceremony for the deceased Desi Phuntsok Namgyal.

20. Taking the Vinaya Vows

In this chapter the Tenth Karmapa describes the approximately three-year period after he was free from Chagmo Lama's control and was able to enjoy the company and learning of his teachers. His account of his relationship with his teachers is told with natural simplicity and great affection and admiration.

10th Karmapa

Bodhisattva[236] Gawey Yang Tsuklak Gyatso (Pawo Rinpoche) took me to Lho Drowo Lung[237] for a retreat (around 1621). I followed his teachings. During[238] our stay there, Bodhisattva Chokyi Wangchuk with five hundred monk-disciples arrived. I enjoyed every day, receiving teachings from both of them.

At that time, the new king[239] (Desi Tenkyong Wangpo of Tsang) was strolling in his park in the palace.

"How long ago was this park built?" he asked the park's caretaker.

236 *KAC*: 166, last line

237 It was Marpa's seat monastery.

238 *KAC*: 167

239 In his wrting, the Tenth Karmapa addressed the Tsang Desi as "king."

"Your father built it so that he could invite Bodhisattva (the Sixth Shamarpa) and his monks here," replied the caretaker. He then recounted the history of every invitation the former king had extended to Bodhisattva and his monks.

The new king, wishing to follow his father's example, decided to invite Bodhisattva Chokyi Wangchuk and his entourage from Lho Drag to the capital. After a year, the king again sent a messenger; but this time, it was to invite Bodhisattva Gawey Yang. However, Bodhisattva Gawey Yang always liked to meditate in peaceful places. He did not like to live in kingdoms,[240] nor did he wish to associate with kings and the general populace.

Bodhisattva Gawey Yang's view was this: If one were verbally abused by people of samsara,[241] one would not take any offense. Why? Because one knows that these people's minds are in ignorance. For the same reason, if one were praised by people of samsara, one would also not feel elated. Therefore, one who is dedicated to the bodhisattva practice does not need to ever conform to kings, ministers, wealthy people or the masses.

Bodhisattva Gawey Yang did not go (to the capital). Moreover, I, Jigten Wangchuk, remained with him. Jigten Wangchuk[242] served and assisted him in every way. I also spent some time painting the Buddhas. In this way, we spent three years here (until 1623).

The king again invited me. I could not leave Bodhisattva Gawey Yang. He had given me the Dharma and all the right directions on the path of Dharma. I wanted to remain with him, so I did not accept the invitation.

However, my administrators and followers wanted to expand my administration – they wished it to grow big and famous. They pressed me to fulfill their wishes. Finally, I relented and accepted the invitation.

---

240 Both the Tenth Karmapa and Pawo Rinpoche called bustling cities "kingdoms" as opposed to the quiet countryside or isolated forests.

241 "The people of samsara" are those caught up in samsara, that is, the realm of cyclic existence characterized by dissatisfaction due to ignorance in the mind.

242 In *KAC*, the Tenth Karmapa usually referred to people by their full names rather than using pronouns. He even did so when speaking of himself. In this translation, however, appropriate pronouns are substituted for the full names of people.

Bodhisattva Gawey Yang thus offered me all kinds of precious items that would support my Dharma activities. He advised me, Jigten Wangchuk, as follows: “When you visit the kingdom (Tsang capital), don’t stay too long with the inhabitants. Don’t get distracted by the parks and palaces. Don’t get too close to the people, for nothing good will come of it. Better stay in the mountains and isolated areas and meditate.”

As for me, Bodhisattva Jigten Wangchuk, I felt that every day was a day closer to being separated from my noble teacher, a day closer to falling into the nest of ignorant living beings. Tears helplessly streamed down my face. In a very soft voice, I replied, “My Guru, I am not going for the beautiful gardens in the king’s palace, nor do I go to seek the support and respect of the king and his people. These monks and the many people who depend on me hold too much hope and ambition. To fulfill their wishes and interests, I will go. However, I shall not stay with the king and his ministers for too long, as you have advised. Afterwards, I shall go to Mount Kailash to get blessings from Bodhisattva Chokyi Wangchuk. Distance cannot carve a separation between us. Please think of me always.” This I did request of him.

I offered Bodhisattva Gawey Yang all kinds of precious things, and then I went to the kingdom of Tsang.

We[243] spent a few months in the palace.

Autumn arrived. I myself took a trip towards Mount Kailash. On the way, I could not cross the rivers, and decided to go to Tsurphu instead where I stayed for a few months.

Bodhisattva Chokyi Wangchuk was teaching in a town near the Horse Mouth River. He had just finished teaching his disciples, and having thus satisfied their wishes, he headed towards Tsurphu. The moment I, Jigten Wangchuk, heard this news, I went to a place not far from Tsurphu, called Neynang Gyalwai Ri (a place of retreat), to receive him. I made all the necessary arrangements.

Neynang was the retreat center of *Mahasiddha* Dragpa Sangye (the First Shamarpa). In this area, the rocks were very smooth like

243 *KAC*: 170

mountain jewels. Crystal streams ran over the rocks on two sides. Flowers were blooming everywhere imbuing the air with mixed fragrances. The fields were flat and a beautiful green. Many cranes gathered there. Such was the place where I received Bodhisattva Chokyi Wangchuk.

Bodhisattva Chokyi Wangchuk gave me teachings on the nature of samsara and impermanence. He gave me teachings on the subject of selflessness. So convincing was he that I fully committed myself to following the Bodhisattva Path straight through, without pausing or wavering. I spent some time at Neynang.

One day after my return to Tsurphu from the medicine hills of Lho Drag, Bodhisattva Gawey Yang arrived. I offered him my prostrations and then served him completely.

Later, Bodhisattva Chokyi Wangchuk also came to Tsurphu from Neynang Gyalwai Ri.

In the temple, and in front of the Buddha statue, (originally brought to Tsurphu by five great yogis of India), I received the full *Vinaya* vows (in 1624). Bodhisattva Chokyi Wangchuk assumed the role of *Khenpo* (Abbot or Master of Studies) of *Vinaya*. Bodhisattva Gawey Yang was the *Lopon* (assistant to the *Khenpo* in the *Vinaya* ceremony). In[244] addition, the required number of sangha (members) as stipulated in the *Vinaya* was fully assembled. In all their presence, I received the complete *Vinaya* vows.

* * *

BL

When[245] Karmapa came to the age of twenty-one, in the year of the Wood Mouse (1624), he received the Full Monk's Vows, or the Full *Gelong*[246] Vows. Shamarpa Garwang Thamchad Khyenpa was the ceremonial *Khenpo* (abbot), giver of the *Gelong* Vows. He was assisted by Pawo Tsuklak Gyatso as the *Leykyi Lopon* (same as

244 *KAC*: 172

245 *BL*: 169b

246 Vows of ethics and conduct for a monk according to the *Vinaya*; they total 253.

Lopon, assistant to the *Khenpo*), and Situ Chokyi Gyaltsen as the *Sangtonpa.*[247] Another seven senior *gelongs* (ordained monks) also presided over the ceremony. In their presence, Karmapa received the full vows given by the Sixth Shamarpa. At that same ceremony, the Fifth Gyaltsab Dragpa Choyang[248] received the Monk's Semi-Vows[249] from *Khenpo* Shamarpa.

Karmapa, Gyaltsab and Situ Rinpoches and their party traveled to Lhasa to see the Jowo Buddha[250] at the temple (Jokhang). There, they offered an elaborate puja.

* * *

247 *Sangtonpa* is the interviwer who privately asks the vow-recipient a list of questions as a prerequisite to the vow ceremony.

248 He was recognized by Karmapa; see end of previous chapter.

249 While the Full Monk's Vows consist of 253 precepts, the Semi-Vows consist of thirteen fewer, thereby allowing the monks greater flexibility in every day life.

250 The Jokhang Temple houses the famous Jowo Shakyamuni statue.

21. Learning the Ways of a Bodhisattva

BL

After[251] the memorial rites for Desi Phuntsok Namgyal were completed (in 1621), Karmapa and entourage (except the Sixth Shamarpa) went on a pilgrimage to a big lake (Namtso) north of Lhasa. Long ago, the Third Karmapa (1284–1339) had left his footprints inside a temple called Tashi Dowori in the vicinity. When the Tenth Karmapa entered the temple, the very sight of those footprints brought back all the memories from his past life as the Third Karmapa.

Another incident took place outside the temple on a road. A fire had ignited the dry grass field nearby. Karmapa uttered a few words of blessings, and the fire was extinguished.

The next stop was Radreng. They visited the monastery built by Dromtonpa, the chief disciple of Atisha.[252]

From Radreng, they travelled to Yangpachen Monastery where the Sixth Shamarpa was awaiting their arrival at his main seat. On

251 *BL*: 169b

252 Atisha, the founder of Kadam Buddhism, taught *the Seven-Points of Lojong* (Mind-Training). The present Shamarpa's commentary on these teachings is published in his *The Path to Awakening* (New Delhi, India: Motilal Banarsidass, 2009).

the tenth day of the fourth month, a performance of Guru Padmasamvara's *mandala*[253] dance took place. Afterwards, Shamarpa joined Karmapa's party, and together they continued on to Tsurphu.

At Tsurphu a sand *mandala* of *Kalachakra* was created. Shamarpa first gave the *Kalachakra* initiation to Karmapa, Situ and Gyaltsab Rinpoches. Then, he gave them the empowerments of the *Red Avalokiteshvara*, and *Two-armed Mahakala.*

During the stay at Tsurphu, Shamarpa painted the sixteen *arhats*[254] on cloth. The figures were cut and pasted onto a special brocade thangka. Shamarpa offered this thangka to Karmapa.

From Tsurphu, Karmapa traveled back to Lho Drag to see Pawo Rinpoche. He wished to finish receiving from him the *lung* transmissions and (various) initiations, which had started earlier. However, Pawo Rinpoche was ill. To remove the obstacles threatening his teacher's health, Karmapa sent a messenger to invite Shamarpa to Lho Drag to help. Shamarpa soon arrived and conducted the *Long Life Initiations of Amitayu*[255] to eliminate all threats and obstacles. Pawo Rinpoche's health recovered completely.

Karmapa and Shamarpa then went to Shamarpa's retreat center in central Tibet. It was located in a beautiful forest. There, Shamarpa gave Karmapa the *Initiations of Drub Thab Gyatso.* Karmapa offered Shamarpa a standing Buddha statue made of red bronze. Its height was one arm's length (measured from the fingertips to the elbow).

After the initiations were completed, Duke Drakhawa of the district invited them to a huge ceremony where he presented a great many offerings to Karmapa, Shamarpa, and Gyaltsab Rinpoche.[256]

* * *

253 A symbolic representation of a Tantric deity's realm. As an offering, it symbolizes the entire universe.

254 An *arhat* is one who has attained a realization of mind such that the causes for rebirth in samsara have been eliminated.

255 One aspect of Buddha Amitabha, Buddha of Limitless Light.

256 *BL*: 170a

10th Karmapa

Probably in the summer of 1624 or 1625, the Tenth Karmapa received many teachings from the Sixth Shamarpa. He also learned from the example and teachings of his guru what it meant to be a bodhisattva.

I[257] rode a beautiful blue horse and went to see Bodhisattva Chokyi Wangchuk. I invited him to go with me to a small mountain retreat where in the past many *mahasiddhas*[258] had successfully accomplished their practices. At that place there were many beautiful flowers, and from time to time it would drizzle.

Bodhisattva[259] Chokyi Wangchuk immediately said he would teach me. In particular, he would teach me the beautiful and poetic verses by Master Satshosgyin. They were stories that described the (past) lives of the Buddha. He reached for some books sitting on his bookcase and handed them to me. I took them. I offered him my blue horse, and off we went together.

Master Satshosgyin was an Indian Buddhist pandit who likely lived in the time of Nagarjuna (c.150 – c.250). His poetic verses are stories that recount the past lives of the Buddha, before his life born as a prince who later attained enlightenment. In those lives, he was a bodhisattva – one who is committed to achieving enlightenment in order to help sentient beings. His help is not restricted to just the people of India, or to the humans and animals of this earth. Rather, the bodhisattva takes rebirth from realm to realm, in the form of beings that he wishes to help. In each life, he immerses himself completely in accomplishing his wishes for beings in the different universes, as it were. The Sixth Shamarpa emphasized this important point to the Tenth Karmapa, who grasped its full meaning. The Karmapa then dedicated himself to working as a bodhisattva just as the Buddha did.

Along the way, as Bodhisattva Chokyi Wangchuk was riding my horse, I thought to myself, "The happiness I feel now is the result of having invited Bodhisattva Chokyi Wangchuk. It is truly great

257 *KAC*: 173

258 Great "accomplished one(s)" in meditation.

259 *KAC*: 174; poems and poetic narratives on pages 173–178 have been omitted.

– so great that it has turned me completely into a true follower of Bodhisattva Chokyi Wangchuk. It is so immense that no other happiness can compare with it. The great happiness of the rich kings in the heavens pales next to my happiness now!"

While we were in retreat, one day Bodhisattva Chokyi Wangchuk sat on a rock, which served suitably as a seat. I sat lower than him. Bodhisattva Chokyi Wangchuk began to teach me the poems of Satshosgyin.

That first day, and for seven whole days, Bodhisattva Chokyi Wangchuk taught me. He taught me the *Lotus Sutra* and the stories contained in the *Vinaya* texts. These teachings showed me how to be a bodhisattva, how to practice the path of a bodhisattva, how to achieve the bodhisattva practice through the practice of the *paramitas,*[260] and so forth. All these practices would develop the noble qualities as vast and as deep as the ocean. I listened.

Rimdrowa, suppose a man found an *indraneela* stone (blue sapphire) and knew it to be a precious stone though he might not know its name. He showed it to an expert gem collector who happened to be a boatman.

Suppose the boatman told the man with the *indraneela* stone, "This is a stone called *indraneela.* And yes, there is a very special island where you can get it. Don't you know? It is that island there across the ocean."

Suppose the man had never seen the ocean, and so he replied, "No, I don't know. Actually, I don't even know what an ocean is? Can you tell me if it is big or small?"

The boatman said, "Ah, the ocean is very big, bigger than a continent. All the water your eyes could see combined would still be too small to be the ocean. And the ocean has so many precious stones and gems, far greater in quantity than what you could find on land. And I've found this special island in the ocean where many precious stones and gems have been washed ashore from the ocean."

"In that case, there must be many more precious stones there on

260 Literally, *paramita* means "to reach the other shore." It is a Mahayana method to transcend concepts of subject, object and action according to the *Prajnaparamita* scriptures.

the island like this *indraneela*." the man surmised.

"Yes, there are so many precious stones there on the island!"

"In that case, why am I working here?" questioned the man. "With the taxes I have to pay on this small farm, I can never be rich. But, if I were to follow this boatman, he can lead me across the ocean to that island. I can become rich like him. Why won't I follow the boatman?"

Bodhisattva Chokyi Wangchuk is the boatman who knows how to reach the precious land of enlightenment. He knows how to cross the ocean of liberation by gathering merits. He knows how by the bodhisattva practice and the practice of the *Perfection of the Paramitas* to grow a tiny amount of merit until it becomes as vast as the ocean. Therefore, Bodhisattva Chokyi Wangchuk is the guide for enlightenment. I should trust and rely upon him to guide me to enlightenment. I[261] should follow him, and I should serve him.

And so it was on that day that I heard such precious teachings from Bodhisattva Chokyi Wangchuk. He knew the boundless qualities of the bodhisattvas. He knew the directions how one can comfortably reach great levels of accomplishment. He also possessed the compassion to lead others to attain the supreme qualities of the Buddhas. Why wouldn't I follow Bodhisattva Chokyi Wangchuk?

I thought to myself, "I am a spiritual teacher. To collect offerings and show off everywhere as a highly revered person holds no meaning for me. From now on, I will follow Bodhisattva Chokyi Wangchuk who possesses the Dharma-ship to cross the ocean of samsara. He[262] can ferry me across to precious nirvana. I am committed to following him from now on."

Rimdrowa, while I was in the retreat house at Neynang Gyalwai Ri, very early one morning, I heard Bodhisattva Chokyi Wangchuk reciting the sutras of the Buddha as I woke up. First,[263] I was very sad upon hearing the conditions of samsara. But then, I was happy again and encouraged by the realization that from time to time,

261 *KAC*: 178

262 *KAC*: 179. Some poems from this point until the middle of page 180 are omitted.

263 *KAC*: 180

day or night, I have the precious opportunity to hear the great sutras recited by the great Bodhisattva Chokyi Wangchuk. That in itself is wondrous happiness that, surely, heavenly beings do not possess.

Rimdrowa, you know, sometimes Bodhisattva Chokyi Wangchuk and I, Jigten Wangchuk, his follower, would be together on the top floor at Tsurphu Monastery. We would create paintings of the Buddha surrounded by bodhisattvas and *arhats*, of Chenrezig and others. Bodhisattva Chokyi Wangchuk, and I, Jigten Wangchuk, exchanged views about how to design the background scenery in the paintings. We both experienced the blessings we were receiving, and the merits we were accumulating.

Rimdrowa, one day, Bodhisattva Chokyi Wangchuk sat on a throne and gave me, Jigten Wangchuk, the *Initiation of Arya Tara*, the protector of the sixteen obstacles. Another day, Bodhisattva Chokyi Wangchuk gave me the books written by Master Satshosgyin, the best among the Indian pandits (scholars) called *The Wish-fulfilling Tree*. He also gave me a book entitled *Riding the Horse of Cloud* by Chandrawati, another great Indian pandit, which told of how the Buddha accomplished the limitless activities of a bodhisattva.

Rimdrowa,[264] on another occasion, a Mongolian king who was very devoted to the Buddhadharma invited Bodhisattva Chokyi Wangchuk and his monk disciples. They went and stayed there for a while. One day in the autumn, I heard that Bodhisattva Chokyi Wangchuk was on his way back. I rode my horse beautiful like a peacock to an area with streams and covered by fragrant flowers. It is near the snowcap of Thanglha (named after a Tibetan god) and Yangpachen. I went there to receive him.

Bodhisattva Chokyi Wangchuk and I settled down in that area. We talked about the Dharma, and the different places we visited. We also told jokes. Every day we saw deer and rabbits playing in the fields. Near the stream, the cranes were singing and playing. Bodhisattva Chokyi Wangchuk explained to the disciples there the

264 *KAC*: 185. Poetic narratives from 181–184 not translated.

verses and poems of Master Satshosgyin – how Buddha Shakyamuni engaged in bodhisattva activities over many lifetimes.[265] I volunteered to hold the umbrella over him to give shade, as it was very hot. He taught for fifteen days. Sometimes we took some days off when we would play and go swimming in the streams.

265 *KAC*: 186

22. Visits to the Seats of Kagyu Sects and to the Tsang Capital

Karmapa travelled together with the Sixth Shamarpa and visited the monasteries of the Kagyu sects. Afterwards, upon the invitation of the Tsang Desi, they went to Shigatse and his palace (Sambdrub Tse).

BL

The[266] three masters and party arrived at Samye Monastery. Shamarpa gave Karmapa and Gyaltsab Rinpoche the Bodhisattva Vow. The next day, they together performed the *tsokor* of Guru Yoga of Guru Rinpoche.[267]

Karmapa and party then continued their pilgrimage in central Tibet. They visited Nyinched Ling in Zatham, a famous Buddhist college founded by Shamarpa. A big *monlam*[268] puja was performed. Karmapa received the *Vinaya* teachings. Shamarpa then offered Karmapa the entire college of Nyinched Ling giving him

266 *BL*: 170a

267 *Tsokor* is a long puja or prayer.

268 *Monlam* is a prayer festival.

all the land title deeds, along with everything valuable there.[269] To Gyaltsab Rinpoche, Shamarpa offered a huge silk thangka which depicted the Buddha's life in Magadha plus many other relics and offerings.

The pilgrims then went to Taglung to visit the main seat of the Taglung Kagyu sect. They performed a large ceremonial rite and made many offerings. Drigung, the main seat of the Drigung Kagyu sect, was their next stop.[270] A famous throne for public teaching called the Red Brick Throne was there. Karmapa sat on it and taught the *Four Dharmas of Gampopa* to the monks and the public.

From Drigung, the party continued on to Yerpa Kagyu. Again, they performed a puja and made offerings at the temple. Karmapa painted a few thangkas, one of which depicted the sixteen *arhats*. He also painted a bodhisattva in the form of a bird.

The Desi of Tsang sent an invitation to invite Karmapa and Shamarpa.

* * *

10th Karmapa

> The Tenth Karmapa writes about his teacher's reaction to the Tsang Desi's invitation.

One[271] day, Bodhisattva Chokyi Wangchuk went to Nyinched Ling to teach many monks there. I, Jigten Wangchuk, followed him. Bodhisattva Chokyi Wangchuk and I read the *Vinaya* to the monks in order to remind them of the impermanence of life, to encourage them to fully commit to the life of a renunciate. Together we did

---

269 The Tenth Karmapa wrote in *KAC* that he declined this offering.

270 At that time, the Sixth Shamarpa was the main holder of the Drigung Kagyu lineage.

271 *KAC*: 187

the purification practice of *sojong*.[272]

One[273] day, Bodhisattva Chokyi Wangchuk and I along with the disciples went to a beautiful forest in front of Tsurphu Monastery covered in white flowers. He began to teach how samsara was an illusion and how worldly life was impermanent – once the present illusion was over, we would again fall into another illusion. We cannot attain enlightenment through the cycle of illusions. Therefore, because this life is short, we must not waste it on meaningless acts. Bodhisattva Chokyi Wangchuk gave us profound teachings on this vast subject.

Many disciples were able to give up their homes that were like the nests of snakes.[274] They chose instead to stay in caves or in tiny huts among the trees, the flowers, the deer, and the birds, which neither irritated nor disturbed them. As a result, they experienced *samadhi*[275] by following Bodhisattva Chokyi Wangchuk's instructions and successfully renouncing worldly life.

One[276] day a messenger from the Tsang king arrived. Bodhisattva Chokyi Wangchuk was invited to teach in the (Tsang) kingdom. However, Bodhisattva Chokyi Wangchuk was unwilling to go. He did not say very much. In his view, kingdoms (i.e., political states) were places of samsara. The messenger waited for his reply for some time.

Then, some caretakers of the monastery, who were responsible for looking after the monks' community, approached Bodhisattva Chokyi Wangchuk. They told him not to ignore the king, or the monastery might encounter problems down the road. They felt that a cooperative relationship with the (Tsang) king would prove helpful in every respect.

Bodhisattva Chokyi Wangchuk took into consideration the pres-

---

272 The Tenth Karmapa and the Sixth Shamarpa both liked to practice *sojong* regularly. It is a short purification retreat. Whenever they were together, every fifteen days, the two masters would practice *sojong*. Sometimes, to keep his discipline as pure as possible, the Tenth Karmapa practiced it in between on his own.

273 *KAC*: 188

274 "Nests of snakes" is a metaphor to depict city-homes as crowded and undesirable.

275 A state of meditation.

276 *KAC*: 189

ent as well as the future. He knew that the staff responsible for the monks and monastery wished very much to receive support from the (Tsang) kingdom. He also thought the people of the kingdom would benefit from being guided in the right direction. When its people follow the Dharma, the kingdom would turn into a place of merits. Thinking thus, he decided to fulfill the wishes of the administrators.

Bodhisattva Chokyi Wangchuk came to me and told me that he was going, and asked, "Would you like to go?"

I answered, "Ever since I was separated from my family and until now, I've never had the opportunity to be in a peaceful retreat away from samsaric problems. Why would I go to the king's house and waste this precious time? I will not go."

Then[277] Bodhisattva Chokyi Wangchuk said, "We should go this once to fulfill their wishes, and then we shall go to Mount Kailash."

"Very well then," I said, "the great Bodhisattva Chokyi Wangchuk had given me these words, and I will follow them."

And so Bodhisattva Chokyi Wangchuk and I, Jigten Wangchuk, went.

* * *

BL

Karmapa[278] and party traveled to the Sambdrub Tse Palace. After a most generous reception, they all camped at Gyaltse Park.

At Sambdrub Tse, when the Earth Dragon year was ending, and the Earth Snake year (1629) was about to begin, Karmapa, Shamarpa and the Desi prepared a very big prayer rite to welcome the New Year. Afterwards, Je[279] Shamarpa gave an extensive teaching on the *Gongchi* text[280] to a huge following.[281] It was written by

277 *KAC*: 190

278 *BL*: 170a

279 This is an honorific appellation.

280 *Gongchi* means unique view. In this context, it refers to the unique way of teaching the Buddha's teachings of the *Tripitaka*.

281 *BL*: 170b

the Drigung Kagyu lineage founder.[282] Afterwards, Karmapa and Shamarpa jointly asked the government officials to release all prisoners from the jails.

While still camped in Sambdrub Tse, Karmapa and Shamarpa took time out to visit a special temple at Narthang. The great Buddhist master of Tibet, Chim Namkha Drag, had once made special prayers to invite the sixteen *arhats*. His prayers were answered at this temple when the all sixteen *arhats* miraculously descended from their abodes and appeared for a short while.

During a *Madhyamaka*[283] conference, Shamarpa and Karmapa engaged in debate with Kadampa *geshes*[284] for one whole day. Karmapa painted a very special thangka of the wrathful deity Achala.[285]

From the capital of Tsang, the party went on to Sakya where Karmapa met Sakya Dhakchen Rinpoche, the head of Sakya sect.

282 The founder of the Drigung Kagyu lineage is known as Skyobspa Wjig Rten Gsungyi Mgonpo, or Kyobpa Jigten Gongchi Gonpo.

283 *Madhyamaka* is considered the highest Buddhist view or philosophy commonly referred to as *The Middle Way.* Scholars, philosophers, and Buddhist masters gathered in the *Madhyamaka* conference to discuss and debate the different views.

284 Scholars from the Kadam sect who follow the teachings of Atisha.

285 *Achala* is "The Immovable One, King of Wrath."

23. Pilgrimage to Mount Kailash

This chapter recounts the Tenth Karmapa's pilgrimage around 1629 to Mount Kailash, which Tibetans also call Tise. Before setting out, he and the Sixth Shamarpa travelled together for a short while after leaving the Tsang capital of Shigatse. During this time the Sixth Shamarpa transmitted the entire Karma Kagyu lineage to him.

BL

The[286] Tenth Karmapa and the Sixth Shamarpa arrived at Gyalgyi Shiri[287] Monastery near the Nepal border. The two masters conducted special prayers at the site of a holy rock called Chutshang Drag (or Water Nest Rock).

One day, Karmapa had a vision of the *Mahasiddhas* of India in the sky, while others around him saw only rainbows.

At Dhingri Lang Khor (in southern Tibet), Karmapa suddenly had a realization of *Dharmakaya* (the unobstructed purity of self and of phenomena). He had a vision of Dampa Kunga, the *Ma-*

286 *BL*: 170a

287 In Gyalgyi Shiri, there used to be a well-developed *Mahamudra* center until recently. It was here that the Drukpa Kagyu Master Togden Shakya Shri organized and taught the profound *Mahamudra* teachings. Distinguished Kagyupa masters from this great monastery are still alive today.

hasiddha of Tibet, dressed in a multi-colored robe and playing the *damaru* (two-sided hand drum) As the land was flat in that region, Karmapa decided to walk the rest of his pilgrimage.

At Labchi Chubar, Karmapa saw Tsering Chednga – the five sister-deities of Mount Everest – in the sky. They were the disciples of Milarepa. Karmapa also saw Milarepa in the sky dressed in a yellow monk's robe with a big smile on his face.

Karmapa and Shamarpa decided to build a temple at a special place called Chojung Teng.[288] Both skilled in geomancy,[289] the two masters selected a perfect spot and placement for the temple. They also took part in its construction. Carrying the bricks and rocks with their hands, they worked alongside the workers.

* * *

BL

The[290] Tenth Karmapa taught at holy places. He explained the basic teachings of the *Samadhiraja Sutra* (known as *The King of Contemplation Sutra*). He taught the *Sahaja Yoga* (on the simultaneous production and union, or innate union). And he gave instructions on *Mahamudra*[291] meditation in the Dhagpo Kagyu tradition.

During the same period, the Sixth Shamarpa explained at length and in great detail why there is not a single difference between the *Mahamudra* teachings and the teachings of the *Samadhiraja.*[292]

One day, a forest fire erupted on the mountain Bonpori. Karmapa prayed to Konchog Sum (or the Triple Gem),[293] and he uttered aloud the words "must rain," and immediately it rained. The fire

---

288 As noted in chapter 22, this land was given by the King of Tsang.

289 Geomancy is called *feng shui* in Chinese; *wastowa* in Sanskrit, or *sached* in Tibetan.

290 *BL*: 170a

291 *Mahamudra*, which literally means "The Great Seal," is the highest view expounded by the Karma Kagyu sect, which can be realized through meditation.

292 Here is the time and place when the Sixth Shamarpa transmitted the Karma Kagyu lineage teachings to the Tenth Karmapa. This special transmission is called the *Karma Kagyu Golden Lineage*. It encompasses the detailed explanations, instructions, and blessings that elucidate and connect the meanings of the *Samadhiraja* teachings with the *Mahamudra* teachings as the same, without any difference.

293 The Triple Gem is the Buddha, Dharma and Sangha.

was extinguished.

On the recommendation of the Sixth Shamarpa, during this period, Karmapa began to paint a set of thangkas depicting the lineage holders of the *Mahamudra*. He also painted the sixteen *arhats*.[294]

* * *

10th Karmapa

The Tenth Karmapa writes of the time when he and the Sixth Shamarpa went to Dengmadring in southwestern Tibet, where the Sixth Shamarpa taught and asked him to paint the sixteen arhats.

After some time in spring, Bodhisattva Chokyi Wangchuk set out for the area where the supreme Milarepa had meditated in the caves called Drin Nyenam. I, Jigten Wangchuk, followed him. One month after we left the (Tsang) kingdom, we reached Dengmadring in the west.

Bodhisattva Chokyi Wangchuk gave teachings to the monks and laypeople on how to commence the precious Dharma practice by fully contemplating on impermanence, the preciousness of life, and the nature of samsara. He explained how to cultivate a peaceful mind, renounce attachment to samsara, and liberate oneself from samsara, like casting a snake out of one's lap or like putting out sparks in one's hair.[295] He explained that in order to control negative attachments, one should practice and recite sutras. The teachings he provided to the sangha were complete. The number of his disciples increased by the day.

Rimdrowa, it was such an opportunity for me. I heard the most profound music of Dharma from Bodhisattva Chokyi Wangchuk in such a great place once blessed by the most supreme enlightened being, Milarepa. This thought occupied my mind the whole time we were there.

294 *BL*: 171a

295 This analogy means to eliminate attachments reflexively, without any thought and very hastily.

One[296] day Bodhisattva Chokyi Wangchuk said to me, "To accumulate great merits, why don't you paint the sixteen *arhats* as you did when you were at Tsurphu in *sithang* style?"

I respectfully accepted this advice and started painting. In five months I completed the thangka.[297]

The term sithang *is derived from two Tibetan words –* si-u *which means brocade fabric and* thang *from thangka that means painting.* Sithang *is an elision of these two words.*

Sithang *is a technique for creating thangkas. The artist first sketches the outline of the image on a piece of cloth (e.g., the deity Avalokiteshvara.) Pieces of brocade are cut to form the desired shapes and colors and sewn onto the image in a patchwork fashion. Prior to the Tenth Karmapa, similar thangkas called by other names were created with silk or other materials. Karmapa's innovation was the use of* si-u. *This was more challenging because the colors of the brocade had to match the colors desired in the design. (For two brief descriptions of the creation of a* sithang *thangka, see chapter 28.)*

The very first sithang *thangka depicted the sixteen* arhats *which first became a popular theme in Chinese art. Chinese historical records*

reveal that the Emperor Taizong of the Tang Dynasty (reigned 627–650) once invited sixteen arhats *to China. They were said to have miraculously arrived and did a summer retreat at the palace. Karmapa made a special* sithang *thangka of the sixteen* arhats *in this Chinese tradition.*

* * *

BL

One[298] day, the Tenth Karmapa asked permission from his guru, Shamarpa, to travel towards Tise (the Mt. Kailash massif). Shamarpa taught him what to do for this special pilgrimage. He gave him

296 *KAC*: 195

297 *KAC*: 197

298 *BL*: 171a

all the background information about the snowcapped mountain, why it was holy, and other details.

Karmapa left for Tise. On his way, he made a stop at the famous lake in Palmopathang where Milarepa once did retreats in a nearby cave. Karmapa stayed in the same cave for some time. Many nomads went every day to see him. They offered him sheep, which he then set free in the mountain. Gold traders paid their respects to Karmapa and offered him a lot of gold.

Karmapa then proceeded to Lake Mapam (today known as Lake Manasarovar). On the south side of the holy lake, he bathed. The sky was a very clear blue, and as he bathed, a rainbow clearly appeared. Through the beautiful rainbow, he could see Tise. He also saw many *yidams* (deities) assembled there, while numerous heavenly beings made supplications and offerings to them. Karmapa's parents were with him at the time, and so he taught them how to supplicate the holy deities.

West of Lake Mapam was Miracle Cave, so named because Milarepa performed many miracles there. Inside it was a beautiful thangka depicting the Buddha and the sixteen *arhats*. There, Karmapa recited the *Vinaya Sutra* to his monk disciples and performed the purification practice of *sojong*.

* * *

10th Karmapa

Below, the Tenth Karmapa recounts his trip to Tise (the Mt. Kailash massif).

One day Rimdrowa asked me to tell of the time when I traveled to Tise.

It[299] was when I had finished my paintings that I told Bodhisattva Chokyi Wangchuk that I would like to visit Tise. He thus instructed me on how to go there. He gave me detailed instructions on what to do at the holy caves, lakes and mountains. He

299 *KAC*: 198–213, poetic descriptions and inconsequential information not translated.

told me to be careful of robbers and to take care when crossing strong waterfalls. I should be careful not to get lost crossing the vast flat lands. He also asked me to bring back some water from Lake Madhro.[300]

To send me off, Bodhisattva Chokyi Wangchuk escorted me quite some distance. Seven hundred disciples volunteered to accompany me on this pilgrimage.

We went first to a very large and flat land called Palmopalthang. There was a beautiful clear lake and a cave used by Milarepa. I spent one night there while constantly thinking of the stories from the life of Milarepa, and great devotion arose in me.

Everywhere I went, people gave me offerings, and I in return gave them teachings. I even met some gold-diggers who offered me gold pieces.

One day, as I was crossing a vast, flat, and sandy land, a man riding a black and white horse suddenly approached our group.

He asked me, "Where are you going?"

"We are going to Tise," I told him.

The man said that behind the mountain, a large group of thieves from India had made camp there. The people in our group, which included many Chinese, were all frightened by this news. I told them not to be afraid, that we would find a way around the thieves. Our group should stay close together to look large in number, and this should deter the thieves. As it happened, the thieves did run away from us because we were greater in number.

Finally one day, we saw Tise in the distance. I proceeded to reach the east side of Lake Madhro and bathed in it. My parents were also with me, and they bathed in the south side of the lake.

Gradually, we approached Tise, which is usually seen with its peak hidden among the clouds. But when we got close, they cleared away so that we could see the peak. My mind was not distracted the whole time from thinking how wonderful it was to be in such a remote area just to do meditation.

We reached a cave that contained Milarepa's handprints. I med-

---

300 Buddha called Lake Mapam by the name Lake Madhro.

itated there. Among the followers were about one hundred who had taken the Full Monk's Vows. Together we performed a special prayer using a thangka of the sixteen *arhats*.

Very early one morning, I started to circumambulate Tise.[301] The moon was still bright in the sky, so I could see the road. I passed by a place where the Buddha once came miraculously and performed a special practice. Five hundred *arhats* left their footprints there on a rock. I reached this rock and offered special prayers while thinking of what had happened in the past. Groups of deer came to greet me. I made many cloth copies of the footprints to give to the people. When I was about to leave, the groups of deer came again to send me off, which was quite out of the ordinary.

Then I climbed to the upper part of the mountain. On a beautiful rock was a footprint of the Buddha. The moment I saw it, I felt how great the Buddha was, and I made special supplication to him and offered him a homage prayer.

I reached a cave called Miracle Cave where Milarepa had stayed. I stayed in this cave. Afterward, I reached a flat land where a rock in the center stood in the shape of an umbrella. At that time, some deer followed me for some way as if seeing me off.

The king of Purang (south of Kailash) sent his ministers with his army to invite me. I told the messengers that we were many in our group and that we had to return before the winter. We would not have time to visit their kingdom. I sent him a message and included some teachings. In my reply, I told him that by the devotion of himself and his people, there was no difference between seeing or not seeing me in person. Their devotion would cause them to accumulate the merits as great as in seeing the Buddha and the bodhisattvas. I told them that praying to me with devotion would be the same as seeing me because I had already dedicated wishes for them all.

I arrived at a village called Mangyul (nowadays Kyid Drong near Nepal) where there was an Avalokiteshvara statue carved

301 Pilgrims from different religions believe that circumambulating Mount Kailasha (a trip of about 30 miles) is a holy ritual that will bring good fortune. Buddhists circumambulate the mountain in a clockwise direction.

from sandalwood. I[302] went to see it.

I[303] received word that Bodhisattva Chokyi Wangchuk was thinking of going to India. All his followers including three kings in Nepal were worried. They thought the journey to India would be difficult, and not good for the health and life of Bodhisattva Chokyi Wangchuk. They knew he wanted to visit Bodhgaya, Varanasi, etc. They told him that India was a place taken over by wrong religious beliefs such as sacrificing humans and animals in worship. There were also many robbers, snakes, and tigers, and so forth, not to mention natural disasters such as forest fires and flooding.

Bodhisattva Chokyi Wangchuk told them that everything depended on his karma. If[304] it were good, he would meet with success in his endeavors. If he had bad karma, he would meet with danger. That was his answer to their concerns.

By that time, I had finished my trip to Kailash and was in Mangyul. Bodhisattva Chokyi Wangchuk knew I was there, and he sent a message to me telling me that he was going to India.

* * *

BL

Messengers[305] came from Mon Dzumlang with an invitation from their king. They offered Karmapa many gold coins. However, Karmapa declined their invitation. This happened when he was on the side of Tise (the Mt. Kailash massif) called Tretapuri.[306]

During his pilgrimage, the Tenth Karmapa once said, "Je Drigungpa (the founder of Drigung Kagyu sect) stated that Tise is Ribo Gangchen[307] mentioned many times by the Buddha in the sutras. Lake Mapam is the lake the Buddha called Lake Madhro.

302 *KAC*: 214; pages 215–235 of *KAC* have been omitted which contained the descriptions of the travels and activities of the Sixth Shamarpa in Kathmandu, Nepal.

303 *KAC:* 235

304 *KAC*: 236

305 *BL*: 171a

306 This is near the northwest border of contemporary Tibet.

307 Ribo Gangchen means Mount Snowcap which today is known as Mt. Kailash.

However, Guru Shamarpa said, "Ribo Gangchen and Tise are somewhat different, yet you can say they are the same. Why? The Hindu doctrine of *Bahadikesara* states that Tise has four horns (i.e., peaks). Ribo Gangchen is only its northern peak, so Tise and Ribo Gangchen are not the same. However, since Ribo Gangchen is one peak of Tise, they are the same mountain."[308]

Karmapa[309] then traveled to Kyid Drong village where there was a very special statue of Buddha Shakyamuni. Karmapa was a pilgrim who traveled like a beggar with the simplest of means. When he arrived in Palmopalthang (near the Nepal border in a village called Kyid Drong today), the villagers discovered that he was Karmapa and went to see him. They asked why he had come to them in such a humble way. "You are even higher than the kings, and they respect you and give you offerings. Why then are you traveling in such a humble way?"

While he was there at the village, Karmapa painted an image of the Buddha Shakyamuni. He also painted a thangka of Milarepa.

While Karmapa was at a cave called Zawog, he received a letter from Shamar Thamchad Khyenpa (the Sixth Shamarpa who was in Kathmandu, Nepal) in order to set in place the small niches[310] on the stupas (in Kathmandu). In his letter, Shamarpa mentioned that he would go on a pilgrimage to India soon.

Karmapa was very saddened by this news. Tears streamed from his eyes. His elder brother Jewon Namkh consoled him, "Don't cry, we should request Shamar Rinpoche not to go."

Karmapa sent a messenger to his guru imploring him not to go to India. He also sent many gold pieces he had received as offerings for the construction of stupas and the golden niches.

---

308 Milarepa noted two views of the snowcap in one of his songs: "From a distance, the Tise Mountain looks like a crystal stupa (to the people) and is thus named. Up close, it is a mountain with a snowcap. However, to higher beings, it is the Chakrasamvara mandala of superior beings (deities)." The Hindu Babas (religious teachers) worship Mount Kailash as the mandala of Lord Shiva. A prediction in Hindu mythology says that one day Lord Shiva and Hanuman, the monkey god, will hold a victory ceremony there.

309 *BL*: 171b

310 These are small, enclosed compartments, or alcoves, set into a stupa that are constructed in copper, and then covered in gold. A statue of the Buddha is usually placed in such an alcove. It is then sealed by a gold mesh, which serves as a screen.

24. A Plea

10th Karmapa

The Tenth Karmapa tells how he asked the Sixth Shamarpa, likely in the late 1620s, not to go to India. As well, he explains why, like the Sixth Shamarpa, he prefers to travel in the simplest manner.

I[311] could not eat. I could not drink. Uncontrollably, tears welled up in my eyes. A relative asked why I was so sad. I said it was because the great Bodhisattva Chokyi Wangchuk, who was already old,[312] was planning to go to India. That place was too far away, and its climate so hot that anything could happen to him. Therefore, I felt quite concerned. My relative suggested that I should write him and ask him not to go.

I sent a letter to Bodhisattva Chokyi Wangchuk by the quickest possible way. Here is what I wrote:

> All the Buddhas and bodhisattvas who are in the bodhisattva practice have no concern for their own well-being. They do not care whether something is good or bad for them. While this is typical of bodhisattvas, nevertheless, Bodhisattva, you are getting on in years.

311 *KAC*: 236–237

312 He was only in his 40's, not old by today's standards.

> Suppose you were here in a meditation house, then we, your disciples, would be able to assist you with everything. However, in the faraway land of the supreme beings (India), you would be without our assistance.
>
> In the aim to liberate many beings, please consider liberating the sentient beings in Tibet, the land of Avalokiteshvara. Also, please have compassion and consider our heartfelt request of you not to travel so far away.

I learned later that the great Bodhisattva Chokyi Wangchuk took my letter, opened it and read it. He analyzed my request in his wisdom. He checked to see if there were still living beings in Tibet, the land of Avalokiteshvara, whom he could help. He also requested a prediction from the Triple Gem, and the answer was yes. Therefore, Bodhisattva Chokyi Wangchuk gave up his plans for India. Everything happened exactly as I had requested.

Bodhisattva Chokyi Wangchuk stayed in Kathmandu. With[313] the help of the best sculptors in Nepal, he finished making all the improvements to the stupas in Swayambhu.

I received a letter from Bodhisattva Chokyi Wangchuk. It said, "There is a stupa in Gomasala[314] that we should help to develop and make beautiful. If you have gold, please send it to me. This would be indeed meritorious."

I sent him all the gold I had. I also wrote him, "When you have finished all your work there, by your compassion, please think of us, and return to us as soon as possible."

I heard that Bodhisattva Chokyi Wangchuk was happy to receive my letter.[315]

Rimdrowa, at that time, I, Jigten Wangchuk, was in Mangyul

---

313 *KAC*: 239

314 Swayambhu of today.

315 The Tenth Karmapa went to great lengths to extol the Sixth Shamarpa's bodhisattva activities. For example, he recounted how the Sixth Shamarpa gave teachings in Sanskrit to large audiences in Nepal. He described how the Sixth Shamarpa provided explanations on profound Buddhist subjects and practices everywhere he went in Tibet and Nepal; how he completed his work on the stupas in Kathmandu, how the kings in the different areas revered him as a Buddha and wanted to invite him to their kingdoms. However, his teacher chose to travel from village to village like a beggar. This very extensive section running many pages in *KAC* has not been translated here but just paraphrased.

(Kyid Drong). The[316] people in that area, including the hunters, came often to give me offerings. They asked me, "You are respected by the king of Tibet, yet you came here looking like a beggar. You gave up that life, why?"

I told them, "Respect and prestige are not good. I do not want them. They are distractions; to pursue them is bad. Therefore, I gave them up as if they were garbage. I choose to go everywhere without a fixed plan."

People were surprised and inspired by my nature. Together as a group, they took up a collection and gave me five hundred coins saying, "For our merits, please accept our offering." I gave them teachings about non-attachment and what is the right path to follow.

Regarding[317] the property of others that had been taken and used wildly (i.e., senselessly), such properties would not make suitable gifts even if they were offered to you.[318]

I gave the people teachings in verses as well as explanations. The people in turn gathered many foods, milk, and butter, and offered them to me. I[319] used their offerings.

I traveled everywhere to meet people, for I wished them to have the seed – one that would enable them to be liberated by me, either now or in the future, because I am a bodhisattva.

My travels then took me to Dhingri where about five hundred people waited. The moment they saw me in the distance, they came forward to receive me. Seeing me as I was, they asked, "You could stay in the palaces of kings and receive offerings from royalty all the time. Yet, we see that you have given all that up. You wander instead in these poor districts like a beggar. Rather than wearing expensive clothing, you are here without a horse to ride on, and without a large following. Your entourage numbers but a few. Why are you doing this?"

---

316 *KAC*: 270

317 *KAC*: 272

318 According to the Tenth Karmapa, property that the kings, dukes, and chieftains have acquired by exploitation of others would not make a suitable gift.

319 *KAC*: 273–274

I replied, “If I distance myself from ignorant indulgences, then I can create a cause for samsara to end. Therefore, I keep the kingdoms and their people at a distance. I go and stay wherever, free.”

People gave me offerings, and I in turn gave them instructions. The many animals offered me would have been destined for the slaughterhouses, but I set them free.

25. Death of the Shamarpa

A year or so before the Sixth Shamarpa's paranirvana *(death of a bodhisattva) in 1630, the Karmapa spent an intense period of time with his guru, gaining last teachings and instructions and tenderly caring for him during his final illness. Upon his death, the Karmapa arranged elaborate funeral rites.*

BL

The[320] Tenth Karmapa arrived at Dengmadring (in the southwestern part of Tibet) and stayed for a while. He started to paint again.

Shamarpa Thamchad Khyenpa arrived from Nepal. Karmapa went to receive him. They met at Trodhe Tashi Gang. Karmapa offered Shamarpa the water of Lake Mapam in a silver pot. Upon receiving the holy water in his hands, Shamarpa sprinkled some over his disciple's head. He in turn offered Karmapa a roll of precious and exquisite red cloth. He also bestowed some elephant tusks, a white scarf from Kashmir, and other wonderful gifts made in India and Nepal.

The two masters then exchanged accounts of all their latest ac-

320 *BL*: 171b

tivities. Shamarpa told of his travels in Nepal and news from India. Karmapa recounted all the details about his pilgrimage to Mt. Kailash and Lake Mapam.

Afterwards, Karmapa carried Shamarpa's bag of books and things on his back, and together they went to Labchi Chubar.[321] There, they rested for some time.

Shamar Thamchad Khyenpa's health then began to deteriorate gradually. When he was ill, Karmapa would serve and tend to him the whole time. A nice cave in the valley proved a suitable place for Shamarpa to stay and convalesce, and so Karmapa accompanied his teacher there.

After a short period, Shamarpa's health improved. He composed a book of poetic verses about the Twelve Deeds of Buddha Shakyamuni. He named it *Joyful Song* and gave it to Karmapa.

Not long afterwards, a message from Lho Drag brought the news that Pawo Rinpoche Tsuklak Gyatso had entered *Dharmakaya* (died). Karmapa was deeply saddened. Soon after Je Garwang Thamchad Khyenpa also passed away.

* * *

10th Karmapa

I[322] went to Dengmadring. During my stay there, I painted the Buddha and the sixteen *arhats*, and Avalokiteshvara. I missed my guru, Chokyi Wangchuk, whom I had not seen in a long time. I decided to write him, "We have not seen you in a long time. Please have great compassion on us. Please think of us and come back."

Then, I received Bodhisattva Chokyi Wangchuk's response, saying that he had finished his work and that he would come soon.

I[323] was very happy. I made ceremonial umbrellas to hold over his head. I arranged a beautiful seat for him. I made an incense pot out of gold. I also arranged to have milk, yogurt, and suitable offerings available for his tea and meals.

---

321 It is situated in west Tibet, near Nepal.

322 *KAC*: 276

323 *KAC*: 278

The next day, a message arrived at Trodhe Tashi Gang where I was living. I knew I would soon have the precious opportunity to see my guru, Bodhisattva Chokyi Wangchuk.

The following morning, I woke up happy and excited. I dressed. Standing and waiting on a large boulder, I was the first to spot Bodhisattva Chokyi Wangchuk in the distance. The moment I saw him, great devotion surged from my heart, and I did many prostrations to him.

When my guru was standing in front of me, the first thing I offered him was the water I had taken from Lake Madhro (or Mapam) near Mount Kailash. I offered Bodhisattva Chokyi Wangchuk a pot filled with that water. He took it from my hands and drank some of it first. Then he sprinkled some droplets over my head. I in turn offered him two silk scarves joined together.

Bodhisattva Chokyi Wangchuk gave me a red shawl made of the most exquisite cloth from Nepal. He also gave me two elephant tusks, a sculpture of a wild boar, and an elephant figurine fully adorned with gold and jeweled ornaments. There was also a piece of the purest white cloth. These were the very auspicious gifts I received from him.

A place for lunch had already been set up. We ate some yogurt and milk. I recounted to Bodhisattva Chokyi Wangchuk my pilgrimage to Mount Kailash.

After a rest, we proceeded to the retreat house. It is usual for bodhisattvas to carry books of the Buddha's sutras, a thangka of the Buddha with the sixteen *arhats*, a white wooden cup, and some sewing threads and needles – all in one bag. I took Bodhisattva Chokyi Wangchuk's bag and placed it on my own back. I then led him to the retreat house in this place of Dengmadring.

We were together for many days. I served him the whole time, and we talked about many interesting things.

Spring arrived. In the forest, trees were blooming with flowers and leaves, while birds and deer became active. Bodhisattva Chokyi Wangchuk only taught from time to time. He stayed neither in the crowds nor with his disciples, thereby engaging in far fewer conversations and discussions.

Usually Bodhisattva Chokyi Wangchuk talked to make people happy. He would do everything to make his disciples happy. However, during that time, he was becoming more isolated and less engaged.

"What is happening?" I wondered to myself, yet I did not dare ask him. I did notice, however, that from time to time, he would gaze at his disciples like a gentle cow in the pasture.

Rimdrowa, what do you think? Why was Bodhisattva Chokyi Wangchuk behaving like that? I think he was reflecting on his accomplishments and his life's work – how he was able to liberate others because he understood the causes and conditions surrounding them. This kind of knowledge and ability went beyond the judgment and capacity of ordinary beings.

One day Bodhisattva Chokyi Wangchuk felt his body was ailing. He said to me, "My body has a sickness due to an imbalance of *lung*[324] – it is too high."

I, Jigten Wangchuk, his attendant, asked, "Should I call the doctor to get you medicine?"

"All right," he replied.

The doctor came and gave Bodhisattva some medicine.

Though Bodhisattva Chokyi Wangchuk knew there was no cure for his condition, he nonetheless allowed the doctor to examine him for three reasons.

First, he (the Sixth Shamarpa) did it out of consideration for me. Seeing that he had told me of his illness, he did not want me to later regret that nothing was done for him. Second, it was for the sake of the doctor, so he would not blame himself for not giving him the necessary treatment. He also did not want the doctor to think me negligent had I not sent for him. Third, he did it for all his disciples, so they would not feel that they were remiss in their care of their rinpoche.

During his illness I, Jigten Wangchuk, dressed Bodhisattva Chokyi Wangchuk. I arranged and changed the cushions for him to sit and lie on. I brought him food, tea, butter and milk. In this way,

324 *Lung* in Tibetan, or *qi* in Chinese, refers to the system of subtle air or wind energy in the physical body.

I served him day and night for quite some time.

Listen, Rimdrowa, as long as the Buddhadharma is here in this world, the *Dharmakaya* will also be present.[325] Bodhisattvas let others see their forms[326] in order that they may realize the impermanent nature of everything. Moreover, bodhisattvas show us the selflessness nature of all phenomena. They will not say anything to the contrary.

One day, Bodhisattva Chokyi Wangchuk looked at me, Jigten Wangchuk, and said, "Tomorrow morning, could you please go to the upper valley and see if you can find a nice rock-cave. It could be near the woods or near a stream, a peaceful and suitable place where I could stay. Please let me know once you've found one."

I, Jigten Wangchuk, said, "I promise I'll do as you've asked."

Early the next morning, I arose and set out to look for a place. I looked everywhere. Finally on the south side of a stream, I found a beautiful blue cave of *indraneela* stone beside a beautiful pine tree. I also happened to see many birds in the small woods nearby.

I returned to Bodhisattva Chokyi Wangchuk to tell him of my find. I told him about the cave, the pine tree, and how I saw the birds flying nearby, and everything.

Upon hearing the details, Bodhisattva Chokyi Wangchuk immediately stood up. He mounted a gentle horse. Caringly, he looked at the devotees in the area and beyond, taking in the landscape and everything in it. Many villagers stared back at Bodhisattva Chokyi Wangchuk, wondering if they would ever see him again. In their hearts they were worried. Tears welled up in their eyes from the depth of their sadness. Suddenly, a forest-spirit in the form of a bird flew down from the sky and looked sadly at Bodhisattva Chokyi Wangchuk.

Guiding his horse ever so slowly, I led Bodhisattva Chokyi Wangchuk to the cave of blue *indraneela*, next to a pine tree. Inside, I had prepared a tent made of a special cloth and a mattress. He was very weak, and I helped him to dismount. With his body half-leaning on

325 *Dharmakaya* is the ultimate enlightenment, which encompasses all the enlightened qualities.

326 This refers to the physical manifestation of enlightenment (*Nirmanakaya*) in the form-realms of living beings.

me, I half-supported and half-carried him into the tent.

Rimdrowa, intermittently during that period, Bodhisattva did feel better. There were days that he was able to walk by himself.

From time to time, he would recite the names of the Buddhas of the millions of universes that I had never heard before. Outside the cave, he would look at the deer and the birds of the forest and the fish in the stream, much like a mother cow gazing at her calf, as if he was seeing them for the last time.

Suddenly one day, Bodhisattva Chokyi Wangchuk remembered that I had once asked him to compose poems of homage conveying the Twelve Deeds of Buddha Shakyamuni. Once Satshosgyin (one of the great masters of India) started to compose such verses but was unable to complete them. The Third Karmapa, Rangjung Dorje, did complete a set. Remembering my request, Bodhisattva Chokyi Wangchuk asked me, "Do you want me to write this?"

"Yes, but since you are not well, you'd better not," I replied.

"No problem. I am physically weak, but I have no pain. Prepare the ink, brush pen, and paper. I will now write for you."

I, Jigten Wangchuk, was so happy that I prepared everything.

Bodhisattva Chokyi Wangchuk began to write about Buddha Shakyamuni's life – beginning with his descent from Tushita (heaven), how he was a fetus in the womb, how he was born as a prince here on earth, how he grew up, how he went to the forest to meditate, how he attained enlightenment, how he taught the Dharma, and how he entered *paranirvana* at the end of his life. Surprisingly, the accounts were not only complete but also detailed. This entire volume thus became an object of reverence to which monks could offer their prostrations and respect. It was also a teaching for all bodhisattvas to follow and to practice.

When the book was finished, Bodhisattva Chokyi Wangchuk gave it to me. Looking at me like a mother cow, he said, "You should also follow the path of a bodhisattva. You must also write stories about the bodhisattvas just as I have written them here for you. If you do, you will be deeply inspired."

We[327] were there for many months. Autumn started, and the flowers and leaves began to fall from the trees.

The Tenth Karmapa gave many details describing the teachings he received every day and the numerous discussions he had with the Sixth Shamarpa that autumn. This section is omitted here. He then continues as follows:

I, Jigten Wangchuk, started to feel sad and worried. Perhaps Bodhisattva Chokyi Wangchuk would enter *paranirvana* soon.

Bodhisattva Chokyi Wangchuk asked me, "Why are you feeling sad?"

"You are a great bodhisattva, yet physically your body is getting weaker and weaker. Outside, the level of the stream is prematurely dropping lower and lower, given that winter has only just begun. In the forest, some flowers are withering, while others are blooming. The animals and birds are gathering food more and more for the winter, yet the green grass on the ground is still growing more and more.[328] Moreover,[329] from time to time, you look at the animals and let them see you. All these outer signs indicate to me that you will enter *paranirvana* soon, so I feel sad."

Bodhisattva[330] Chokyi Wangchuk then said to me, "In the past, I've likened samsara to bubbles in the water. Please do not feel sad, Jigten Wangchuk. Can the lotuses in a lake stay ever together without separating?"

I replied, "No."

Bodhisattva Chokyi Wangchuk continued, "That's right. Sometimes, the lotuses will disappear first, while the lake remains. Sometimes the lake will dry up first. Likewise, some people die poor, while others die rich. Some die young, while others die old. Nevertheless, like flowers, all humans and beings of the universes

327 *KAC*: 289

328 In the sutras, it is said that conflicting signs in the environment forecast the passing of a bodhisattva.

329 *KAC*: 292

330 *KAC*: 293. The Tenth Karmapa composed many poems about this time, which have not been translated here.

go through the cycle of birth, aging, and death. Death cannot be reversed, etc."[331]

I, Jigten Wangchuk, continued to take care of him for a long time. I changed his clothes. I brought water to wash his face. I lit incense in his tent. I served him yogurt and milk. Like this, I tended to his every need. As I cared for him, Bodhisattva Chokyi Wangchuk gave me many examples and metaphors about impermanence, birth, aging, and the inevitability of death.[332]

Rimdrowa,[333] every morning, I prostrated to him. After prostrating to him one morning, I asked, "How was your night?"

He told me that he had a comfortable sleep and a nice dream. "I will tell you," he said.

Curious, I prostrated to him and listened.

"When there is drizzle and sunshine, then a beautiful rainbow will appear. This early morning, I dreamed that I was walking through the colorful lights of the rainbow. I felt very comfortable and happy. That feeling is still with me now."

I was unhappy to hear this, as it showed that he would soon pass away.[334]

Rimdrowa, then I was very sad. Usually when bodhisattvas have finished their work in one planet, they will go to another planet to help. There are two reasons for their passing. The first is to teach people about impermanence; to teach them about the problems of self-clinging due to ignorance and how to solve them through the teachings of selflessness and meditation. When the teachings have been given, the bodhisattvas show the impermanence of physical form and life by their own passing. The second is to further engage in bodhisattva activities for sentient beings elsewhere, as they wish to liberate limitless sentient beings.

I[335] requested Bodhisattva Chokyi Wangchuk to live longer and not to pass away yet.

---

331 The Tenth Karmapa cites many examples of this cycle. They are not translated here.

332 The examples are not translated here.

333 *KAC*: 297

334 Many of the Karmapa's poems from this point on are not translated.

335 *KAC*: 299. Poems on page 300 have not been translated.

Bodhisattva Chokyi Wangchuk then looked at me with his two hands joined together at his heart. He said, "Your asking me not to die is very good. It is going to all the Buddhas in the ten directions asking them not to pass away and to turn the wheel of Dharma for the sake of all sentient beings."

At[336] that time, Bodhisattva Gawey Yang (who was in Seykhar Monastery in south Tibet – months away in distance) understood that Bodhisattva Chokyi Wangchuk, who was as great as the Buddha's regent, the *Arhat* Kashyapa, would soon leave this world. He[337] sent a letter via a messenger requesting Bodhisattva Chokyi Wangchuk to live longer. He also wrote that he, Gawey Yang, had completed his activities just as past bodhisattvas had done and that he would not be able to bear the passing of Bodhisattva Chokyi Wangchuk.

By the time the monk-messenger arrived, a few months had passed. The moment I received the letter, I was very sad. I understood by my own wisdom that Bodhisattva Gawey Yang had passed away. The monk messenger also gave me Bodhisattva's yellow robe. At the same time, I was worried and hesitant to show the letter to Bodhisattva Chokyi Wangchuk. He was already in poor health.

I went to his tent and said a monk from southern Tibet had arrived with a letter. I could not continue as I started to cry. Immediately Bodhisattva Chokyi Wangchuk took the letter and told me not to be sad. He said, "Bodhisattva Gawey Yang must have heard I was ill and sent this letter."

Bodhisattva Chokyi Wangchuk then said that because we were jointly engaged in bodhisattva activities together that we would forever be each other's helper. I knew then that it was Bodhisattva Chokyi Wangchuk's last teaching to me – that he would also pass away very soon. As I cried, Bodhisattva Chokyi Wangchuk kept quiet and looked at me.

One day Bodhisattva Chokyi Wangchuk said to me, "When I pass away, please don't worry. Please remember the teaching that

336 *KAC*: 301. The Karmapa's poems describing the bodhisattvas taking birth in the different realms to liberate beings have not been translated from pages 301 to 306.

337 *KAC*: 306

all phenomena are impermanent. The[338] moment I heard those words, I started to cry.

I said, "Please give us your instructions, your intention for the future. Will you be in a different realm, or in Amitabha's realm, etc.? Is there a chance that you will return here to this human land? Please tell me now."

"Where[339] would you like me to go next?"

I said, "If living beings still have the fortune to receive your bodhisattva activities, please take rebirth in my homeland in Mar. The reason is because people in that area are very pure in devotion."

"Yes, I will do that."

I told Bodhisattva Chokyi Wangchuk, "After you pass away, I will build a stupa to contain your remains for the sake of human beings. Then I will not associate with people, and I will go to remote areas to meditate."

"Very good, you should do that."

Later I received word that Bodhisattva Gawey Yang had passed away.[340] I felt very sad.

Rimdrowa, early one morning, I asked the great Bodhisattva Chokyi Wangchuk, "How are you feeling?"

He[341] answered, "I do not have any pain, and I feel rested."

I offered him the morning tea. He looked more joyful than ever before. He took tea. Moments after sunrise, Bodhisattva Chokyi Wangchuk entered *paranirvana* without any pain or suffering.

I was in tears. At the next moment, I lost consciousness. An assistant threw water on my face. I recovered and became clear again.[342]

Near streams, rivers, and lakes,

---

338 *KAC*: 312. Poems in the previous few pages have not been translated.

339 *KAC*: 313

340 Karmapa intuitively already knew that Pawo Rinpoche had passed away before the message actually reached him.

341 *KAC*: 315

342 From his sadness, Karmapa composed many poems. The following is one example.

near mountains, hills, and trees,
near forests, and flower fields,
wherever in front of you,
the happiness I've experienced
is ne'er experienced by beings,
not even those in the heavens.
Seeing Bodhisattva you,
the time I had close to you,
'tis too soon to be ending –
like a beautiful yet withering flower.

I prostrated innumerable times to the body of Bodhisattva Chokyi Wangchuk. For[343] one whole week, I treated his body with sandalwood powder, saffron leaves, flowers, and scented water. I lit the lamps.

Bodhisattva Chokyi Wangchuk was like the moon in this Dark Age. He[344] passed away and left us with only his teachings written by his hand. Therefore, disciples, you should follow them.

As I shared my thoughts and poems with my attendant, he broke down in tears. "You[345] are a great bodhisattva who had assisted Bodhisattva Chokyi Wangchuk. You transcend all happenings and every imagination," said Kuntu Zangpo (the Karmapa's attendant), and then he prostrated to me.

Again tears streamed down my face as I was overwhelmed by the memories of Bodhisattva Chokyi Wangchuk. We cried together.

"I cry when I see you cry," my attendant remarked. We stopped crying, and for a while we remained silent without uttering a word.

During that period, my attendant and I were ever mindful of impermanence and the constant state of flux in all phenomena. Life passes and fluctuates like the waves of the ocean. Our wealth and possessions will one day dissipate like a dewdrop on a blade of grass in the early morning. In this way, we reflected on impermanence.

343 *KAC*: 316

344 *KAC*: 317

345 *KAC*: 318; some poems after this point are not translated.

Rimdrowa, I took Bodhisattva Chokyi Wangchuk's body to Tsurphu Monastery to give people the opportunity to accumulate merits through their offerings and prostrations.[346]

Every week I changed the cloths for the dressings of the body to a pure new white cloth, a new yellow cloth, a new red cloth, a new green cloth, and a new blue cloth.

Then I sent messages to the contented[347] monks who lived in the mountains, valleys, either alone like a rhinoceros or in a group like parrots.[348] I told them all to come to Tsurphu where they could give offerings and accumulate great merits.

This was my message to them:

> Bodhisattva Chokyi Wangchuk, who has successfully helped sentient beings of this world, has entered paranirvana. He departed his physical body in the valley of Dengmadring in a cave near a pine tree and a forest of trees and flowers. Now I have brought his body to Tsurphu and placed him among all the offerings, flowers, incense, and lamps.
>
> You meditator-monks with your contemplative minds should all be here. In the past, whenever a great bodhisattva passed away, his wishes made for sentient beings would be heard by the supreme beings in the heavenly realms, in the semi-heavens, and in the human and naga realms. These beings would then memorize and repeat the bodhisattva's wishes in the human tongue. All of you know these wishes. Therefore, you should similarly make wishes for sentient beings in front of the wishfulfilling jewel that is Bodhisattva Chokyi Wangchuk's body.

And they all assembled in the valley of Tsurphu. On both sides of the river in the valley, the contented monks filled the space like red lotuses in the River Ganges. They did prostrations and made wishes. I, in turn, gave them shelter, food, and drink every day.

---

346 *KAC*: 319

347 Monks characterized as contented likely were staying in isolated places and practicing the Dharma either alone or in a group.

348 In the sutras, a *pratyekabuddha* – someone who meditates in solitude – is likened to a solitary rhinoceros, whereas meditators in a group are likened to parrots, which congregate in groups.

I invited the best silversmiths and artisans from Nepal.[349] I built a stupa to contain Bodhisattva Chokyi Wangchuk's body.

I hired very experienced builders to construct a temple for the stupa. I, too, participated in building it.[350]

BL

Karmapa performed an elaborate puja[351] at the site where his teacher's body (called *Kudung)* lay and made many offerings. Afterwards, the *Kudung* Rinpoche (a respectful reference to the body) was brought to Tsurphu Monastery where Karmapa made splendid offerings every day. During the funeral ceremony, he personally carried the silver teapot for the monks.[352] He travelled especially to Lhasa and presented great offerings to the Buddha Shakyamuni in the temple there. He also sent offerings to all the big monasteries in central Tibet.

Karmapa received many silver coins, pearls, and gold from the King of Lijiang. He used them to build a stupa to contain the body of his guru. Just as the First Shamarpa's body was placed in a stupa, the Tenth Karmapa built a golden stupa to hold the *kudung* of the Sixth Shamarpa.

In addition, Karmapa built a special temple to house the gold en stupa. The temple became an extension of Tsurphu Monastery. Karmapa participated in the construction of the temple, carrying the stones and bricks by hand. To fulfill the wishes of his guru, he sculpted statues of Chenrezig, Manjusri, Vajrapani, Hayagriva, and others. He also created a painting of the Buddha and the sixteen *arhats* for the temple wall.

Near Chubar where Shamarpa had passed away, Karmapa sent a group of messengers and building materials to establish a retreat center that would accommodate one hundred and eight retreatants.

During the funeral of the Sixth Shamarpa at Tsurphu, Karma

349 *KAC*: 325. Pages 322–324 about the stupa's construction have not been translated

350 *KAC*: 327

351 *BL*: 172a

352 This shows Karmapa's humility.

Chagmed[353] burned one of his fingers[354] as a light offering to the *Kudung* Rinpoche. He was in a meditative state and made infinite bodhisattva wishes. At that time, Karma Chagmed attained the essence of wisdom realization.[355]

353 A student of the Sixth Shamarpa, the first Karma Chagmed, was an erudite Buddhist scholar and abbot of Yangpachen Monastery. He wrote in colloquial Tibetan to make the Dharma accessible to ordinary people. He started the Namcho lineage, which holds the collection of *terma* teachings called "The Dharma Buried in the Sky" by the *terton* Tulku Mingyur Dorje. Today, the Namcho lineage is a subsect of the Shamarpa lineage.

354 Karma Chagmed likely wrapped his finger first in cloth and tied a string around it to secure the wrapping. He then dipped the finger in butter and burnt it.

355 This means Chagmed attained enlightenement.

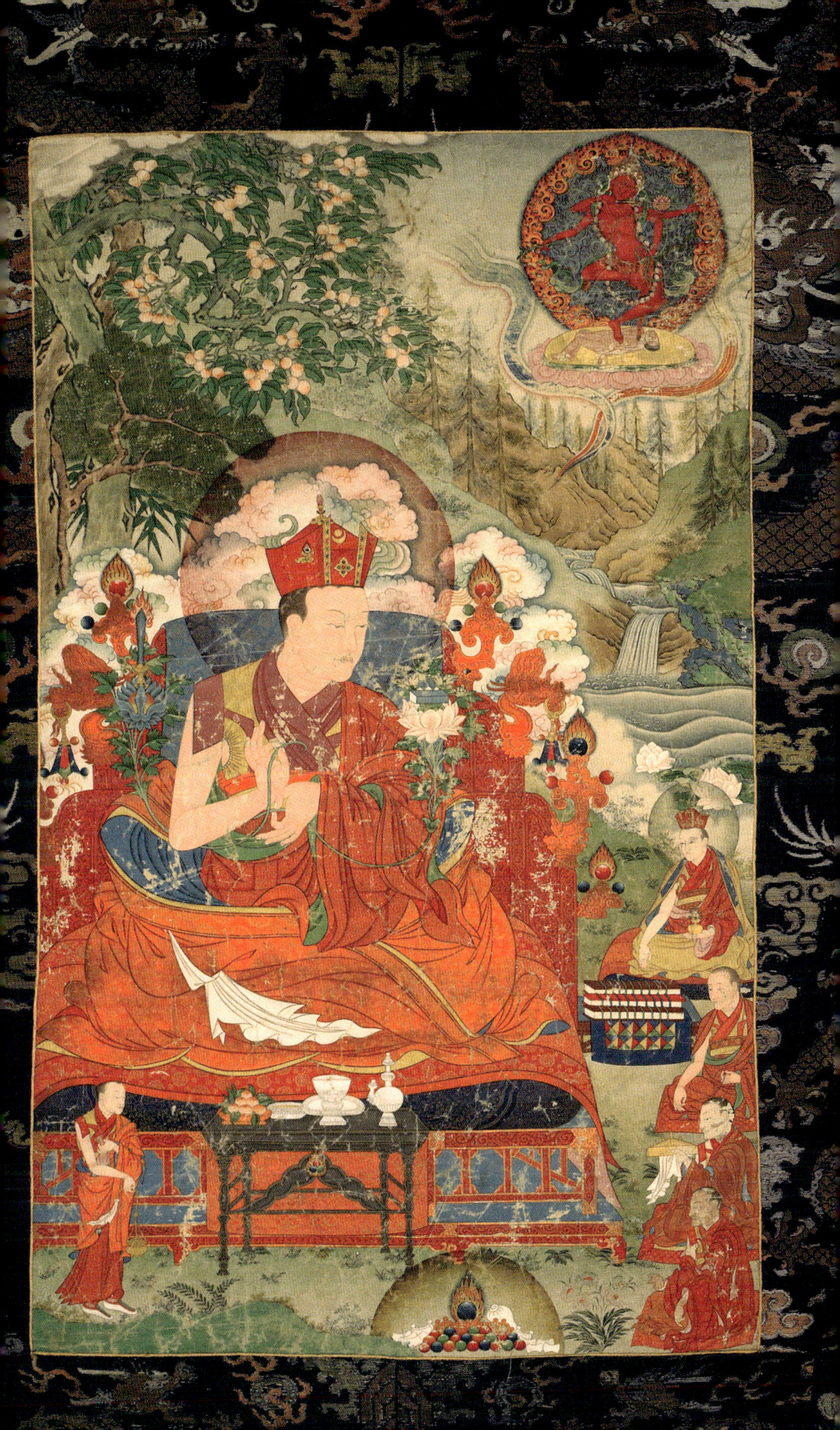

Sixth Shamar, Mipam Chokyi Wangchug (1584–1630).
Kham Province, Tibet.
18th century.
Mineral pigment on cloth.
38¾ x 23 in. (98.4 x 58.4 cm).
Rubin Museum of Art C2007.34.1 (HAR 65804).

The Sixth Shamarpa was the Tenth Karmapa's guru. To the right of the Sixth Shamarpa in this thangka are four 17th-century Karma Kagyu teachers. The Fifth Gyaltsab Dragpa Chogyang (1618–1658), a disciple of the Tenth Karmapa, is the topmost of the four figures. Shown in the top right hand corner of the thangka is the meditational deity Kurukulia, goddess of power.

Fifth Dalai Lama, Ngagwang Lobzang Gyatso (1617–1682), *with episodes from his life*
Tibet. 18th century.
Mineral pigment on cloth.
33 x 21 5/8 in.
Rubin Museum of Art C2003.9.2 (HAR 65275).

Among other scenes from the life of the Fifth Dalai Lama, this thangka depicts his meeting with the Qing Emperor Shunzhi in 1651. See the scene on the right side, middle (next to a white flower).

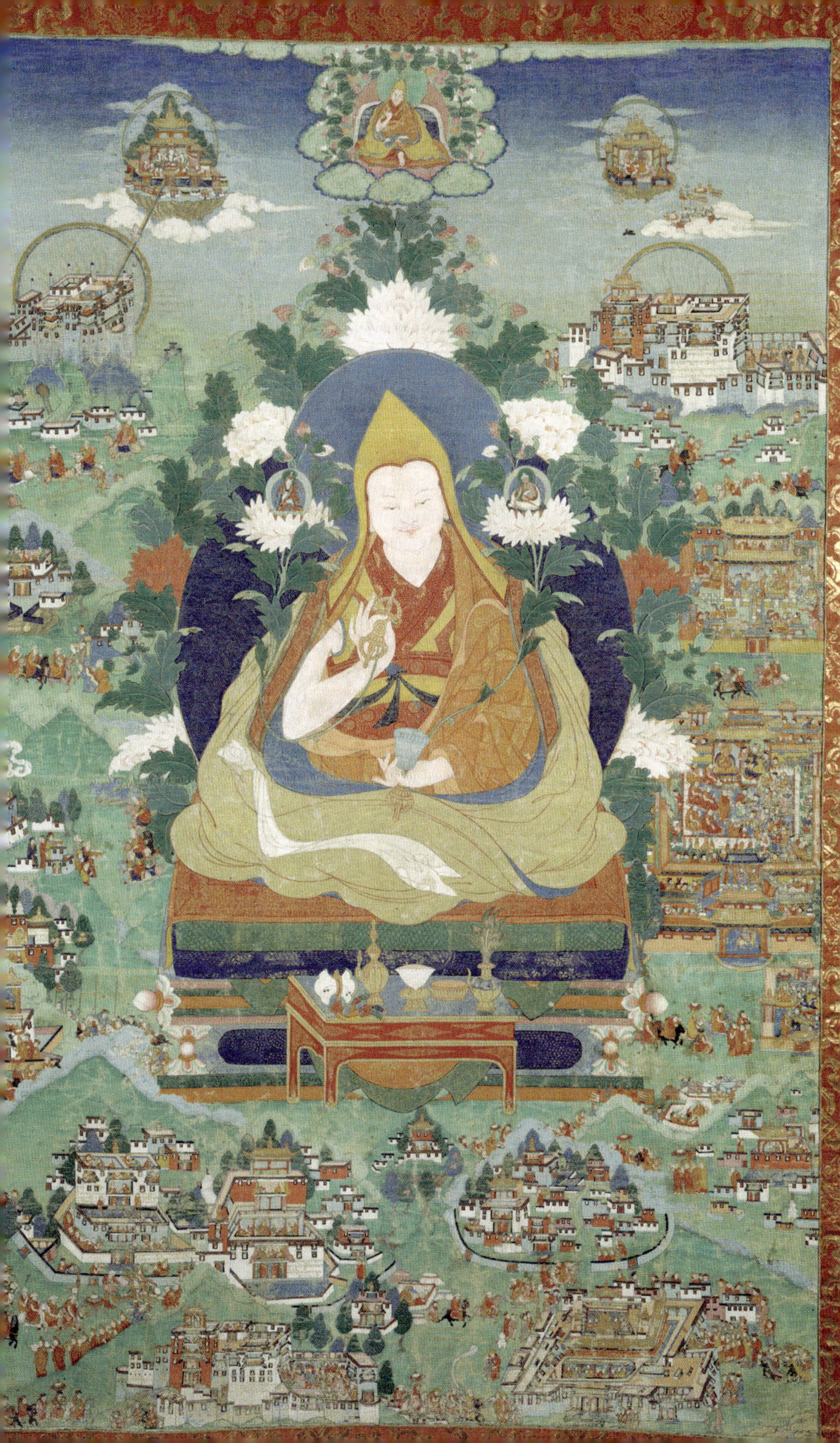

26. In Memoriam

To commemorate the death of his guru in 1630, the Tenth Karmapa composed prayers, erected a temple and stupa, and began to write a reverential biography of the Sixth Shamarpa (The Bountiful Cow: Biography of a Bodhisattva) *which he completed in 1648.*

During the Sixth Shamarpa's funeral, the Karmapa made the following supplication to his guru.

I[356] take refuge in the Red Hat Holder Amitabha, Chokyi Wangchuk. With limitless devotion in my heart, I prostrate.

In general, we are in the Kali Yuga (Dark Age). People have tremendous anger and jealousy. The chiefs of provinces are fighting one another for power and position. By their weapons, innocent people are dying. The poor are dying of sickness and starvation. Under these dark conditions, I trust no one. I rely on no one regardless of class – high, medium, or low, it makes no difference. Therefore, this is the right time for Dharma practice. Practice it from the depth of one's heart.

I am a lama who can be considered "the tenth" of the Rosary of the

356 *Collected Writings of the Tenth Karmapa* (Chengdu, Szechuan, 2004) volume 1, 399.

Deep Blue (i.e., black) Crown-holder.[357] In any case, I would say this is my last life on the whole.[358]

Young men, now is the time to supplicate and to pray. You might understand what I mean if you look through an angle, you will know the surface.[359]

It is time to show a face.[360]
Do you understand, dear mothers, that which has no face?
Do you understand, dear mothers, that which has no fear?361
I am telling you, think again!

A-la-la, the blessing of my Guru!
I could wander without a place to stay.
I could give up being the guru of lords.
I am fully aware that this is the blessing of the Kagyu
Dharma.[362]

Renounce sectarian attachments and resentments.
Be free of ambitions to attain accomplishments.
This, I understand to be the blessing of the Kagyu Dharma.

I could renounce the enemy that is self-clinging.
I could renounce the inherent discrimination in sentient beings.
I understand this to be the blessing of the Kagyu Dharma.

When one gets close to Tongkun (China), there is an opportunity

---

357 "The Rosary of the Deep Blue Crown-holder" refers to the line of Karmapas.

358 The Tenth Karmapa means he will not be reborn as a reincarnation. Why his followers later recognized an Eleventh Karmapa cannot be explained.

359 To look through an angle is a Tibetan expression that means to exercise smart judgement, an ability much encouraged in Tibetan culture. Karmapa is saying here that if you look through an angle, you will know the surface, which means you will understand what is really happening – that given Gushri Khan's aggression, there is no longer good fortune in Tibet.

360 It is from the next two lines that the Tenth Karmapa shows us that "to show a face" means to meditate in order to reach enlightenment. Because there is nothing more that can be done for the future of Tibet, it is best to seek enlightenment.

361 That which has no face and no fear is enlightenment.

362 The Tenth Karmapa is expressing his non-attachment to a home. He has no wish to be like those spiritual lamas who act like powerful lords over others. He attributes his non-attachment to home and power to be the blessing of the Kagyu Dharma.

for me to help living beings.[363]

Dear people of Tibet, recite the six-syllable mantra[364] and meditate on Avalokiteshvara on top of your head.[365]

Meditate on the self-realizing and clear nature of mind.

* * *

10th Karmapa

At the very end of the biography of his guru, the Tenth Karmapa explains his reasons for building the temple honoring his guru and describes The Bountiful Cow.

Rimdrowa,[366] the reason why I built the beautiful temple to contain the precious Bodhisattva Chokyi Wangchuk's body is to benefit human beings. By going to offer respect to the stupa, people will accumulate many merits.[367]

Some years had passed since Bodhisattva Chokyi Wangchuk passed away. While I was in a forest in Tsari meditating, I had a dream. I dreamed that I met Bodhisattva Chokyi Wangchuk in the Pureland of Buddha.[368] I told Kuntu Zangpo my dream, and he asked me to write a book about him.

Kuntu Zangpo and I were staying in a forest. Every day we reminisced about the past.[369] Then we learned that some thieves had camped nearby, and they were robbing the villagers. We left and went to Powo. War was going on there.

We proceeded to an area called Khawakharpo. The Ngulchu

363 The Tenth Karmapa is apparently making a prediction here. It was not realized because there is no record of his ever going to China.

364 The mantra is: *om mani padme hung*.

365 It means to visualize the deity above one's head.

366 *KAC*: 327

367 The long descriptive list of merits is omitted here.

368 *KAC*: 329

369 This was the period when the Tenth Karmapa wrote the biography of the Sixth Shamarpa (*KAC*) at the request of his attendant and friend Kuntu Zangpo. They were traveling together and would often stop to rest at different places. During those rests, they spent time talking to each other, writing, and doing retreats.

River runs through it. We stayed in a beautiful but remote area where white ducks gathered. Later we went to Lijiang (in present day Yunnan Province, China). There is a nice lake there in Gyalthang[370] called Milky Lake. While we were there, I finished writing this book, *The Bountiful Cow: Biography of a Bodhisattva.*

I told Kuntu Zangpo that it is a holy book that I wrote while thinking of Bodhisattva Chokyi Wangchuk and his wonderful deeds and activities. Be respectful to it.[371]

I, the humble servant-poet, the Tenth Holder of the Black Crown, finished this book on the fifteenth day of the eleventh month of the Earth Mouse year.[372]

The Karmapa's biography of the Sixth Shamarpa, in which he interwove autobiographical accounts of his own life, concludes with the year 1630. Consequently, after this point, there are no more autobiographical writings of the Karmapa to include in this study of his life. The remainder of this biography of the Tenth Karmapa relies on a translation of Bey Lotsawa's biography supplemented by a few passages from the Fifth Dalai Lama's autobiography.

---

370 Gyalthang is the Tibetan name for the Chinese county and town in Yunnan Province formerly known as Zhongdian but in 2001 renamed Shangrila in order to attract tourists.

371 *KAC*: 330; poems before and after this page have not been translated.

372 *KAC*: 333. According to the Western calendar, this date corresponds to December 29, 1648.

27. Pilgrimage en Route to Kham

Following the death of the Sixth Shamarpa in 1630, the Karmapa went on extended travels and a pilgrimage to several regions in Tibet. (Unless otherwise noted, all passages in this and subsequent chapters are from BL.)

Karmapa understood that the prosperity of central Tibet was beginning to decline. He decided to go to Kham in east Tibet to benefit sentient beings. He gave instructions to his attendants to prepare for the trip east.

At[373] that time in Tibet, many high lamas were eager to associate with powerful warlords from Mongolia. The Tenth Karmapa was an exception. He refused to meet them, Lord Chogthu being a case in point. The Chieftain of Beri in east Tibet caught news of this and sent Karmapa a message. Being a Bon follower, the Beri Chieftain openly revealed his disdain of Buddhist teachers on several occasions. However, his message to Karmapa was quite the opposite, declaring his respect for someone who had shunned Chogthu. He also apologized for having denied Karmapa passage through his territory in the past.

---

373 *BL*: 172a. Some of the Tenth Karmapa's many travels during this period have not been translated here.

Karmapa was studying the teachings of *Mahamudra* along with Yogi Jatangwa Tenpa Namgyal. During this period, Karmapa sought to stay in remote and isolated areas. He handpicked a few attendants who happened to be meditators as well. In his despair over the deterioration of morals and virtues at that time, he composed many poems expressing his disappointment.

Arsalang (son of Mongolian warlord Chogthu) requested an audience with Karmapa, who refused him. Instead, the Buddhist master predicted that a disaster would soon befall the warlord's family.

In the meantime, the King of Chagar sent a messenger to present Karmapa with a rosary made from expensive pearls.

Karmapa started a pilgrimage. He went to Tsaritra. By[374] then he was travelling by foot. The main stop on this part of his pilgrimage was the *mandala* of Chakrasambhava. Some scholars told of an early time many centuries before when a huge *mandala* was built there. However, natural erosion had taken its toll on the structure, and it fell apart without proper maintenance. Later, a forest had overgrown it, and natives came to inhabit the land. Remnants of bricks and rocks from the ancient structure still lay scattered on the ground.

Karmapa's pilgrimage took him to many places: Gongkarwa, Khishupa, Namsey Ling, Dhol Cho Dzong, Gendun Gang, Drache Tharpa Ling, Samye, Gyalched Ling, Tsethang, and Tseythang.[375] Everywhere Karmapa went, many monks and lay people came out to greet him and pay their respects, bearing gifts and offerings. Karmapa gave them all his blessings and satisfied everyone.

In Tseythang, Karmapa saw the famous Buddha statue from Serling (Sumatra, Indonesia) brought to Tibet by Atisha. After that, this statue became the model for all of Karmapa's sculptures.

Karmapa met Rechung Rinpoche when he visited the Rechungphug Temple. He then visited Yertod, Gatshal Zhunglug Ling,

---

374 *BL*: 172b. Tsaritra is located in southeast Tibet. It is the upper part of the Tsari region where the locals were followers of the Drugpa Kagyu and Karma Kagyu sects. Natives or aborigines inhabited the lower part of Tsari.

375 These places are all in the general region of central Tibet under control of Tsang rulers.

Samde, Yazang, and Chudo.[376]

During that time, Mongolian cavalry, whose horses were multi-colored, arrived in the Yardrog area of Tibet. The Tsang government prepared for a confrontation.

Karmapa went to Go Rabten Ling. The local chieftain offered him all his properties. Karmapa distributed them among the monasteries.

Karmapa then proceeded to Dhagpo Shedrub Ling, a Karma Kagyu college. Afterwards, he visited Dhag La Gampo, the seat of Gampopa. Karmapa's pilgrimage in that area was comprehensive. Many rainbows appeared. He did a one-week meditation retreat in which Gampopa appeared to him riding a lion surrounded by Indian *sadhus*.[377] Karmapa also gave teachings to the monks there.

Karmapa visited Tsati Gang,[378] and other places where there were holy lakes and temples. At Zimpoling, Lama Nyingpowa showed Karmapa all the relics of the *terton* Sangye Lingpa.

When Karmapa arrived in Zurudong and Tayul, the local chieftain, Jaba Shabdrung, appealed to him for help. He was about to be attacked by the Tsang Desi. Apparently, it was because the Shabdrung could not get along with one of his wives granted him by the Tsang Desi. Karmapa interceded accordingly and stopped the fight.

376 These places are in central Tibet closer to the southeastern side.

377 Yogis.

378 *BL*: 173a

28. Activities in Kongpo and Lhasa before the Mongol Invasion

At[379] Ga Mamo Monastery in Kongpo (a region in southeastern Tibet), the monastery of the Fourth Shamarpa,[380] Karmapa celebrated the New Year of the Fire Ox[381] by offering many prayers.

Near Ga Mamo Monastery, Karmapa designed the layout of a thangka. He made the outline from silk patchings. The thangka depicted the Buddha and the sixteen *arhats* surrounded by another 16,000 *arhats* and disciples. Ten tailors were employed, dividing the work among them.[382]

As was his custom, Karmapa continued to personally distribute to beggars the gifts he received and to release all the animals offered to him. He gave the same teachings to the monks and lay people. To anyone who wished to do a retreat, Karmapa would give a small thangka of the Buddha painted by him. To anyone who wanted to practice the recitation of Chenrezig, Karmapa would give a thangka of Chenrezig, also painted by him.

Karmapa also made many renovations to stupas that contained

379 *BL*: 173a

380 After the Fifth Dalai Lama became the ruler of Tibet, Ga Mamo Monastery was converted into a Gelug monastery.

381 This was 1637, seven years after Shamarpa's passing. Karmapa had reached the age of 34.

382 This describes the process of creating a *sithang* thangka. Another example can be found later in this chapter.

the bodies of the Second Shamarpa Kha Chod Wangpo and the Third Shamarpa Chopar Yeshe.

Being a complete vegetarian himself, Karmapa encouraged others to become vegetarians too. He urged the people in Kongpo not to kill animals.

In Kongpo, Karmapa visited a special retreat cave of the Third Karmapa Rangjung Dorje.[383] He also visited a temple at Zhagkha and made renovations to it as well. A chieftain of Zhagkha offered Karmapa one hundred horses and fifteen mules.

At that time, Salanee (a representative of the Tsang Desi) went to Ga Mamo Monastery in Kongpo. He was rude and a bully and was killed while he was there. To avert revenge, Karmapa advised the residents of Kongpo to confess their crime to the government. As penance, they should perform a grand puja for the deceased. This appeased the government, and Ga Mamo Monastery was not blamed.

Karmapa continued his travels in the Kongpo region. In Nyangpo Gyaldo, he met the great Nyingma *terton* Rigdzin Jatshon Nyingpo, who offered Karmapa two texts. One was a Guru Padmasambhava practice called *Konchog Chidus*. The other was a joint practice of Hayagriva and Vajrayogini.[384] He then announced to Karmapa, "According to Guru Rinpoche's own prediction, you will come to own this collection of his *termas*." Karmapa accepted ownership and became the lineage holder of the Jatshon *Terma*. This happened in the year of Fire Ox (1637).

Following *Terton* Jatshon Nyingpo's suggestion, Lama Dzochenpa, one of Jatshon's chief disciples, was sent to Tsurphu Monastery specifically to perform a puja to dispel any evil attacks on Tsurphu.

During the time of the Eighth Karmapa (1507–1554), Rigdzin Zhigpo Lingpa offered the Eighth Karmapa all his *termas*, but the transfer did not go well due to some obstacles. Living beings just did not have enough positive merits to receive the profound Dharma.

Tagtse Namgyal Gang was Karmapa's next stop where a statue of Shamarpa was known to talk and give teachings.

---

383 BL: 173b

384 A *yidam* practice of the Kagyu sect.

On his way to Lower Kongpo, Karmapa arrived at Buchur Temple.[385] There was a beautiful statue of Chenrezig in the temple. Karmapa painted the image of that statue in a beautiful thangka.

While he was at Tse Lha Gang Monastery in Kongpo, he painted the sixteen *arhats*. He hired ten tailors to embroider them and created a special Chinese brocade in three pieces. The three pieces were so large that they hung like curtains covering one wall in the temple. Karmapa also designed twelve angel-like females holding offerings, which were also embroidered by tailors on a piece of fabric. It was then placed on top of the beam that hung the curtains. During that time, Karmapa gave teachings to the people. He gave the *Upasaka* vows, and he also did a lot practice.

Then Karmapa went and stayed at Lho Drag Seykhar.[386] He did one hundred thousand prostrations there. Dhitsha Tulku[387] went to see him. In jest, Karmapa asked him, "Could you please recite the supplication prayer to Avalokiteshvara written by Chandrakirti?"[388] Dhitsha Tulku recited the whole prayer from memory. Karmapa gave him a present – a thangka which was his self-portrait sitting on an elephant.

Paksam Wangpo (head of the Drugpa Kagyu sect) sent a messenger with many gifts including a very old statue of the Mahakali Dusolma. He requested that he might meet with Karmapa in the near future. He also asked for a thangka of the sixteen *arhats* by Karmapa's hand. Karmapa proceeded to paint one. As he was working on the colors of this thangka, some signs showed up which Karmapa interpreted as an omen that Paksam Wangpo Rinpoche would not live long.

Lhasa

Karmapa[389] travelled to Lhasa. Dressed as a layman, he went to Nakartse temple. The owner of the temple offered Karmapa a beautiful

385 *BL*: 174a

386 *BL*: 174b

387 Historically, Dhitsha Tulku was a lama of the Nyingma sect.

388 Chandrakirti was a great 7th-century Indian master.

389 *BL*: 174b

ivory statue of Buddha defeating the *maras* (evils); it also depicted heavenly boys and girls holding up offerings to the Buddha. This statue was believed to have been created by the Indian master Nagarjuna.

While Karmapa was in an area called Tshal Min, a group of Muslim businessmen offered him an emerald *mala* worth a million gold coins. Karmapa gave many coins to the local community there and asked them to build a temple to house a Buddha statue for the benefit of the local people. Yolmo Tulku arrived to see Karmapa and offered him a bronze Buddha statue in Kashmir style.

When Karmapa arrived in Lhasa (around 1638), he visited the Jowo temple, which housed the famous statue of Buddha Shakyamuni.[390] He offered three scarves to the Jowo Buddha symbolic of the body, speech, and mind of enlightenment. When he went back the next day, all three scarves were knotted together and fell on him. Karmapa accepted them as a gift from the Buddha and wore them.

The Fifth Gyaltsab Dragpa Choyang and Dragpa Palzang, the head of Riwoche Monastery in Kham, came to see Karmapa. He gave them teachings on a text called *A Letter to a Friend* written by Nagarjuna.

Karmapa visited an area called Chalpo Zhika. While there, a messenger from the King of Lijiang arrived with many offerings and an invitation to visit his country. During this time, Karmapa made two beautiful tables with curves to offer to the Jowo Buddha.

Karmapa also received a message that his elder brother had passed away. He then invited Gyaltsab Dragpa Choyang to join him in performing a puja of liberation for his deceased brother. In addition, he painted a thangka of the Buddha and the sixteen *arhats* on that occasion. Karmapa also made sculptures of Shakyamuni Buddha, Chenrezig, and others. Not long afterwards, a message arrived that said his other brother, Abum, had also passed away. Karmapa performed a liberation puja for him as well. During this period, Karmapa allowed Gyaltsab Rinpoche to stay with him. It was the Earth Tiger year (1638), and Karmapa turned thirty-five.

Gushri Khan's armies entered Tibet and later waged war (1639–1642) against the Tsang government and its allies.

---

390 *BL*: 175a

29. Wartime

Many[391] evil people carried out devious schemes. Their actions brought on war in central Tibet between a Mongolian warlord and the Tsang ruling government. In the end, the Tsang Desi and the ruling government lost.

The Tenth Karmapa requested the Panchen Rinpoche to arrange a meeting with the Fifth Dalai Lama. (The Tenth Karmapa probably made his request shortly after the war ended in 1642.)

"I, Panchen Lama, will vouch for you. I can attest for the fact that you, Gyalwa Wangpo Karmapa, are entirely blameless for any conflict between the Karma Kagyu sect and the Gelug sect."[392]

The Panchen Lama declared Karmapa's innocence to the Fifth Dalai Lama, "Karmapa is free of any blame. I bear witness to his being faultless and give you my personal guarantee on it. The Karma Kagyu administrators, on the other hand, have not dealt with the situation skillfully."

The Panchen Rinpoche went on to advise the Fifth Dalai Lama how to manage the situation. He also procured an order from the Fifth Dalai Lama to his followers not to act against the Karma Kagyu.

---

391 *BL*: 175a

392 *BL*: 175b

Lho Drag

From central Tibet, Karmapa and his party, including the Fifth Gyaltsab Rinpoche, traveled again to Lho Drag. On their way, they visited Legshed Ling, a Karma Kagyu college. They stayed in Lho Drag for some time. Karmapa did a retreat. He also made many thangkas of Chenrezig, White Tara, etc. He recognized the reincarnation of the Third Pawo Tsuklak Gyatso.

It was during his stay in Lho Drag that Karmapa appointed his disciple Kuntu Zangpo[393] to be his personal attendant. Symbolic of this appointment, Karmapa put his yogurt in his disciple's cup and asked him to eat it. He then gave him 1,000 rolls of paper, some bamboo paintbrushes, and the necessary materials for making ink and colors.

Meanwhile, the Tsang ruling government sent messengers to Kongpo. They wished to enlist the Kongpo army to fight the Mongolians, specifically Gushri Khan and his men. Along the way, the recruiters took horses from the Tsurphu Monastery farm. A fight broke out with the locals, and lives were lost. As a result, Karmapa was extremely upset with the government. The Tsang ministers tried to appease him by claiming that they neither started the fight nor encouraged it. Karmapa kept his distance and did not want to support the government. However, this incident caused a rift in Karmapa's camp.

When the soldiers of Kongpo arrived in central Tibet, Karmapa sent them a letter: "Go back, and don't make war! Otherwise, you will bring disastrous consequences to all Karma Kagyu monasteries including Tsurphu, and you will be responsible. I have already surrendered to the Fifth Dalai Lama." Many Karma Kagyu followers criticized Karmapa for abandoning the Tsang government and his responsibilities for the Karma Kagyu sect.

The Gyalwa Wangpo (Karmapa) always likened kingdoms to honey laced with poison. This was why he maintained a separation between the Karma Kagyu sect and the Tsang ruling government. Nevertheless, he still got all the blame.

---

393 Kuntu Zangpo is the same attendant-friend referred to as Rimdrowa in *KAC*.

From time to time, Ogyen Guru Rinpoche, who knew the past, present, and future, gave predictions. He foretold that Tibet would split up; foreign soldiers would flood the monasteries.[394] He predicted that the lineage of pure Dharma would decline – that it was already happening.

Once he (Ogyen Guru Rinpoche) predicted what would become of the four Kagyu sects when the birth or emanation of Lord Tsangpa Lhayimetog – the Fifth Dalai Lama of the Gelug sect – took place. The Karma sect (Karma Kagyu) would be like a cushion;[395] on the other hand, the Taglung (meaning land of the tiger) Kagyu sect would preserve its stripes; the Drigung (*dri* means female yak) Kagyu's horn would be broken; and the Drugpa (*dru* means dragon) Kagyu would find its own future.[396] In any event, dire times were inevitable for Tibet because of collective karma.

After the Mongols placed the rule of Tibet in the hands of the Fifth Dalai Lama and Gelug sect in 1642 (see chapter 7 for more about this), the Dalai Lama's secretary Zha Ngo *Sonam Chopal made the Karma Kagyu sect his main target of elimination. Many Karma Kagyu monasteries were forcibly converted into Gelugpa monasteries. As Ogyen Guru Rinpoche predicted, the Karma Kagyu sect was flattened like a cushion.*

In 1618 when the Sera and Drepung monks allied with Duke Kyisho Depa and fought the Tsang ruling government, they lost (see chapter 5.) The rebel monks found refuge at the monastery of Taglung, because the head of Taglung Kagyu, Tashi Paldrub, sheltered them. Moreover, he later persuaded the government to allow the monks to go back to their monasteries. To return this favor, the Gelug government did not attack the Taglung monasteries. Taglung Kagyu thus survived the war.

The Drigung followers lived in a region called Drigung. Unlike the Taglung, they did not help the Sera and Drepung monk soldiers, and so were awarded some farms by the government. For that dis-

394 *BL*: 176a

395 This means Karma Kagyu would be squashed like a cushion.

396 This last part of the prediction became true because at that very time, Shabdrung Ngawang Namgyal, one of the heads of Drugpa Kagyu sect went to Bhutan, took it over, and made the country independent as it remains today.

> pensation however, the Drigung had to pay very heavy taxes. Thus figuratively speaking, the horn of "dri" was broken as foretold by Ogyen Guru Rinpoche.
>
> Drugpa Kagyu, on the other hand, did not join either side in the war. They were neither for nor against the Gelug sect. As a result, they survived.
>
> The events, indeed, unfolded as Guru Rinpoche had predicted.

Then Karmapa went to Tsurphu Monastery. New Year had started (not specified, but probably 1642), and Karmapa went to Tsang, where he visited Ga Dong Monastery. He made two statues, one of Avalokiteshvara and the other Maitreya, both in bronze. He also made a thangka of Chenrezig surrounded by sixteen *arhats*.

The administration of Karmapa sent a message to the Panchen Rinpoche asking him to help avert an impending war.[397] However, he responded that there was nothing he could do. He could neither cooperate nor support the Karma Kagyu since everything was then under the control of Sonam Chopal (the Fifth Dalai Lama's chief administrator) and the Mongol warlord Gushri Khan. The Karma Kagyu administration therefore failed to present their case to Gushri Khan or the Fifth Dalai Lama.

Karmapa went to central Tibet and stayed in Legshed Ling Monastery. He then went again to Lho Drag. While he was in retreat in Marmephug, in his spare time, he made a thangka of Chenrezig in Chinese style in the form of "a protector from eight disasters" as a present for Dhitsha Tulku.

From his attendant, Kuntu Zangpo, Karmapa received the *lung* transmission of a collection of sutras including the *Lotus Sutra* (the last sutra taught by the Buddha before his *paranirvana*).[398] He also received the transmission of *The Hundred Thousand Poems* composed by Milarepa.

During that period, Karmapa distributed to beggars every offering he received. Before leaving for Kham in east Tibet, he per-

397 *BL*: 176a

398 *BL*: 176b

formed a prayer ceremony with Kuntu Zangpo.

On the way to Kham, Karmapa stood on a rock and recited the *Lotus Sutra* aloud. Then he declared, "We have to practice the bodhisattva wish for sentient beings." He then meditated on the bodhisattva wish and left his footprints on the rock.

Taglung Tashi Paldrub, head of Taglung Kagyu, met Karmapa and offered him auspicious prayers of long life. He gave him a letter from the Fifth Dalai Lama that said that the Sakya, Kagyu,[399] and Gelug sects should be in peace. This letter was distributed everywhere. Karmapa in turn asked Tashi Paldrub to deliver a letter of reply to the Fifth Dalai Lama.

In the Water Sheep year (1643), on the eighth day in the month known as the Buddha's demonstration of miracles (the first month), Karmapa went to Zang Phuk. He gave the Full Monk's Vows to the Fifth Gyaltsab and Dhitsha Rinpoches. He gave the Monk's Semi-Vows to the Fourth Pawo, who was the reincarnation of his teacher, Pawo Tsuklak Gyatso.[400]

Karmapa was forty years old when he and his party traveled to Kham. Sonam Chopal led Gushri Khan's army and set out to capture Karmapa. Taglung Tashi Paldrub managed to intercept the army and stopped it at Khamda (in the southeastern part of central Tibet). Gushri Khan was also there. Sonam Chopal said to Tashi Paldrub, "You must talk to Karmapa and make him swear that he will not do anything to the Gelug sect in the future."[401]

399 In those days, the Nyingma sect was aligned with Kagyu, so the Fifth Dalai Lama included Nyingma under Kagyu.

400 *BL*: 176b

401 *BL*: 177a

30. Karmapa Attacked

On[402] the tenth day in the sixth month of the Wood Monkey year (July 14, 1644), Karmapa was in Dorkha Pang Shang. Taglung Tashi Paldrub met with Karmapa. He asked Karmapa to give in to Sonam Chopal's demand. Karmapa said, "There is no need for me to swear for the future. I can swear that I never did anything bad to the Gelug in the past." This message was relayed back to Sonam Chopal and Gushri Khan.

Sonam Chopal twisted Karmapa's response by saying, "We are not talking about the past. We want his guarantee for the future. Seeing that he fails to promise not to harm us in the future, it must mean that he will." The army was then ordered to attack Karmapa and his group. Sonam Chopal led Kyisho's[403] army as well as Gushri Khan's soldiers and surrounded Karmapa, his monks and followers.

Ambushed, Karmapa sat on a rock and meditated while he played a guitar. He invoked the special power of Saraswati so that all his people disappeared into his guitar of Saraswati.[404] For several days, the soldiers could not see them. They looked everywhere

402 *BL*: 177a

403 This is most likely the same Kyisho Depa Sonam Namgyal who collaborated with the administrators of Sera and Drepung monasteries. See chapter 4 for details.

404 Saraswati is a deity of knowledge, music, and the arts.

and became quite confused. Some of them started to quarrel among themselves, while others became devotees of Karmapa.

After a few days, many of Karmapa's monks were able to escape to safety. However, some were killed, and others were injured. Karmapa and Kuntu Zangpo pressed south towards a hidden area called Khenpa Jong. The soldiers futilely tried to find Karmapa. He appeared to them sometimes as a deer, sometimes as an eagle flying in the sky. As a result, he was never captured. That happened.

For twelve days until they reached Khenpa Jong, Karmapa and Kuntu Zangpo had no food. However, every day they saw Guru Padmasambhava who gave them *amrita* (nectar). As a result, they did not experience hunger or the cold temperatures of the ninth month.

Eventually, Karmapa and Kuntu Zangpo reached Tsari (a land of tribal natives in southern Tibet situated to the northeast of Arunachal, India).[405] People recognized Karmapa and came out to pay him respect and to give him offerings. The party of two kept to a path through an area inhabited by natives (in nowadays Arunachal, India). From time to time, when they came upon a suitable cave, the two travelers would do a retreat. Karmapa also continued to sculpt statues of Tara, Vajrapani, Hayagriva, etc.

In some areas, the natives gave them honey. One native gave Karmapa a deer. The deer followed Karmapa everywhere. In another area, one hundred monkeys encircled Karmapa. They played and danced right in front of him. It was their way to pay respect to him.

405 *BL*: 177b. *Tsari is situated today in a remote area area disputed between China and India.*

31. Flight to Safety

Tso Kar Chung Dzong

It[406] was already spring in the year of the Wood Bird (1645). Flowers were in bloom everywhere. Karmapa and Kuntu Zangpo arrived at Tso Kar Chung Dzong (Tso Kar is a lake located in Tsari) where they stayed for about four months.

At Chung Dzong, Karmapa saw in his meditation many Buddhas in their respective nirvanas. One day a white man on a white horse appeared and said to him, "Please go to Kham, and everything will be perfect."

On another day, two women donning only green skirts were holding hands in the distance. They were singing, "You should have a consort, then everything meaningful will be achieved (enlightened)."[407]

Karmapa again made a statue of Tara.

At a small lake called Shining Lake, the upper torso of a *naga* woman from her waist up appeared to Karmapa. She was shining like a pearl shell. Karmapa read many Dharma verses to her.

---

406 *BL*: 177b

407 This means that the Tenth Karmapa should take a wife who can be his partner in Vajrayana practice to speed up his progress in meditation.

Karmapa wrote a book titled *Ganga of Milky Amrita*.[408] In it, he described a dream he had of *Dewachen*.[409] Karmapa composed a small text especially for Kuntu Zangpo's solitary meditation retreat. He also composed another book called *Super Horse Balaho: Directions of the Path to the Nirvana of Avalokiteshvara* (no longer extant). Karmapa wrote these two books when he was with Kuntu Zangpo during that period.

Afterwards, they went to lower Kongpo. People recognized Karmapa and heaped many offerings upon him. He in turn gave them to the monasteries in the area to support the monks and residents.

By his power as the Karmapa, he blessed and revived an old, dried-up spring. Subsequently the spring produced healing water.

Powo

It was the year of the Fire Dog (1646), and Karmapa was forty-three years old. He and Kuntu Zangpo arrived at Kanam Sewa Gang in Powo district.[410] Karmapa conducted a big *monlam* puja. A great many monks in the Powo area came to participate in it. The offerings made to Karmapa were splendid. As usual, Karmapa distributed them all to the impoverished and to various monasteries.

Karmapa taught the Powo people, including the Lord and nobles, the practice of Chenrezig. He emphasized this practice and encouraged everyone to do it.

Because he was so adept in painting and sketching, Karmapa was able to finish a thangka of the Buddha and the sixteen *arhats* in just sixteen days.

During his stay in this part of Powo, many assistants attended him, though not by his wish. Everywhere he went, people served and honored him.

From his wisdom, Karmapa understood that the emanation of

---

408 *BL*: 178a. This book is no longer extant. "Ganga" is the River Ganges.

409 *Dewachen* is the Pureland of Buddha Amitabha.

410 The Powo Duke Kanam Depa and his people were tribesmen who wore caps made from leaves. They were devotees of Karmapa. This Indo-China border region enjoyed some independence until the 1940s. It is located in southeast Tibet now under China's control, not far from the northern tip of today's Myanmar.

the Sixth Shamarpa Garwang Chokyi Wangchuk had been reborn in the far eastern district of Golok. He composed a recognition letter and a long life prayer for Shamarpa. He selected a *mala* and some auspicious cushions. For Shamarpa's parents, he set aside some gold coins. Karmapa then sent two messengers with these things he had prepared.[411] They were Karma Nyinched and Karma Thondrub. From his wisdom mind, he was able to draw a map so the two would know how to get to the village and how to locate the family of the young Shamarpa incarnate.

Further, Karmapa understood that Karma Sonam Rabten, the King of Lijiang, would pass away soon. He made prayers especially for him. Within a month, the King passed away in the seventh month.

411 *BL*: 178b

32. Exile in Lijiang

In the year of the Fire Pig (1647), Karmapa was forty-four years old. He traveled towards the lower part of Kham. His attire was simple, yet in spite of his humble appearance, people recognized him. They came out to pay him respect and to give him offerings.[412]

When Karmapa was at a sand hill in an area called Gemala, he had a vision. It was in the morning when he heard a human voice cry out, "The fortune of Tse Lha Gang (in Kongpo) is finished." Later, Karmapa found out that it was at that time that Kongpo was destroyed by Gushri Khan's armies.

Karmapa reached Phuntsok Gephel Ling (monastery near Lijiang) in the ninth month. Messengers of the King of Lijiang arrived to invite him to Lijiang. It was around this time that Karmapa finished the biography of his guru (the Sixth Shamarpa), *The Bountiful Cow: Biography of a Bodhisattva.*[413]

At Pongdzira, Karma Thubten, the senior minister (of Lijiang), and his entourage of over a hundred people stood ready to receive Karmapa at a riverside.[414] After the reception, they escorted him to

412 Karmapa also visited some renowned monasteries – Ranyag Gonpa, Shugdhe Gonpa, for example. Bey Lotsawa's description of these visits is not translated.

413 Karmapa continued with his travels, visiting Khawakhar, Ju Tashi Dhargye Gongpa, Dro Shong Gonpa. The details of these visits are not translated.

414 *BL*: 179a

Gyalthang[415] (or Victory Field). The Losar celebration of the Earth Mouse year (1648) began and spanned many days.

When Karmapa was forty-six years old, messengers from the royal family of Dokhar Moko arrived.[416]

Karmapa visited Phelgye Ling (monastery) and gave teachings there.

Karmapa visited a printing house that contained the woodblocks of the *Kanjur*.[417] He made wishes there and blessed the woodblocks. He also visited some nearby temples.

The art of fireworks is a Lijiang tradition. To honor Karmapa, the Lijiang people specially staged a grand and fantastic fireworks show.

After the celebrations, a long procession of soldiers, Lijiang monks, and Chinese monks escorted Karmapa to the capital of Lijiang. They crossed the Bala River by boat. As they neared the capital at the top of Mount Kungala, the late king's brothers, Prince Karma Phuntsok Wangchuk and Prince Bukhu Zol, were already waiting to receive him in an elaborate procession accompanied by music. They escorted Karmapa all the way up (to the capital at the top of Mount Kungala).

At the top of the mountain, Jang (King) Saddam Gyalpo Karma Chimed Lhawang sat waiting on a palanquin flanked by his external and internal ministers and officials. A huge white tent had been set up complete with thrones and everything for an elaborate reception. The king as host led Karmapa all the way to a throne. Once Karmapa was seated, the king proceeded to prostrate to him on the ground.[418]

First, the king offered (to Karmapa) a golden *chakra*[419] and a

415 Present-day Zhongdian (recently renamed Shangri-la) in Yunnan Province, China.

416 A *dokhar* is a small region ruled by a duke or a chieftain-king. The chieftain-king is referred to as the Dokhar followed by his family name as in Dokhar Jacko, Dokhar Moko, and so forth.

417 The King of Lijiang commissioned the creation of these original woodblocks of the collection of Buddha's teachings called the *Kanjur*. He requested the Sixth Shamarpa to oversee the whole project.

418 *BL*: 179b

419 A wheel signifying the Buddha's teachings.

white, spiraled conch shell adorned with golden wings. He also presented many other auspicious offerings. The king touched the Karmapa's feet with his forehead and made many supplications. He requested prayers for his deceased father and prayed aloud to Karmapa.

The next day, the king escorted Karmapa and his party in a huge procession to Baisha, the capital of Lijiang. On the way, thousands of people lined both the left and right sides of the road. Dressed in fine garments, they knelt on the ground. Offerings of incense and flowers, among other things, were gathered on tables set out for the occasion. Rows of guitarists, flutists, and cymbal players performed celebratory music.

Karmapa and his party stayed at the capital for a brief period. Afterwards, they descended the mountain capital and proceeded to a holy site. The Eighth Karmapa Mikyo Dorje and the Sixth Shamarpa Chokyi Wangchuk had both given their blessings there. A throne was prepared for Karmapa, and a fine reception took place.

After the reception, Karmapa was escorted to the Palace of Lijiang. Seated on a lion throne, Karmapa donned his Black Hat. The palace residents offered Karmapa the eight auspicious symbols and seven jewels of royal power, all crafted in gold. They also offered him sacks of gold and silver as well as rolls of brocade stacked up high. Karmapa gave a short teaching on Avalokiteshvara and a short recitation of the mantra.

Another day, Karmapa gave extensive teachings to the king, the royal family, the ministers, and the people. He began with the chapter on "The Doors on All Sides" from the *Lotus Sutra*. He gave instructions on the importance of Bodhisattva Avalokiteshvara, the importance of this practice, and the recitation of the six-syllable mantra. He also gave instructions on karma, impermanence, the suffering of samsara, and the preciousness of human life. He gave advice on how to renounce the negative karmic activities, and how to develop the merits through virtuous practice based on the text *Letter to a Friend* by Nagarjuna.

At different places in Lijiang, Karmapa gave many teachings

and blessings. The king's younger brother took the *Genyen* Vows[420] from Karmapa. He received the name Karma Rinchen Nyingpo.[421] Karmapa gave many teachings on *Mahamudra* and the practices of Chenrezig and of Chakrasambhava. Afterwards the king invited Karmapa to his Ngalokir Palace.

In China (i.e., region east of Lijiang), there were three small kingdoms named Gedang, Dotsame, and Yungnge. Their kings separately sent messengers with offerings to Karmapa. They could not come themselves due to the dangers posed by Liu Chi and his army.[422]

> [*Bey Lotsawa comments*]:[423] The kings of Lijiang believed that they were descendants from the gods. Up until then, there had been fifteen kings. Before they met the Eighth Karmapa, the people of Lijiang were sky-worshippers.[424] They sacrificed animals in their worship of ancestors. The illustrious Eighth Karmapa, who once declined an invitation from the Ming emperor of China, chose instead to accept the invitation from the King of Lijiang. During a reception, the Eighth Karmapa was asked to climb the steps to mount an elephant. But the elephant gently lowered its body to the ground in prostration. Having witnessed this amazing incident, the king thought Karmapa a god. His pride was completely squashed. By his own initiative, the king promised that he would do anything Karmapa asked of him. The Eighth Karmapa told him that a country should follow the ten virtues and refrain from the ten non-virtues. Ever since then, the people of Lijiang became Karma Kagyu followers.

At the time when the Tenth Karmapa was in Lijiang, there were about 121,000 households.

---

420 Five vows of conduct that can be taken by a lay Buddhist.

421 *BL*: 180a

422 Liu Chi is the Tibetan transliteration for a Chinese military figure who cannot be identified. In the fifteen or so years following the creation of the Qing dynasty in 1644, Yunnan became one of several bastions for remanants of the Ming dynasty. It is possible that Liu Chi was part of this band of loyalists. In the late 1650's the Qing dispatched an army to eradicate the Ming loyalists from Yunnan.

423 *BL*: 180a

424 *BL*: 180b

The king gave Kuntu Zangpo many offerings to thank him for serving Karmapa so well. In addition, he offered him more attendants to assist him in his duties.

Karmapa visited a temple called Chunakotra that housed a special statue of Kashyapa.[425]

The Lijiang king offered Karmapa one hundred gold coins and requested him to do a very special puja for his deceased father. He wanted to know where his father had been reborn. Karmapa explained that because his father had practiced great generosity towards the very poor and sick in his kingdom, he had already been reborn in one of the heavens.

Karmapa declined the king's invitation to stay longer in Lijiang. He did not wish to stay among the wealthy. He would rather be alone and free. He soon set out for Gyalthang, Lijiang.

Karmapa visited a Chinese Mahayana temple called Shangtoli[426] where many Mahayana and Vajrayana monks were staying.

At Ketse Dzong, Karmapa did a summer retreat with the monks there.

Afterwards, Karmapa went to Yang Thang. The local landlord-duke was mentally ill. By the blessings of Karmapa, he became normal again.

When Karmapa was at Gyaja Gonpa, people from all parts came to see him. He performed the New Year celebration for the year of the Earth Ox (1649).[427] He organized a very large group recitation of the Chenrezig-Mani mantra.

Karmapa then proceeded to Chagra Monastery built by the Sixth Karmapa.

Karmapa visited Atro Gonpa, the monastery of Atro Rinpoche.[428] A fire broke out. Karmapa blessed some water and simply tossed it in the air, and the fire was extinguished.

In the area of Gangkar Chedsum, Karmapa constructed a tem-

---

425 This is likely the Buddha Kashyapa.

426 This is a Tibetan transliteration of a Chinese name.

427 *BL*: 181a

428 The current Atro Rinpoche is in his seventies today and lives in Cambridge. The Sixteenth Karmapa placed a great deal of trust in him and respected his honesty.

ple of Chenrezig. He stayed there for some months and taught the resident sangha.

Karmapa and Kuntu Zangpo then returned to Gyalthang. At the Khangsar Monastery, they did the summer retreat of the Earth Ox year. He gave teachings during his stay in that area. He also made and painted many statues to give to the monasteries and people. He also organized the communities of the practitioners. Many offerings were given. As usual, he distributed them among the poor.

Having accomplished everything for the people there, Karmapa and his attendant slipped away to practice meditation on the other side of Lijiang's mountain.

At that time, rebels in that area called Dolpa[429] were challenging the Lijiang government. Karmapa and Kuntu Zangpo were there and tried to stop the fighting. However, the Lijiang soldiers would not listen. Instead, the Lijiang general and soldiers asked Karmapa to do a puja to defeat the rebels. Karmapa's response was, "I am one who does not disturb even a tiny bug. I will not do anything to anyone."[430] The army went on to attack the rebels, but the rebels won.

Kuntu Zangpo gave much food to the defeated soldiers, and they went home to Lijiang. The rebels did not stay in Lijiang either. They moved to another province and settled there.

Karmapa and Kuntu Zangpo went to the mountains where the natives lived (near the northern tip of Burma, or Myanmar, today). They stayed there for a year.

429 *Dolpa* literally means a large group of barbaric hunters.

430 *BL*: 181b

33. Recognition of the Seventh Shamarpa

One[431] day (likely in 1649), Karmapa told Kuntu Zangpo that he would go to invite the reincarnation of Bodhisattva Chokyi Wangchuk (to Lijiang). From his wisdom, he knew that the reincarnation was in Golok (in east Tibet).

Karmapa wanted to go there by himself. He asked Kuntu Zangpo to remain behind and to continue his meditation practice. Though Kuntu Zangpo would very much have liked to accompany him, he finally gave in and listened to Karmapa.

For his journey, Karmapa took one horse, a walking stick, and a few staples, which he tied to his horse. He left for Golok with the meager provisions of a beggar. On the way, he had to pass through jungles inhabited by many tigers, but he did not encounter any.

Karmapa crossed over a very rocky mountain and came to farmland on the other side. The land was quite bare and flat. Karmapa stopped for a break and had something to eat beside a river. His horse was scared to cross the river because it was haunted, but Karmapa crossed it anyway. Later, he was able to find a cave where he could stay and rest.

From a shepherd Karmapa bought yogurt and milk. The shepherd introduced Karmapa to Tharlam, the head of a small local

431 *BL*: 181b

group of families. He treated Karmapa very well but could not convince Karmapa to stay.

Karmapa pressed on towards his destination. He arrived at a region that had many rice fields, unlike central Tibet that had none. One day his horse slipped in a rice paddy. Karmapa took this to be a bad omen. He decided to stop and spent the rest of the day and night there.

At that same time, Kuntu Zangpo dreamed that his tooth was falling out and his head was struck by lightning. In the morning Kuntu Zangpo felt worried and hired two men to catch up to Karmapa. But they encountered so much trouble along the way that they had to turn back.

Meanwhile, Karmapa continued on his way. He ran into robbers along with their stolen livestock. They robbed Karmapa, too – his horse, clothing, and whatever else that was tied to the horse.

Karmapa was then left with nothing, but he pressed on. His shoes soon fell apart. It was winter and snowing. The skin on his feet cracked so he had to find a place to rest. He came upon a family who took him in. They gave him food and shelter and treated him very well. He stayed with this family until the wounds on his feet healed.

Karmapa started on his way again. He had no cup. Someone gave him a broken wooden cup bound together by some cords. Another gave him a shawl to cover his shoulders.

Karmapa filled the wooden cup with soil and mixed in some butter. He patted down the dough-like mixture in the cup. On this surface, he then created a picture from one of the stories about the Buddha's past lives (*The Jataka Tales*). It told about Buddha as a prince who gave up his body to feed a hungry mother tiger.[432] With this picture in the cup, Karmapa offered it to the Buddha and made a wish that he would be able to accomplish the bodhisattva practice.

Karmapa reached the retreat house-temple of a Sakya lama.[433]

---

432 This is an extreme example of bodhisattva action that the Tenth Karmapa used for inspiration to perfect his own bodhisattva practice.

433 *BL*: 182a

The lama was very happy, for he recognized Karmapa and asked him to stay. Karmapa remained at the temple for some time. He read sutras and wrote poems about the Twelve Deeds of the Buddha.

Later, Karmapa passed by the White Stupa of China near a village. A tea merchant from the village offered him a package of tea leaves. "This is very helpful," Karmapa said to him. Back at the village, the tea merchant told the villagers how he had met a beggar who must be special.

When Karmapa arrived at an area called Bo, people felt something about him, that he was special. Though Karmapa was like a beggar, they respected him.

Karmapa went to different areas such as Rabgang and Dartsedo. He sent a detailed message to Kuntu Zangpo letting him know where he was and what he was doing.

Whatever Karmapa received as an offering, he gave away. He continued to travel as a beggar. He reached an area with nomads who had gathered in great numbers. They offered Karmapa one hundred horses, food and many things.

Karmapa traveled from Rabgang to Washul. He took a break and taught the local people the Dharma. He gave them his blessings. After a few days, he moved on and arrived at Domed Thagku.

> [*Bey Lotsawa comments*]: When Karmapa passed through Domed Thagku, he learned about a man called Juzhag who knew how to do a mo (prediction or divination) in the Bon tradition. Juzhag told his friends that his divinations around that time all revealed the auspicious birth of Buddha Shakyamuni. His thinking was that Karmapa would come from somewhere. That very afternoon, Karmapa arrived at their village, so everyone was quite surprised. My guru (the Eighth Situ) told me that this story is still being recounted in that area today.

Meanwhile, the reincarnation of the Sixth Shamarpa, now a young child, knew from his superior wisdom mind that Karmapa had come to find him. He sent his relative to go and receive Karmapa at his birthplace in the area called Machu.

Karmapa crossed the big river Ngo Cho and arrived at Jobri. There he built a small temple and a big prayer wheel. He then proceeded to Zirka Lhamo Darthang. This was the place where a famous Dharma throne was especially constructed for public teaching. It was made of bricks and stones. The Gyalwa Konchog Ban (the Fifth Shamarpa) and Je Chokyi Wangchuk (the Sixth Shamarpa) had both taught from this throne.

When Karmapa reached Mar Yul in Golok, the child Shamar Tulku, who had already arrived previously, was waiting to receive him.[434] The young child prostrated to Karmapa and offered him a pearl *mala*. He then invited Karmapa to his parents' house, which sat in a field where the river meandered in the pattern of the Tibetan letter "A." The house sat right in the center of the letter. Karmapa in turn offered many gifts to the very young boy and his family.

434 *BL*: 182b

34. From Golok to Lijiang (1650–1658)

Birthplace Revisited

After[435] he met with Shamar Tulku (likely in 1650), Karmapa wished to visit upper Golok, where his own family used to live. The trip must have taken a few days. Upon his arrival, he discovered that his family no longer lived there. The house was gone, and in its place, a small temple had been erected. Inside there was a thangka of the thirty-five Buddhas on the wall. Karmapa performed a prayer ceremony there.

He met a grey-haired man who was his childhood neighbor. They used to play together when they were children. The man remembered Karmapa.

Karmapa decided to stay and do a meditation retreat. The child Shamarpa who had accompanied him on this trip then returned home.

During his stay, Karmapa composed many poems about the meaninglessness of samsara. In his retreat, he remembered that Kuntu Zangpo, who was also in a retreat in Lijiang, had asked for some poems by him. He wrote the poems and sent them by messenger to Kuntu Zangpo.

---

435 *BL*: 182b

People again went to greet him. He was paid the highest respect and given many offerings. As he had done in the past, he gave away everything, mostly to beggars, the poor, and the needy.

It was winter. Karmapa stayed in the lower part of a forest called Dhi Yi Dragkar, which is the name of Manjusri's mantra. He missed his horse which the robbers previously had taken, and he asked some people to look for it. He found out that the robbers had sold the horse. Apparently, one of the thieves had lost his hut to a fire shortly after he had taken the horse. He thought this a bad omen and sold the horse. By the time Karmapa's people found it, the horse was terribly weak, and it cried when it was finally reunited with Karmapa. Karmapa wrote a poem about it.

Karmapa understood that Kuntu Zangpo missed him very much, so he sent word for him to come together with Karma Rinchen, Karma Kalzang, and others. They arrived, and Shamar Tulku also went, so they were all gathered there.[436]

Many people were gathered, and many things were offered, and they in turn received blessings. Afterwards, the young Shamarpa returned home. Karmapa and Kuntu Zangpo remained for some time. Karmapa painted the Black Hayagriva and also Dorje Namjomma.[437]

The Iron Hare Year (1651)

After the Losar celebrations for the Iron Hare year were finished, Karmapa began to teach. (Shamar Tulku came again.) He taught Shamar Tulku the *Mahamudra* teachings and the *Lotus Sutra* together with many disciples. Upon completion of the teachings, Shamarpa returned home.

Karmapa then visited many places and monasteries in Menang (in the district of Golok). For one whole year, he met with the people – lamas from the Bon monasteries, local lords, and people in this eastern part of Kham. At the request of Kuntu Zangpo, Karmapa began to write his autobiography, *The Story of My Trip, Song*

436 *BL*: 183a

437 Dorje Namjomma is a Tantric form of meditational deity for the cure of illnesses and diseases.

of a Bird of Paradise Along Its Journey.[438]

When he was in Shel Khog, Karmapa visited many temples.[439] He taught the teachings of Guru Rinpoche and gave the sangha and lay communities the related *lung* transmissions. Kuntu Zangpo performed a special long life ceremony for him. Karmapa then confirmed that he would live out his life to its full term. To the public, he taught in detail on the topic of the four Dharmas of Gampopa. It was here that Karmapa recognized the reincarnation of Pawo Rinpoche.

During that time, the young son of Chieftain-king Beri came to Karmapa for help because his life was at risk. Gushri Khan had already defeated and killed his father. Though the father had been disrespectful to him, Karmapa felt only compassion and repaid the son with kindness. He made arrangements so that the young man could seek refuge in Gyalrong where the local lord and his people were the Karmapa's devotees.

From memory, Karmapa made a copy of a thangka that was in Gangkar Chodhe Monastery depicting the Buddha and the sixteen *arhats*. He gave the painting to Phagmo Shabdrung, a high Karma Kagyu lama who followed Karmapa from time to time.

Then Karmapa made a White Tara statue out of sandalwood. At the end of the Iron Hare year, Karmapa and Kuntu Zangpo took turns teaching the *Lotus Sutra* to many disciples.

The Water Dragon Year (1652)

At the Bo Gangkar Monastery, Karmapa performed the Losar celebrations for the Water Dragon year. The high lama Ralung Thuchen Chogyal and Duke Dopa Minyagpa[440] both held Karmapa in great esteem. They invited him (to their monastery) and showered him with offerings and elaborate services.

Karmapa conducted a special enthronement for his attendant Kuntu Zangpo to recognize him as one of the lineage holders of

438 For more about this work, see this book's Introduction.

439 *BL*: 183b

440 This means lord of Minyag province.

Karma Kagyu. In front of a large gathering of lamas and monks from the different temples in the vicinity – mainly Karma Kagyu and Nyingma followers – Karmapa presented Kuntu Zangpo with the seal of a lineage holder.

At the request of Kuntu Zangpo, Karmapa painted a self-portrait, in which he was dressed as a layman. His hair was tied back in a knot, and he wore earrings of large round loops.[441]

The young Shamar Tulku again traveled from his home to see Karmapa. They met at a temple called Pal Lhakhang built earlier by a Chinese princess on her way to marry a Tibetan king. It was also here that a man named Sengye Gonpa offered Karmapa a very holy statue of the Second Karmapa.

In this year of the Water Dragon, Shamar Tulku aged twenty, received the Full Monk's Vows from Karmapa. During the vow ceremony, the required number of monks as prescribed by the *Vinaya* was fully assembled. Karmapa was the acting *khenpo*, Kuntu Zangpo the *lopon*. Karma Zabsal, a famous Karma Kagyu lama, was one of the assistants. Yung Rab Jampa, also a learned Karma Kagyu lama in the Kham area, was the timer.[442]

The seventh incarnate Shamarpa was given the name Yeshe Nyingpo. It was selected from among the Shamarpa's names given in Guru Padmasambhava's predictions.

Two famous tulkus also received the Full Monk's Vows at the same time. One was Shagom and the other, Nangso of Tse Lha Gang Monastery.

All the rinpoches and monks who had just taken the Monk's Vows together did a *manghalam sojong*[443] led by Karmapa. Karmapa gave teachings on the *Vinaya*. Kuntu Zangpo recited the sutra called *Praising Vinaya Sutra*.

On the tenth day of the month of *Tha Kar* (the tenth month of the lunar calendar), Karmapa led a special ceremony to endorse and honor the Seventh Shamar, which included an offering ceremony.

During that period, countless visitors came to pay respects to

441 *BL*: 184a

442 According to *Vinaya* tradition, the timer records the time when the last vow is transmitted.

443 A very auspicious purification practice.

Karmapa and Shamarpa, who in turn gave them the initiations of the *yidams* and protectors.

Karmapa painted a famous thangka of the White Umbrella deity to eliminate evils, to bring peace to sentient beings, and to protect the Dharma. This happened at the end of the Water Dragon year.

The Water Snake Year (1653)

Losar of the Water Snake year was celebrated with many prayers and rites performed by many monks.

In China, Phing Tong,[444] the regent-general who had gained control of half of China, sent an invitation to Karmapa. Karmapa who was fifty years old at the time refused to go. The general's messenger later returned with a great many offerings and a letter stating that he was fully confident that Karmapa was the real god of the sky.

Shamarpa returned home to prepare for his departure from his birth home.

Karmapa said, "On the art of poetry and painting, I can say that I am one of the best in Tibet and its nearby regions. Avalokiteshvara is happy with me, and he likes me the most. I came into this world to paint stories of the Buddhas, the bodhisattvas, and the *arhats*."[445]

The Wood Horse Year (1654)

Karmapa celebrated Losar at Gorapang Temple. He made a thangka of the Buddha's Twelve Deeds. The reincarnation of the Fifth Situ Rinpoche and his monks arrived with many offerings.[446]

Karmapa spent the whole year here creating many paintings of the Buddha, which he gave to different tulkus and rinpoches.[447]

444 Tibetan transliteration of a Chinese name. The person cannot be identified.

445 *BL*: 184b

446 In those days, Situ Rinpoche was in charge of Karma Gon Monastery. Situ's seat of Palpung did not yet exist. Karma Gon was geographically the middle seat of Karmapa.

447 Everywhere he went, Karmapa continued to paint. He gave away his paintings to temples and others. The list of his paintings and their recipients is not translated here.

The Wood Sheep Year (1655)

At Shayul (near the Yunnan/Tibet border, close to the northern border of Yunnan, China) Karmapa gave full ordination to the Sixth Situ Rinpoche. Karmapa was the *Vinaya Khenpo*, Kuntu Zangpo the *lopon*, Shagom Rinpoche the questioner, and Nangso Rinpoche the timer. All (religious roles and rites) were in accord with the *Vinaya* tradition. A very long name was given to Situ – Chogyal Mipham Thrinlay Rabten.

Karmapa also enthroned Situ as one of the main activity holders[448] of Karma Kagyu. He gave him a thangka of Avalokiteshvara and protector Vajrasadhu, which he had created.

Karmapa conducted a big puja for the anniversary of (the death) of Je Chokyi Wangchuk (the Sixth Shamarpa).

Karmapa stayed the whole year in this area.

The Fire Monkey Year (1656)

Karmapa started out to Lijiang. First, he visited Gangkar, then Do Shod, and Gyalthang. He visited all the temples and monasteries in those places. He made two Guru Rinpoche thangkas, one of which he gave Kuntu Zangpo.

A prediction by Guru Rinpoche stated that when a temple was built at Melong Teng, an emanation of Padma Jungney (Guru Rinpoche) would come to Lijiang. While Karmapa was staying in that temple (at Melong Teng), one day as he was painting, he mentioned this prediction and stated that he was that emanation.

When he arrived at Lijiang, Karmapa gave the *Vinaya* vow to about one thousand monks. At the time, people were still sacrificing animals as offerings. Karmapa was successful in making them give up this practice completely.

At Legdo Palace of Lijiang, King Saddam gave an elaborate ceremony with splendid offerings in honor of Karmapa. Karmapa stayed in Lijiang that whole year. One of the princes was a serious practitioner. Karmapa taught him the *Six Yogas of Naropa* and the *Vajrayogini* teachings.

448 An activity holder is one who helps spread beneficial activities of the lineage.

The Fire Bird Year (1657)

Losar[449] was celebrated at the Legdo Palace.

In that year, Karmapa taught, sculpted, and painted as usual. He made an Avalokiteshvara statue and a statue of himself and gave them to the King.[450]

Two of Karmapa's teeth came out. Kuntu Zangpo commissioned two stupas to be built in gold to contain them. He paid one hundred gold coins for each. He also built a silver stupa to hold Karmapa's hair.

In that year, there were many rumors of an impending war. Karmapa prayed to his *yidam* for a prediction as to what would happen. The prediction came in his dream: on the field free of drought, take care of the sheep of your meditation experiences.[451] Karmapa then told the Lijiang people that there would not be any war at that time. The rumors stopped.

Then, an infectious disease spread throughout the area. In a dream, Karmapa saw the famous Dromtonpa, one of two main disciples of Jowo Atisha, reading a homage prayer to Atisha. Dromtonpa turned to Karmapa and said,

> Flowers are blooming in the field of truth.
>
> The angel is drowning in the water.

Accordingly, Karmapa made a thangka of a female deity dressed in leaves sitting on the backs of evil diseases.[452] He then blessed the thangka. The disease was eradicated.

The Earth Dog Year (1658)

Losar celebrations were conducted. Later, Kuntu Zangpo's mother

---

449 *BL*: 185a

450 Debreczeny (2009), (2011) and (2012) discusses, in part, some of the paintings by the Tenth Karmapa while he was in Lijiang.

451 A field free of drought is a field free of contamination such as wrong views and doubts. The sheep symbolize meaningful experiences of meditation. The meaning of the dream is to stay relaxed, as there is no need to worry.

452 Karmapa understood that he should paint a thangka of the female bodhisattva known as the "Leave-dressed Goddess."

passed away, and Karmapa made a thangka.

Karmapa had a dream.[453] In it, he saw the Fifth Gyaltsab Dragpa Choyang, who came to him on a white horse and talked with him. Karmapa knew that the Fifth Gyaltsab Rinpoche had passed away in Tibet. Later, he learned that he died on the 3rd day in the month of *O-dha* (second month in Tibetan calendar). Karmapa made a thangka of the Buddha and the sixteen *arhats*. He performed a special prayer ceremony for the deceased Rinpoche. He also understood that the reincarnation would be reborn in Lijiang.

The Lijiang prince Takzhi invited Karmapa to his palace. Karmapa gave a very long lecture on the subject, "The Four Thoughts That Turn the Mind from Samsara." He also taught in detail the *Mahamudra* based on *The Three Cycles of Dohas of Saraha*.

Then Karmapa went to Tala in Lijiang and did a retreat.

Shunzhi, the first Qing Dynasty emperor, conquered China when he was just sixteen years old. Karmapa had a dream of a huge red snake surrounding Gyalthang. He told everyone about it and then decided to move to Gangkar with his entourage. Later, General Liu Chi[454] indeed arrived suddenly with an army of seventy thousand. In addition, a bad disease ravaged the population, which people called "the ghost of Qing." Karmapa painted a thangka of Wod Zerchenma, the Glowing Goddess, and he made many wishes. He composed and conducted many prayers to remove disease and war. Subsequently, the Chinese army left, and the disease subsided.

When the Seventh Shamarpa went to see Karmapa, the latter paid him homage by singing the Seven Branch Prayer while playing a guitar.

---

453 *BL*: 185b

454 See footnote 421 for an explanation of Liu Chi.

35. Free of Politics

After[455] more than a year in Tala, Karmapa and Kuntu Zangpo left. Shamarpa and many other rinpoches later joined their group.

The Iron Mouse Year (1660) in Gyalthang

Karmapa and Shamarpa together conducted a big ceremony for Losar of the year of the Iron Mouse. Situ Tulku, Pawo Tulku, Palmo Shabdrung, Tserlha Tulku, and Shagom Tulku, together with the Lijiang king, also participated in the pujas.

In the area of Gyalthang, there were many poor people and refugees after an attack by a Chinese general. Karmapa helped the homeless and the displaced. The Chinese had set fire to some monasteries, and Karmapa helped to rebuild them.

Karmapa recognized the son of a family in Gyalthang to be the reincarnation of Gyaltsab Dragpa Choyang. He was born the seventh day in the month of *O-dha* (second month of Tibetan calendar), Iron Mouse year, and was named Norbu Zangpo.

At that time, Karmapa received a letter with an offering from the Emperor Shunzhi of China.

During this time Karmapa taught extensively on the *Six Yogas*

455 *BL*: 186a

of Naropa, the *Five Teachings of Mahamudra* in the Drigung Kagyu tradition, the *Mahamudra* transmission and written instructions of the First Karmapa Dusum Khyenpa, *Chekawa's Seven-Point Mind Training* of the Kadampa lineage, as well as the *Eight Verses of Lojong,* plus many *lungs* of the *Diamond Sutra,* and other *lungs.*

Karmapa made a red crown by his own hand, which he described as "a red crown extraordinarily shaped and adorned." He then conducted a special ceremony during which he offered it to the Seventh Shamarpa.

Karmapa painted a thangka of the sixteen *arhats* and gave it to Prince Tagzhi. Karmapa printed a set of the *Kanjur* (the collection of the Buddha's texts). He also ordered a very special set of Chinese-style boxes for each volume. By his own hands, Karmapa sewed the straps for the boxes, decorating them with precious stones.

Two Chinese generals, Pi Chu Wang and Fi Pi Wang,[456] arrived with a small band. The Emperor of China had sent them to deliver a gold letter to Karmapa. The two generals became devotees of Karmapa. They even advised him how to write an appropriate reply to their Emperor.

Karmapa undertook many restorations in the Gyalthang area. He also sculpted some statues. Among them were human-size statues of the Five Buddhas; the statues of the Three Buddhas (past, present and future); and one standing two-armed Avalokiteshvara statue.

The King of Tharlam, Karma Tenzin, received from Karmapa instructions on how to meditate on the nature of mind.[457] He later gave up his family life and became a very good meditator-lama.

A reply from Emperor Shunzhi in a gold letter arrived together with many offerings, including some from the empress and crown prince.

In the letter, the emperor stated, "Now I will make you a new seal. I will also designate a permanent messenger between us. He will relay the correspondence between us every year."

---

456 These are Tibetan transliterations of Chinese names.

457 *BL*: 186b

The emperor wanted to offer Karmapa the title "The Spiritual Leader of Tibet," the same title offered to the Fifth Karmapa by the Ming emperor (in 1407).

Karmapa replied, "I have no interest in worldly titles. I don't need them."

Situ Rinpoche (the Sixth), however, beseeched Karmapa, "You must accept!"

"I don't need these things," Karmapa scolded him. "You people are after the Chinese silks and brocades. As for me, in my wisdom, I see the lakes in China filled with human blood."

> [*Bey Lotsawa comments*]: The Fifth Dalai Lama wrote in his autobiography, "Karmapa ran away. He went to China to bring Chinese soldiers." Now here, even this incident can prove whether Karmapa had such interests or not.

> This record shows that the Tenth Karmapa had the opportunity to be guru of the Emperor of China, who would restore his rank and status in Tibet. This would be undesirable for the Fifth Dalai Lama and his administrators who treated him badly. But Karmapa turned down the Chinese emperor.

> *The Fifth Dalai Lama writes: "The Karmapa* Yab Sey[458] *stayed in Lijiang. I have confidence that the Eastern King (emperor of China) will not change his mind, and therefore I am not afraid (i.e. of Karmapa)."*[459]

> *The Fifth Dalai Lama means that the Chinese emperor will continue to favor him alone. He did not realize that the Chinese emperor had indeed offered a prestigious title to the Karmapa who could have used it for his own political gain. Furthermore, the Dalai Lama did not realize he had nothing to fear from the Karmapa who had no interest in political power.*

> *The Sixth Situ Rinpoche Mipham Thrinley Rabten recognized the opportunity to regain the spiritual status and influence the Karma Kagyu had lost. He tried to impress upon Karmapa that he must accept the offer from the emperor of China. On a worldly level, Situpa seemed right. However, Karmapa turned down the title offered him.*

---

458 See footnote 213 for an explanation of *Yab Sey.*

459 *DL*: Volume 1, 559

In the biography of the Sixth Situ also written by Bey Lotsawa and published in The Garland of Omnipresent Wishfulfilling Crystal Gems, *there is additional detail about Situ's appeal to Karmapa. He told Karmapa that he must grab the opportunity and accept the Qing emperor's title. The Sixth Situ said he wanted to be reborn as a prince of China, so he could help the Karma Kagyu. The Tenth Karmapa naturally stopped him. He scolded him saying he should focus more on taking rebirths in the millions of universes to help sentient beings.*

In Palpung Monastery library, there are two separate woodblock editions of The Garland of Omnipresent Wishfulfilling Crystal Gems (BL), *which, among other biographies, included those of the first twelve Karmapas and other lineage-holders up to the Tenth Shamarpa. The only difference between these two editions is the biography of the Tenth Karmapa. One edition, the original, has a detailed biography of the Tenth Karmapa on which this translation is based.*[460] *In the variant edition, Bey Lotsawa's original text is completely excised and in its place is substituted a simplified biography written in verse by the Seventh Shamarpa Yeshe Nyingpo. At the conclusion of this biography is added a note: "The Thirteenth Karmapa Dudul Dorje recommended that the verses written by the Seventh Shamarpa Yeshe Nyingpo should be inserted."*

The Seventh Shamarpa wrote the new and very different biography because of "recent unexpected circumstances," so says an explanatory note. The actual reason for this substitution is not known today. However, it seems likely that the Gelugpa government was troubled by Bey Lotsawa's criticism and contradicton of the Fifth Dalai Lama who wrote in his diary (DL) *that the Karmapa ran away to China to bring troops. Bey Lotsawa challenged and disproved this assertion.*

460 *BL*: 161a–190b

36. Lineage Teachings Transmitted

Karmapa[461] continued to teach and paint. He made a thangka of the Chakrasamvara surrounded by five deities. Above the main figure were Atisha and Dromtonpa, Panchen Sakya Shiri with his disciple, and an Indian *mahasiddha.* Underneath Chakrasamvara were the six-armed Mahakala, Dzambala, and Norzinma. Karmapa painted this thangka in Nepalese style.

After Losar (likely the Iron Ox year, 1661) celebrations were over, the youngest prince of Lijiang, Mipham Tenpey Nyinma, renounced family life. He became a very good meditator monk choosing to do a life-long retreat.

Karmapa met with monks from Tibet and China. He met with everyone who came to see him – lay people, local kings, ministers, dukes, and lords.

At that time, some visitors traveled all the way from India. They were Indian *acharyas*[462] Subhi, Bahiragi, Sanyeshi, and Jaghama. When the Indian *acharyas* heard their native tongue spoken from the lips of Karmapa,[463] they were so astonished and happy that

461 *BL*: 186b

462 An *acharya* is a scholar.

463 The Tenth Karmapa spoke common Sanskrit, which was the Indian language of the day. The Sixth Shamarpa taught him Sanskrit when they were together near Nepal during the late 1620's.

they touched their heads to his feet.[464] Karmapa gave gold coins and footwear to these travelers from a faraway land.

At that same time, some Chinese monks arrived from China. In their company were also Chinese scholars and professors. They were very learned on the teachings of the *Lotus Sutra*. Chinese *bhikhus*[465] from Ching Ley[466] also journeyed to meet Karmapa. The written characters of Ching Ley are very similar to *Wartu* (a form of written Sanskrit). Chinese *Taoshi*[467] also arrived. These groups from China addressed Karmapa as *Siphu*.[468] Karmapa gave them hats, shoes, and clothing for their travels.

Gyalthang Rignga Lhakhang

In Gyalthang Karmapa built a temple.[469] The architecture closely followed the Lijiang style. It had a beautiful roof surrounded by twenty pillars all around the outside. Four pillars stood in the center of the shrine hall. Inside the temple were five Buddha statues. As they were being made, Karmapa carried the stones with his own hands as well as on his back.

Karmapa declared, "Whoever visits this temple will not go to the lower realms, I guarantee it. Moreover, the person will connect to Avalokiteshvara." The temple is Gyalthang Rignga Lhakhang.

Karmapa also said, "By the blessings of this Lhakhang (temple), may diseases, famines, conflicts, and wars not happen in this area."[470] When the reincarnation of Gyaltsab Dragpa Choyang was three years old, he was enthroned in this temple. He was named Norbu Zangpo.

---

464 *BL*: 187a

465 This is the Sanskrit word for a layman who gives up everytrhing to become a fully ordained monk.

466 Tibetan transliteration of a Chinese place name, which cannot be identified.

467 *Taoshi* is a Tibetan transliteration of the Chinese term, *Daoshi*, which means Daoist master.

468 *Siphu* is a Tibetan transliteration of the Chinese term, *Shifu*, which means master-instructor.

469 See Figure 14 and its caption for more about the Rigna Lhakhang.

470 Indeed, ever since then, the area of Lijiang has suffered less from disasters than other regions in East Asia, even human disasters like the Cultural Revolution.

Some time later, Karmapa contracted the flu. His appetite started to wane, and he became thinner.

Karmapa wrote a letter of prediction for his future reincarnation. In addition, Karmapa appointed Gyaltsab saying, "Gyaltsab Norbu Zangpo should take care of Tsurphu, my seat monastery. If you can continue to maintain and take care of it properly, then the lineage of genuine Dharma will not completely disappear. In order to make this happen, I now make an auspicious act by declaring officially, here and now, that you, Gyaltsab Norbu Zangpo, are my son."[471]

Karmapa gave Gyaltsab his prayer beads, a full set of his clothes, and his religious relics, among other things. He then told Gyaltsab's mother, "Act like you are now my consort. Kuntu Zangpo shall support Gyaltsab Norbu Zangpo."

Karmapa then wrote in full a letter what he had declared. He gave this letter to the King of Lijiang.

However, Kuntu Zangpo requested Karmapa not to leave yet. "It's not yet time for you to go. Please live." He then gave Karmapa the empowerment of Dorje Nampar Jompa (a water purification to expunge the contamination of sinful people). Karmapa recovered and became well again.

In response to Kuntu Zangpo's request, Karmapa made an orange hat. When Gyaltsab Norbu Zangpo became eight years old, Karmapa enthroned and crowned him with this orange hat. He gave him the *Genyen* Vows as well as the Bodhisattva Vow.

Karmapa and his entourage were invited to Gyaja Monastery nearby. Later, the people of Chathrinpa as well as Torma Rongpa came out to pay their respects to Karmapa in huge numbers. Karmapa gave them the Chenrezig teachings and blessings.

Lineage Transmissions Given at Gyalthang Rignga Lhakhang

Gyalthang Rignga Lhakhang (temple) was completed.

At this newly completed temple, Karmapa started to give the

471 *BL*: 187b. Gyaltsab's administration was kept separate from the Karmapa's administration. See chapter 37 for more details.

lung of the whole set of *Kanjur* which he had received from Pawo Gyalwa. This *lung* was given to the Seventh Shamar Yeshe Nyingpo, the Sixth Gyaltsab Norbu Zangpo, the Sixth Situ Thrinley Rabten, the Fourth Pawo Thrinley Gyatso, Palmo Tulku, Karma Rinchen, Tulku Chokyong Zangpo, Tulku Kalzang Nyingpo, and so on, as well as many monks.

Karmapa said, "I am doing this exactly as my guru, Je Tsuklak Gyatso (the Third Pawo Rinpoche) did."[472] The transmission (*lung*) of the *Kanjur* began with the concise verses of *The Sutra of Prajnaparamita.*

During the period of transmission, Karmapa gave teachings in three separate sessions: *The Contemplation on the Four States of Mindfulness, The Thirty-Seven Practices of the Bodhisattva Path,* and *The Shunyata (*Emptiness*) View of Asanga and Nagarjuna.*

Karmapa also explained in great detail the meaning of the *Samadhiraja Sutra.* He explained how the advanced *Mahamudra* teachings of Kagyupa matched all the points and meanings expounded in that sutra. He showed that there was no difference between the two.[473]

Karmapa completed the *Kanjur* transmission after two years and nine months. He was then about sixty-one years old in the year of the Wood Dragon (1664).[474]

> This account clearly illustrates a historical example of how Karma Kagyu lineage teachings, called the "Golden Lineage," are passed on intact from guru to disciple between the generations of incarnate masters. Such a process ensures that the lineage is continued through the generations complete and unbroken.
>
> *When the Tenth Karmapa was young, he received the* lung *of the* Kanjur *from the Third Pawo Tsuklak Gyatso at Pa Nam. In the passage above, he is shown transmitting the same* lung *to the next Pawo reincarnate and to the Fourth Pawo Thrinley Gyatso.*

472 In *KAC*, the Tenth Karmapa referred to this Pawo Rinpoche as the Bodhisattva Gawey Yang.

473 *BL*: 188a

474 The *lung* transmissions began in 1662, the year of the Water Tiger.

The Tenth Karmapa also received the transmission of the Karma Kagyu Golden Lineage from the Sixth Shamarpa at Chojung Teng. The account above records how the Tenth Karmapa transmitted the very same lineage teachings on to the Seventh Shamarpa.

* * *

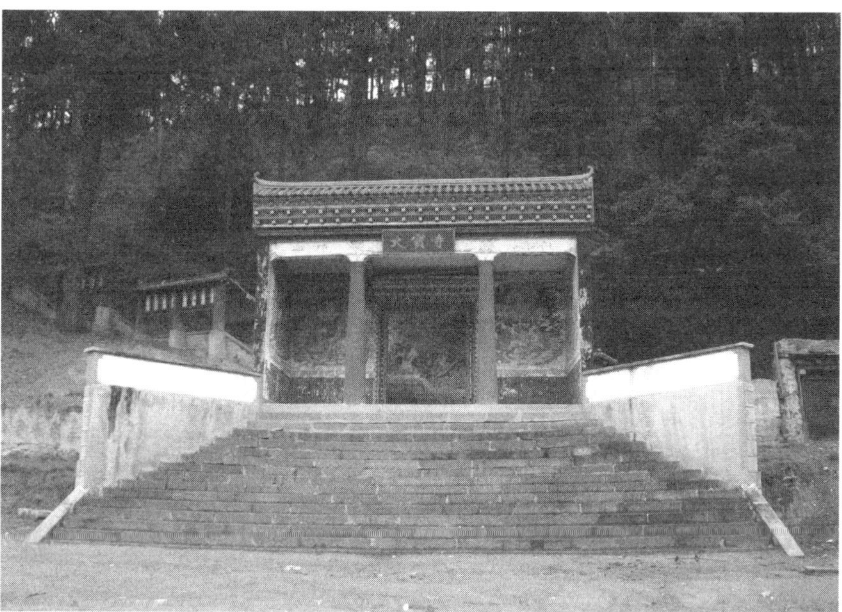

Figure 14.1

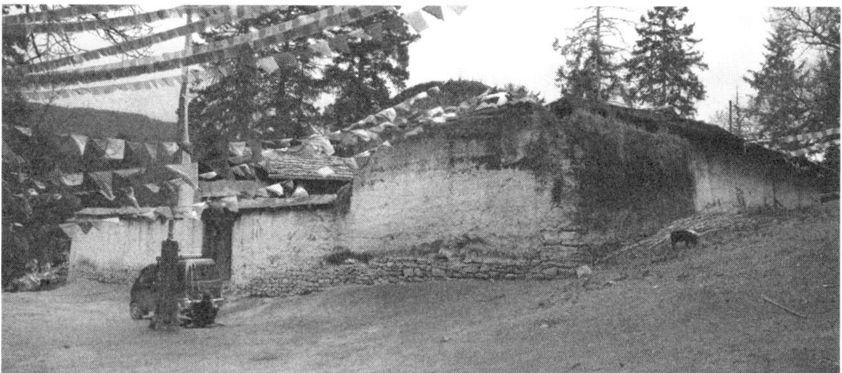

Figure 14.2

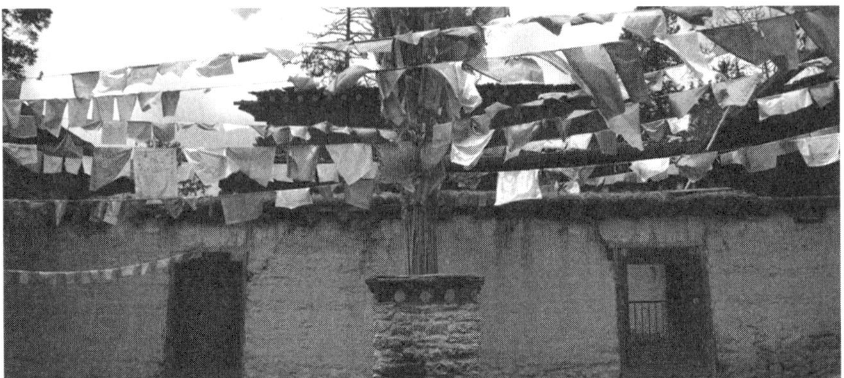

Figure 14.3

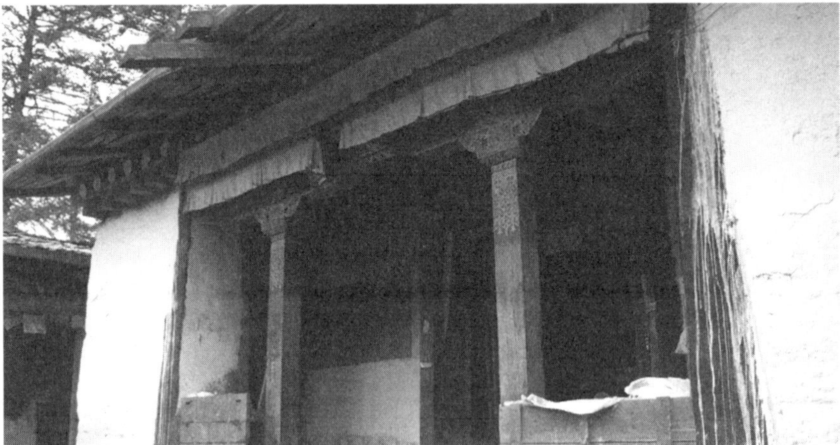

Figure 14.4

The Tenth Karmapa built with his own hands the Gyalthang Rignga Lhakhang in 1661–1662. The original 17th-century temple no longer stands as it burned during the first half of the 20th century and was further destroyed during the Cultural Revolution.

The Karmapa conducted important lineage transmissions at this temple. Soon after the Karmapa's death, it was forcibly converted to the Gelugpa sect. Today it is under the administration of Ganden Samtse, a large Gelugpa monastery.

The temple site is located on top of a hill outside Gyalthang (the Tibetan name for the town now known as Shangri-la, Yunnan). The entrance gate to the complex at the bottom of the hill has the

Chinese name Dabao Si (Figure 14.1). In the 1980s, a structure was rebuilt on the site (Figure 14.2). Inside the courtyard (Figure 14.3) is a chapel (Figure 14.4).

Photographs by Shahin Parhami.

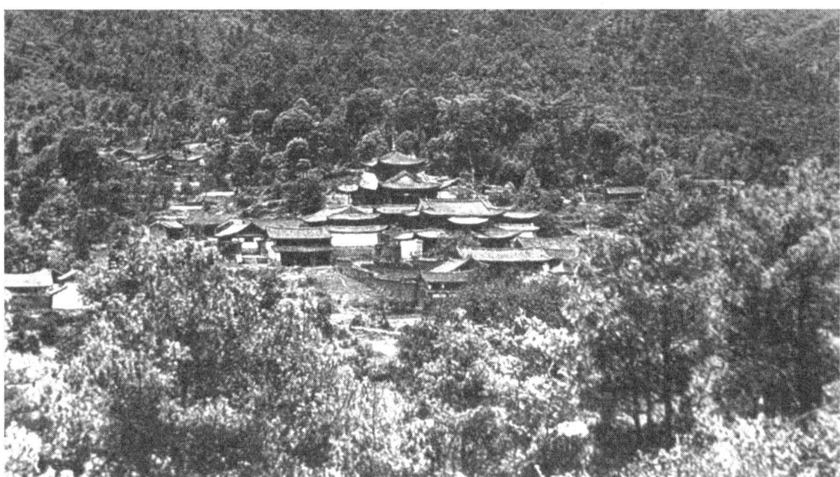

Figure 15.1

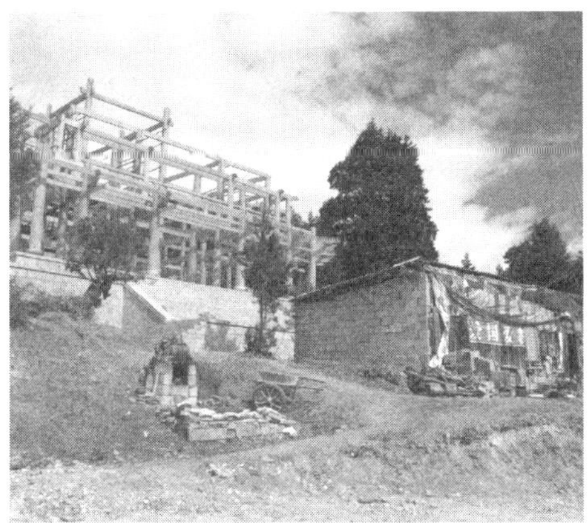

Figure 15.2

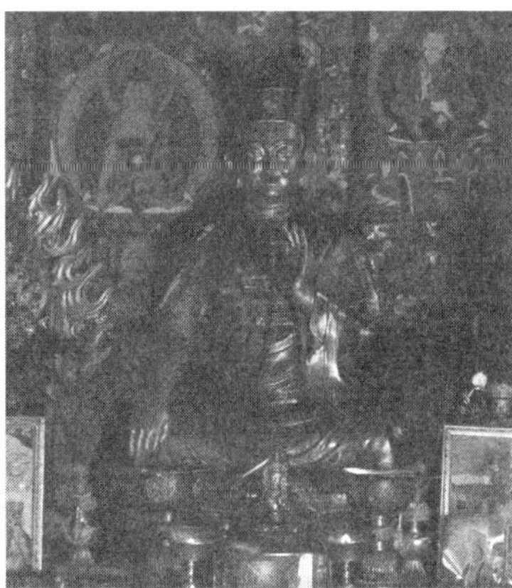

Figure 15.3

The *Fuguo Si* (Kingdom of Blessing Temple), built by a Lijiang king, was once Lijiang's most prominent and active monastery. It did not escape the ravages of the Cultural Revolution. Figure 15.1 shows temple and monastery complex before the Cultural Revolution. Today a new temple is under construction (Figure 15.2). Only a handful of monks live there. A shrine (Figure 15.3) – one of the monastery's few remaining treasures – is inside a brick bunker (structure in Figure 15.2 where prayer flags are hanging) and displays a large statue of the Tenth Karmapa.

Photographs by Shahin Parhami.

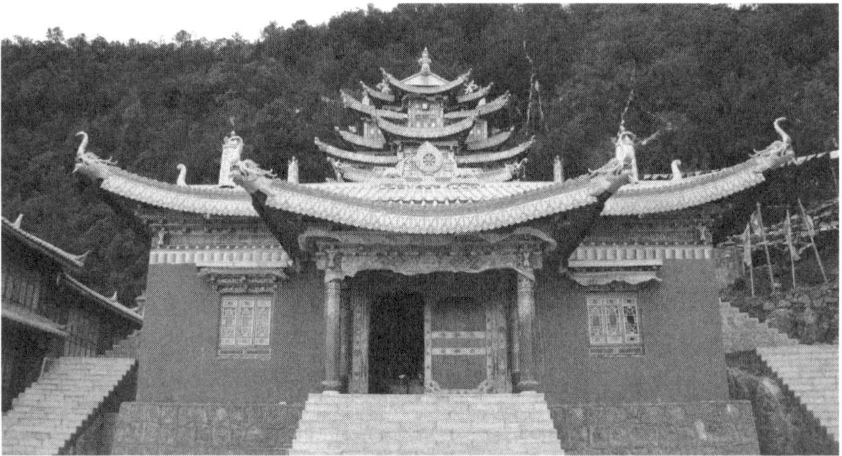

Figure 16.1

Located on a mountain a short distance south of Lijiang, the *Wenfeng Si* (Peak of Culture Temple) is a site where the Tenth Karmapa visited and meditated in a cave. During the Cultural Revolution, the Red Guards destroyed much of the temple complex, but parts have been rebuilt. Figure 16.1 is a chapel that houses the Tenth Karmapa's meditation cave behind an altar (Figure 16.2). His footprints are in a rock inside the cave, which is locked and closed to the public except for one day a year.

Photographs by Shahin Parhami.

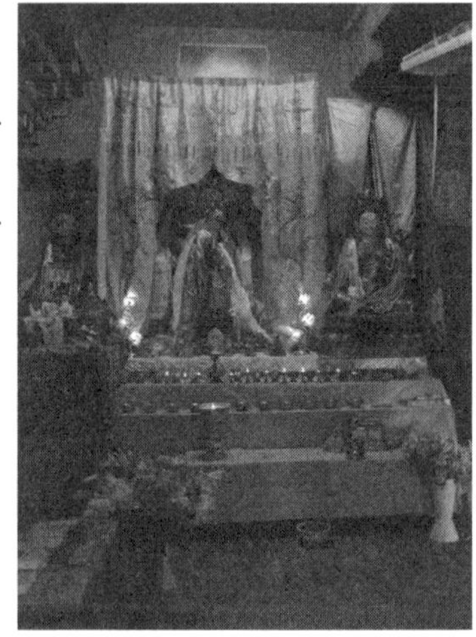

Figure 16.2

37. Peaceful Passing

When Karmapa and the young Gyaltsab went to Dro Gang in Bayul, Mongolian warlords and the Qing emperor were at war with each other. This war spanned the Fire Horse, the Fire Sheep, and part of the Earth Monkey years (1666–1668). The Mongolian general's name was Khandro Lozang Tenkyong. Karmapa served as a mediator and was able to end the war. He sent the Mongols back to their own land.

At the end of the Earth Monkey year (1668), inauspicious omens appeared to Karmapa. He saw the Vajradhatu protector whose hair was falling to the ground riding a goat. He also had a vision of a dead goat with its head turned outward showing a mournful face. He also dreamed that the whole valley of Gyalthang was very empty.

Some time later, Situ Rinpoche (the Sixth) and Palmo Shabdrung both passed away in China from small pox.

At the port of River Balen, a large, evil ghost of China[475] donning a black hat and dress appeared. Karmapa defeated it by his *samadhi*[476] power.

---

475 In those days in the region of River Balen, the local Tibetans believed that there was a ghost from China that appeared to them from time to time. The ghost would cause harm by toppling boats in the river so that people would drown.

476 A state of undistracted concentration and meditative absorption.

Karmapa and his party then returned to the Gyalthang Rignga Lhakhang (temple).

Warlord Khandro Lozang Tenkyong[477] came all the way from Mongolia to see Karmapa. Karmapa said this of him, "This man is very ambitious and very proud of his military power. He wants to conquer China." Karmapa told him to give up his ambition. He gave him many teachings on how not to commit evil acts anymore. However, the warlord still tried to attack the Chinese territories, but failed to defeat even the Chinese police.

Khandro then returned to Karmapa. This time, he wanted to build a temple at his own house. Karmapa told him not to build there, but to find a cleaner and more suitable place. Again, the advice fell on deaf ears. Digging began at his house, and a very poisonous snake came out – a bad omen.

One day Karmapa dreamed that a big bird dove down from the sky and carried away Khandro with his body hanging upside down. Later, the warlord was captured and killed by Dalai Hung Taigee,[478] another Mongolian warlord.

Around[479] the same time (probably in the first part of 1669), the government of Tibet invited Karmapa back to central Tibet.

* * *

DL

Regarding Khandro's actions, the Fifth Dalai Lama writes:[480]

Lord Khandro's heart was possessed by evil and he brought disaster to the area of Gyalthang. As a result, Karmapa's party could not remain there. Dalai Hung Taigee sent Mongolian troops led by Zhalpon Drophen and Dargye Tashi[481] to invite Karmapa to central Tibet.

---

477 He was a follower of the Gelug sect.

478 Dalai Hung Taigee was a pro-Gelug warlord, an ally of Gushri Khan.

479 *BL*: 188b

480 *DL*: Volume 2, 359

481 Zhalpon and Dargye are civilan government titles.

This invitation undoubtedly came from the Fifth Dalai Lama. Records do not reveal why the Fifth Dalai Lama invited the Tenth Karmapa back to central Tibet. However, it is possible that he wanted to remove the Tenth Karmapa from Lijiang and its neighboring area since Mongolians troops were going to convert Karma Kagyu monasteries and temples to Gelugpa. Under those circumstances, Karmapa would face serious danger.

* * *

In[482] the year of the Iron Pig (1671), *Terton* Rigdzin Mingyur came to see Karmapa. He stayed until the beginning of the year of Water Mouse (1672). *Terton* Mingyur gave Karmapa all his *termas*,[483] and Karmapa was recognized as the genuine *terton* of this lineage.

Karmapa then traveled to Lhasa to meet the Fifth Dalai Lama. On the eleventh day of Nagpa Dawa (the third month of the Tibetan calendar), he started his journey.

On the way, he visited Lithang and came upon some Tibetan soldiers. Their general asked Karmapa, "Is this Gyaltsab Rinpoche (the Sixth Gyaltsab Norbu Zangpo) really your son?"

"Yes, he is my real son."

The previous Gyaltsab, the Fifth Gyaltsab Dragpa Choyang (1618–1658), was devoted to both the Sixth Shamarpa and the Tenth Karmapa. He was able to prevent twenty-one Karma Kagyu monasteries, including Nyinched College belonging to the Sixth Shamarpa as well as the Taglung and Shabdrung monasteries, from being converted into Gelug monasteries.

Gyaltsab's ability to shield the monasteries and their residents from Gelugpa takeover was due to the fact that he and his family were relatives of the Fifth Dalai Lama. More importantly, Gyaltsab Dragpa Choyang knew how to skillfully maintain a good friendship with the Fifth Dalai Lama. As a result, after the Dalai Lama became the head of the Tibetan government, he issued a letter supporting the Tenth Karmapa's appoint-

482 *BL*: 188b

483 His *termas* consisted of these practices: a Guru Padmasambhava practice; a practice of the Buddha of Long Life; Thabshey Khajor (or The Union of Methods and Wisdom); and the practice of Dorje Dro Lok (Wrathful Guru Rinpoche).

ment of Gyaltsab as the regent of Tsurphu Monastery.

However, the good rapport between the Karmapa and the Gyaltsab incarnates did not last. Gyaltsab's role as regent naturally dissolved towards the latter part of the Sixth Gyaltsab Norbu Zangpo's life (1660–1698). The Sixth Gyaltsab had by then set up his own administration and monastery completely separate from the Karmapa's. From that point on, the two administrations have remained separate and distinct, and the close relationship between the two lines of incarnates also ended.

Gyaltsab[484] and Pawo Rinpoches traveled together with Karmapa. The whole party arrived in Chamdo.[485] Phagpa Lha of Chamdo Monastery of the Gelugpa sect very respectfully hosted Karmapa.[486] Afterwards, Karmapa and his party went on to Riwoche.[487]

When Karmapa arrived in the large district of Drigung, people came from all over to greet him. The head of Drigung Kagyu sect met him. When Karmapa arrived in Taglung, Shabdrung Rinpoche, head of Talung Kagyu sect, met him. They were very happy to be together and exchanged detailed views about the Kagyu sect.

After visiting many monasteries and meeting people along the way, Karmapa and his entourage finally arrived in Lhasa.

The Fifth Dalai Lama met Karmapa. The two had long discussions together. Karmapa was then seventy years old. His hearing was weak. The conversation had to go through another person, Kuntu Zangpo, who would repeat the Dalai Lama's words into Karmapa's ears.

* * *

DL

About his meeting with the Tenth Karmapa, the Fifth Dalai Lama writes in his autobiography:

---

484 *BL*: 188b

485 Chamdo is today a border town of Tibet.

486 One of the Phagpa Lha's previous incarnations was a disciple of the Fifth Karmapa.

487 *BL*: 189a

Karmapa[488] then arrived in Lhasa. On the sixth day of the eleventh month, Karmapa was received at the Potala Palace. I received him with all the pomp and decorum due someone of his rank, just as I did for Shamarpa Tulku in the past.

There was a reason why the Red Hat Karmapa (Shamarpa) was so highly honored. Up until the Third Shamarpa Chopal Yeshe, the Shamarpa was just a chief disciple of Karmapa. However, ever since Je *Chen-nga* Thamchad Khyenpa Chokyi Dragpa (the Fourth Shamarpa) ascended the throne of the Phagdru dynasty, there was no longer any difference between the Red Hat and the Black Hat Karmapas. This was the reason why I afforded them both equal status.

The Dalai Lama's treatment of the Tenth Karmapa upon his return indicates that the Karmapa's prior status was fully restored. The Dalai Lama's Desi, Sonam Chopal, did not believe that the previous Gyalt-sab Dragpa Choyang and the Sixth Shamarpa had opposed the Gelugpas. Both had passed away before Gushri Khan's invasion of Tibet. However, Sonam Chopal considered the Tenth Karmapa to be anti-Gelugpa.

The Tenth Karmapa Choying Dorje is undoubtedly the head of the *Vinaya* lineage of monks and all the doctrines of Karma Kagyu-pa up to (i.e., including) the Fifth Gyaltsab Dragpa Choyang. But he has long hair and wears Mongolian dress (layman's clothing). He travels with *jomo*[489] and a son and is in the company of many male and female followers.[490] Some people are disrespectful for this (reason), but now they are changing their minds. I am not sure whether this change of mind is (the flow) of compassion upward or whether they are praying that the rain of hot ashes, charcoal and weapons in hell is turning into a rain of flowers.[491]

The Karmapa presented high-profile gifts to me in keeping with

488 *DL*: Volume 2, 359

489 *Jomo* can mean either a lama's wife, or a nun. In this case, it means most likely a wife.

490 People looked down on the Karmapa for including females in his entourage because at that time women were considered inferior in Tibetan society.

491 This prayer comes from Shantideva's wishing prayers.

protocol.[492] Unlike some people whose hands tremble when holding a silk roll, the Karmapa was not like that.[493]

At tea time I asked him, "How was your trip? I hope that you are not too exhausted by it." I asked him all the suitable questions in keeping with a meeting of great bodhisattvas. The Karmapa asked his attendant to answer for him. In this way, we conducted quite a lot of exchanges.

At one point in the meeting, Karmapa told me sarcastically, "When a book of Buddha's teachings descended from the sky and landed in the lap of King Lha Thothori,[494] it made only one impression, namely, a good omen for his longevity. There was no one who could read or explain the book, so it was useless. And so it is the same with the earth Dharma and rock Dharma of the Nyingma tradition.[495] They no longer have any use." I thought to myself, "He's mocking me, but this really ridicules his own blind disciples like hitting them over the head with a *dorje*."[496]

When the Gyalwa Karmapa held some incense in his hand and waved it in front of us, people thought him truly skillful![497] Ever since he was a boy, the Karmapa has been meeting kings, high dukes, and high lamas of central Tibet and of Tsang. Obviously, his diplomatic liaisons were all at a very high level.

It is also widely known that he is authorized in his role as the

---

492 The Fifth Dalai Lama was indirectly saying that other lamas did not offer him such high-class gifts.

493 The Fifth Dalai Lama here mocks those people who are reluctant to give expensive gifts, as shown by their trembling hands grasping the gifts. By contrast, the Karmapa was genuinely generous.

494 Lha Thothori was the King of Tibet in the 5th century before Tsongtsen Gampo (7th century) during a time when Bon was the main religion.

495 Karmapa, who was the head of both the Karma Kagyu and the Nyingma sects, knew that the Gelugpas those days made fun of the Nyingma *tertons* and their *termas* by calling their teachings "earth Dharma and rock Dharma" because Nyingma *tertons* found Dharma teachings hidden underneath rocks. So Karmapa was being sarcastic in this instance by repeating the Gelugpa's view in front of the Dalai Lama.

496 In Tibetan, when you defeat your opponent in an argument with a cutting remark, then it is said to be like delivering a blow on the head with a hammer, or *dorje*, stunning the opponent senseless. The Fifth Dalai Lama is saying that it is the Tenth Karmapa who has blind devotees who do not need any explanation in the same way that King Lha Thothori's followers superficially interpreted his receipt of a Dharma book as simply a good omen.

497 The Fifth Dalai Lama was again mocking Karmapa here.

Karmapa by his own prediction.[498] Therefore, he is definitely worthy of our devotion. Even in the general view of the Vajrayana, one should view the universe as a *mandala*, and living beings as deities. Of course, Karmapa undoubtedly deserves our devotion. There are those on my side who would say bad things about him. But I myself control my mind so as not to have any disrespectful thoughts towards Karmapa.

* * *

The Dalai Lama asked many Dharma questions.[499] Karmapa answered them all. On the subject of *Mahamudra*, the Dalai Lama asked if the realization of the fourth initiation in Vajrayana is the genuine *Mahamudra* practice or not.

Karmapa answered in a restrained manner. Later, he told a close friend, "Because of my guru's training, I could have gone into a great and elaborate instruction on the subject. But as it was not the right time, I, therefore, tried to avoid going into the details during our conversation."[500]

The Dalai Lama provided Karmapa with gifts to assist his travels, plus an escort. It was also during this visit that he gave his permission for Karmapa to return and stay at Tsurphu Monastery.

While in Lhasa, Karmapa again visited the Jowo Buddha. He also visited the Eleven-faced Avalokiteshvara temple.

After a year at Tsurphu, the Fifth Dalai Lama requested Karmapa to do special pujas at Drag Gyalched Tshal near Lhasa.[501]

Karmapa went there. He caught the flu.[502] He dreamed of a

---

498 In the line of Karmapa-incarnates, every Karmapa would predict the circumstances of his next rebirth. Therefore, every Karmapa-incarnate is validated if the circumstances of his rebirth correctly match his predecessor's prediction.

499 *BL*: 189a

500 *Mahamudra* teaching means the direct pointing of mind's nature through very advanced instruction. Therefore, it is only taught to qualified devotees and is not a subject for casual conversation.

501 Drag is an area with a *ngapa*, which is a retreat monastery led by a lay lama. Drag Gyalched Tshal originally belonged to the Karma Kagyu but at some unknown point from the Fifth Dalai Lama's time on was converted to Gelug. It is about a day's trip from Tsurphu.

502 *BL*: 189b

mountain in the east where there was a round cave and a bridge that he had to cross.

While Karmapa was there, he stayed in a room at the side of the monastery. He said, "We don't have to stay here for very long."[503]

He made a thangka of Vajrapani holding a hawk and gave it to Gyaltsab Rinpoche. He sculpted a statue of Wod Zerchenma out of sandalwood for Gyaltsab's mother. Then as the year of the Water Ox (1673) was ending, he performed pujas. During that time, he saw bad omens. He saw a huge Mahakala looking very weak with the objects in his hand dropping to the ground. He told his attendants that the signs were very bad omens for the Dharma. He also saw that the external signs spelled bad news for the Dharma.

By then, the Gelug government previously had given the order that all the monasteries and farmlands that were taken over should be returned to the Karmapa. He also gave permission for Karmapa to stay at Tsurphu Monastery. Before he returned to Tsurphu, Karmapa dreamed that he was riding a white horse going towards the northeast. He then told his disciples that he would not live long.

From the ninth day of the month of *O-dha* (second month of the lunar calendar), in the Wood Tiger year (1674), Karmapa's health began to decline. On the eleventh day of the same month, the whole house where Karmapa was staying was filled with light for all to see.

Then on the fifteenth day, in the morning, after he took morning tea and soup, he passed away quite comfortably.

> [*Bey Lotsawa comments*]: That day should be counted as the sixteenth day (April 2, 1674) though known as the fifteenth because Karmapa passed away at an early hour. To a Tibetan, the early morning of the sixteenth is still called the fifteenth until full daylight. However, I, Bey Lotsawa, consider the change of a day to occur at midnight. On that basis then, the early morning of the

503 Karmapa chose to stay at the side of the monastery because he knew his stay would be brief.

fifteenth really was the early morning of the sixteenth.[504]

* * *

DL

In his autobiography, the Fifth Dalai Lama mentions the passing of the Tenth Karmapa:

From[505] Drag, I received a message about the Karmapa's death. Therefore, I made many offerings and prayers to fulfill the wishes of Je Karmapa who had dissolved his manifestation in this world.[506] I made my wishes to the Triple Gem to accomplish all his great wishes for the limitless sentient beings in the oceans of realms, and I made great offerings. I also sent delegations to Tsurphu to assist and to distribute offerings to the monks who participated in the funeral rituals.

* * *

The[507] Fifth Dalai Lama was notified of Karmapa's passing, and he wrote that his government had commissioned the funeral rites.

The body of Karmapa was taken back to Tsurphu on the twenty-seventh day of the same month. Pawo and Gyaltsab Rinpoches led the procession with the monks from Tsurphu Monastery and from Wozer Ling and Samten Ling.[508] All the monks were there in full attendance. They began the prayer rites in the second month. On the sixth day of the third month called *Nagpa*, the cremation took place.

In the same year, construction of a silver stupa with gold plat-

504 Bey Lotsawa and his guru, the Eighth Situ, were both very good in astrology. In the Western calendar, the 16th day of the first month of the Wood Tiger year corresponds to March 3, 1674.

505 *DL*: Volume 2, 384

506 A highly courteous way of saying he passed away.

507 *BL*: 189b

508 *BL*: 190a

ing began and took eight months to complete. Kuntu Zangpo then invited the Seventh Shamarpa, Gyaltsab and monks to perform the prayers consecrating the stupa.

> [*Bey Lotsawa concludes*]: The Tenth Karmapa's compassion was such that he had not the slightest anger towards those who harmed him or those who would harm him. Just as he had done every time, he always reciprocated harm with help. To the beggars, dogs, and animals alike that came his way, he gave them food and protected them. He did everything he could for them.
>
> He saw all phenomena as a mirage, and he was not attached to anything. Therefore, he was not excited when he was famous, and influential. He was not depressed when he was poor. He remained in constant equanimity and was evenly joyful.
>
> Day and night, Karmapa was in the mind and speech of Avalokiteshvara.[509] He never used any form of (evil) curse on anything or anyone. He did not perform any malediction pujas. He did not recite malediction mantras. And he did not perform fire pujas to put a curse on others, which many did in his time.
>
> Karmapa was completely vegetarian. Bi-monthly, he did a sojong practice in order to set an example for others.
>
> Throughout his life, with his own effort and by his own hands, he built statues, temples, and thangkas, countless in number.
>
> The powerful storehouse of merits that he accumulated through his vast generosity in the past and present, he dedicated to the welfare of all living beings. All the offerings he received from the people, politicians, and dukes, he consistently gave away to the poor and needy. He kept away from political leaders who harbored ulterior motives harmful to the people.
>
> Throughout his entire life, whenever he met people, animals, and other living beings during all his travels, his sole purpose was to lead every single one of them to the path of Dharma.
>
> I,[510] Bey Lotsawa Tshewang Kunkhyab, to fulfill the wish of my guru, Situ the Eighth, may I be a follower of Karmapa life after life in all my lifetimes.

---

509 This means his mind was always in the realization of the nature of mind without any thoughts and he was always reciting the mantra of Avalokiteshvara.

510 *BL*: 190b

Afterword

After the passing of four centuries, what are we to make of the Tenth Karmapa's life? First and foremost, he is the ideal bodhisattva, like a golden swan graceful and serene even in turbulent waters. The swirling currents of politics and military aggression in 17th-century Tibet did not divert him from the path of a bodhisattva. Nor was he deterred from carrying out bodhisattva activities and fulfilling his primary responsibility as the head of the Karma Kagyu sect, namely passing down the lineage transmissions intact to the next generation.

The only times the Karmapa interjected himself in the turmoil of his day were to act as a peacemaker. This was in keeping with his bodhisattva nature of nonviolence and protecting lives. As early as age seven when he urged the Mongolian warlord Dai Ching to stop killing, he evidenced his commitment to pacifism. Much later in his life when he was in exile in Lijiang, the king offered to dispatch his army into Tibet to attack the Gelug government and regain the many Karma Kagyu monasteries and temples that the government had converted to their sect. In declining this offer, the Karmapa remarked that further fighting would only bring on negative karma.

The Karmapa consciously avoided becoming entangled in the

affairs of state. He did, however, perform religious ceremonies for political leaders such as the Tsang Desi, but only upon their request. He did not always comply with these requests, though, especially if he thought that the political figure did not deserve the benefits of a religious ritual. For example, he and the Sixth Shamarpa initially refused to perform funeral rites in 1621 for the Tsang Desi Phuntsok Namgyal who had ignored the Shamarpa's request not to invade several smaller kingdoms.

Perhaps the most telling example of the Karmapa abstaining from politics occurred in 1660 when he turned down the Qing emperor's offer of the same title that a Ming emperor famously bestowed on the Fifth Karmapa. When the Sixth Situ urged him to accept the title, the Karmapa berated him, saying: "I don't need these things. You people are after the Chinese silks and brocades. As for me, in my wisdom, I see the lakes in China filled with human blood." For the Karmapa, titles such as this and political power were a distraction from his bodhisattva mission.

In worldly terms, Karmapa was not street-smart or diplomatic. He was honest and forthright to a fault. A case in point is the exchange between him and the Dalai Lama's chief administrator Sonam Chopal after the Mongols invaded Tibet and installed the Fifth Dalai Lama as the political leader of the country in 1642. Sonam Chopal asked the Karmapa to swear that he would not oppose or take any future action against the Gelug sect. Instead of agreeing to this, the Karmapa responded that there was no need for him to swear for the future, but he could swear that he had never done anything bad to the Gelugpas in the past.

In his diary as extensively quoted in this book's final chapter, the Fifth Dalai Lama portrayed the Karmapa in terms that clearly reveal the Karmapa's true nature. According to the Dalai Lama, he dressed in simple layman's clothing, and he wore his hair long. In other words, he had no pretensions. This conforms to Bey Lotsawa's description of the Karmapa who in many instances chose to travel as a beggar rather than in a style commensurate with his high status.

The Dalai Lama also recounts that contrary to the custom of

other religious leaders of the time, the Karmapa travelled in the company of nuns and young men and women. For this he was scorned, because women were generally looked down upon. The Dalai Lama, however, interprets the Karmapa's unusual practice to be an act of compassion. The Dalai Lama's interpretation substantiates the many instances Bey Lotsawa cites of the Karmapa being generous to beggars, common people and animals alike.

From an early age, Karmapa studied the deeds of past bodhisattvas. He wanted to emulate their achievements of helping sentient beings regardless of whether they respond to the bodhisattva's acts of compassion. Throughout his life he seemed to be very conscious of his responsibilities as a bodhisattva. One small example demonstrates this point. In 1650 when he was searching for the reincarnation of the Shamarpa, he lost everything to a band of robbers. He did not even have a cup, and so a poor person offered him a broken wooden cup tied together with string. Rather than use it to drink, Karmapa filled it with soil upon which he drew an image of the Buddha. He offered this to the Buddha with the wish that he would be able to accomplish the bodhisattva practice.

In some ways, the Karmapa romanticized the life of a bodhisattva as one who wanders in the forest communing with nature, is in harmony with the universe, and shows compassion to all sentient beings including animals. Many of Karmapa's poems and art works reflect this sentiment. Two of his gurus encouraged his inclination to retreat into the isolated purity of the natural world. Pawo Rinpoche Gawey Yang advised him, when invited to visit the Tsang capital in the early 1620's, not to stay long there for fear that he would be corrupted and distracted from his bodhisattva activities. The Sixth Shamarpa was similarly wary of contact with political states and urban areas which he considered "places of *samsara.*"

In sum, the Tenth Karmapa was very much true to himself and to the Dharma. In other words, he was not a man of his time. He did not abide by normal customs. His manner of dress, his habit of travelling in the company of women, and his disdain of politics were all as eccentric by worldly standards as were his highly original works of art.

Instead, Karmapa was a man for all times. His focus was directed toward being a bodhisattva and acting only for the benefit of all sentient beings. From his early years studying with the Sixth Shamarpa, nothing fulfilled him more than practicing bodhisattva ways.

With his boundless compassion and unparalleled artistic talents, the Tenth Karmapa was, indeed, a glorious golden swan for the ages.

Glossary

Abhisheka (Sanskrit) An empowerment or initiation.

Achala (Sanskrit) The Immovable One, King of Wrath.

Acharya (Sanskrit) A scholar.

Amitabha (Sanskrit) Buddha of the Pure Land, which is also known as *Sukhavati*, *Dewachen*, or Western Paradise.

Arhat (Sanskrit) One who has attained a realization of mind such that the causes for rebirth in samsara have been eliminated.

Atisha (Sanskrit) Indian pandit and abbot of the renowned Buddhist college, Vikramasila. He spent the last twelve years of his life in Tibet teaching the Dharma – most famous are his teachings of *Lojong* and *Lamrim*.

Avalokiteshvara (Sanskrit) Bodhisattva of Loving Kindness and Compassion.

Bhikhu(ni) (Pali) A fully ordained monk (nun).

Bodhisattva (Sanskrit) Someone who is motivated by love and compassion to seek enlightenment and to help liberate other living beings from suffering.

Bon (Tibetan) Ancient religion of Tibet, predating the introduction of Buddhism.

Buddha Kashyapa (Sanskrit) Buddha Kashyapa was the third of one thousand Buddhas of the Fortunate Eon to teach the Dharma. Shakyamuni was the fourth in the series of one thousand Buddhas.

Chakra (Sanskrit) A wheel signifying the Buddha's teachings.

Chakrasamvara (Sanskrit) (Wheel of Union) An important meditational deity – a *yidam* belonging to the Anuttara Yoga Tantra – of the Kagyu sect.

Chandrakirti (Sanskrit) A great 7th-century Buddhist master.

Chen-nga (Tibetan) The title Chen-nga, meaning "the one in the presence," originated from the time of **Drigung Jigten Sumgon** (1423–1217) when Drakpa Jungmo of the Lang clan served him for 16 years without ever leaving his presence. Later when the family ruled Tibet, the term became an address for the sovereign of the Phagdru dynasty.

Chenrezig (Tibetan) A meditational deity who embodies the nature of love and compassion also known as Avalokiteshvara in Sanskrit.

Damaru (Tibetan) A small two-sided hand drum used in prayer rites.

Dewachen (Sanskrit) The Pureland of Buddha Amitabha.

Desi (Tibetan) Ruler, prime minister, or the head of government.

Dharma (Sanskrit) Derived from the Sanskrit root *dhr*, meaning to uphold, to carry, or to sustain; the Buddha's teachings and methods are referred to as the Dharma. In philosophy, dharma refers to the defining quality of an object—for example, heat is an essential dharma of fire. In this context, the existence of an object is said to be sustained or defined by its essential attributes, which are called dharmas.

Dharmakaya (Sanskrit) (Literal meaning: Truth Body) The unobstructed purity of self and of phenomena that is enlightened mind.

Doha (Sanskrit) A form of poetry usually sung spontaneously by masters like Milarepa and Saraha that expresses a profound view of mind, commonly referred to as "songs of realization."

Dorje (Tibetan) (*Vajra* in Sanskrit) A handheld metal implement used in prayer ceremonies.

Dorje Namjomma (Tibetan) A Tantric form of meditational deity for the cure of illnesses and diseases.

Dromtonpa (Tibetan) Foremost Tibetan disciple of Atisha.

Drugpa Kagyu (Tibetan) A lineage-sect of the Kagyu sect of Tibetan Buddhism.

Dzambhudib (Sanskrit) The term originally means our world but is often used to mean the Asian continent.

Dzogchen (Tibetan) The highest view of the Nyingma sect of Tibetan Buddhism, also known as the Great Perfection, or Ati Yoga.

Dzong (Tibetan) A district with its own administration or government. In 16th- and 17th-century Tibet, there were thirteen *dzongs*.

Eight auspicious symbols Representing the qualities of the Buddha, the symbols are: the parasol, two goldfish, the treasure vase, the lotus flower, the white conch shell, the knot of life, the victory banner, and the wheel of Dharma.

Empowerment or initiation A ceremonial initiation into a Buddhist practice.

Enlightenment An all-knowing, purified state of mind that is completely liberated from negative emotions, habitual tendencies, and erroneous views.

Gampopa (Tibetan) A progenitor of the Kagyu sect; he was the foremost disciple of Milarepa and guru of the First Karmapa.

Garchen (Tibetan) A big encampment.

Garpa (Tibetan) Encampment.

Gelong (Tibetan) A fully ordained monk who commits to all the precepts in the complete *Vinaya*.

Gelong Vows (Tibetan) Vows of ethics and conduct for a monk according to the *Vinaya*, 253 in total.

Gelug(pa) (Tibetan) Also known as The Yellow sect, the Gelug sect is the latest of the four major sects of Tibetan Buddhism. Founded by Tsongkhapa (1357–1419), it emphasizes a dialectical approach to Buddhism. The Dalai Lama is its most influential temporal head. The Gaden Tripa is its highest spiritual authority, who is appointed by the Dalai Lama based on competitive scholarship rather than reincarnation.

Genyen Vows (Tibetan) Five vows of conduct for a lay Buddhist.

Geshe (Tibetan) An academic degree in Tibetan Buddhism.

Goshri (Tibetan) An honorific title first given by Ming emperor to the 7th Karmapa's secretary. Subsequently, Karmapas bestowed the title on special lamas or rinpoches. In Chinese the title is *guoshi*.

Guru Padmasamvara (Sanskrit) (Literal meaning: The Lotus Born) Also known as Guru Rinpoche, or Padma Jungney, he was from Orgyen in the 8th century and established Tantric Buddhism in Tibet.

Hayagriva (Sanskrit) A Tantric meditational deity deemed as the wrathful manifestation of Avalokiteshvara.

Indraneela A blue sapphire.

Jokhang Temple (Tibetan) Founded in Lhasa in the 7th century by King Tsontsen Gampo whose Chinese wife, Princess Wenchen brought with her as a dowry, the statue of Shakyamuni Buddha – the Jowo Buddha. It is enshrined inside the temple and is regarded the holiest object in Tibet.

Jowo Buddha (Tibetan) Statue of Buddha Shayamuni enshrined in the Jokhang Temple of Lhasa.

Kadam(pa) (Tibetan) A Buddhist sect that follows the teachings of Pandit Atisha. The most renowned teachings are *Lojong* (Mind Training) and *Lamrim* (The Way of Meditation).

Kagyu(pa) (Tibetan) Literally, the "lineage of the word," or "oral transmission." The Kagyu sect is one of the four major sects of Tibetan Buddhism: Nyingma, Kagyu, Sakya, and Gelug. The Kagyu school places particular emphasis on meditation as the means to achieve enlightenment grounded in the right view of the nature of mind and of phenomena.

Kalachakra (Sanskrit) Kalachakra is a Buddhist Tantric practice; the name means "Cycle of Time."

Kali Yuga (Sanskrit) The last of Four Ages in the Great Time Cycle described in Indian scriptures, which is considered to be a Dark Age.

Kanjur (Tibetan) The translated words and teachings of the Buddha in Tibetan, about 108 volumes in all.

Karma Kagyu (Tibetan) The Karma Kagyu is one of several branches of the Kagyu sect. It is also known as the Black Hat sect because its spiritual head, the Karmapa, wears a black hat.

Karmapa (Tibetan) Spiritual head of the Karma Kagyu sect of Tibetan Buddhism; often referred to as the "Karmapa Black Hat" because he wears a black hat that was given to the Fifth Karmapa by a Chinese emperor of the Ming Dynasty.

Khenpo (Tibetan) (Literal meaning: Learned one) An academic degree for scholars of Buddhist philosophy in the Kagyu and Nyingma traditions.

Kudung (Tibetan) The body of a deceased Buddhist master.

Lhakhang (Tibetan) A temple.

Lama (Tibetan) A title reserved for experienced and/or learned Buddhist meditation teachers who are authorized to transmit Buddhist teachings to disciples. In modern usage however, people often loosely address all Tibetan Buddhist monks as lamas.

Lamrim (Tibetan) The Way of Meditation; the practice of the stages of the path to enlightenment.

Lojong (Tibetan) The practice of mind-training to attain enlightenment.

Losar (Tibetan) Tibetan New Year.

Lopon (Tibetan) A high-ranking monk who presides over rituals.

Lung (Tibetan) A reading transmission where a teacher reads aloud the text of a particular practice to the disciple(s).

Madhyamaka (Sanskrit) A Mahayana philosophy of "The Middle Way" expounded by the Indian master Nagarjuna, which explains that all phenomena are empty of self or essence, and that these phenomena arise due to causes and conditions.

Mahakala (Sanskrit) A protector-deity of Dharma in Vajrayana Buddhism.

Mahamudra (Sanskrit) (Literal meaning: The Great Seal) The highest philosophical thought or view expounded by the Karma Kagyu sect that can be realized through meditation.

Mahasiddha (Sanskrit) A great "accomplished one" in meditation.

Maitreya (Sanskrit) A bodhisattva revered as the next Buddha to come.

Mandala (Sanskrit) (Literal meaning: The center with its surrounding) A symbolic representation of a Tantric deity's realm. As an offering, it symbolizes the entire universe.

Manghalam Sojong (Tibetan) A very auspicious purification practice.

Mantra (Sanskrit) A set of sounds or syllables for recitation, which embodies the nature of a meditational deity.

Marpa (Tibetan) Marpa the Translator is a main forefather of the Kagyu sect, and guru of Milrepa.

Milarepa (Tibetan) A revered saint of Tibet, primogenitor of the

Kagyu sect, and guru of Gampopa.

Monk's Vows (See Gelong Vows.)

Monlam (Tibetan) A prayer festival.

Myriarchy An administrative district in Tibet.

Naga (Sanskrit) A deity/Dharma protector/guardian of treasures and secrets that takes the form of a snake.

Naropa (Sanskrit) An Indian *mahasiddha* and a major forefather of the Kagyu sect famous for his "Six Yogas;" guru of Marpa.

Ngapa (Tibetan) A retreat monastery headed by a layman lama.

Ngon-she (Tibetan) Power to know the future.

Nirmanakaya (Sanskrit) (Literal meaning: Emanation body) The form-aspect of enlightenment that can be perceived by sentient beings.

Nirvana (Sanskrit) A state of mind that is liberated from the cyclic existence of suffering (or samsara) due to the extinction of the notion of a self.

Nyingma(pa) (Tibetan) An original sect of Tibetan Buddhism closely connected with the Kagyu sect.

Nyungney (Tibetan) A purification practice.

Om Mani Padme Hung (Tibetan) The six-syllable mantra of the "Bodhisattva of Loving Kindness and Compassion" known as Chenrezig.

Panchen Rinpoche (Tibetan) The second-ranking lama of the Gelug sect.

Paramita (Sanskrit) Literally, *paramita* means "to reach the other shore." It is a Mahayana method to transcend concepts of subject, object and action according to the *Prajnaparamita* scriptures.

Paranirvana (Sanskrit) (Literal meaning: Passing beyond suffering and entering *nirvana* or enlightenment.) Respectful reference to the passing of a fully accomplished master.

Prajnaparamita Sutra (Sanskrit) The sutra known as "The Perfection of Transcendental Wisdom".

Puja (Sanskrit) Devotional rites of offerings, prayers, meditation, and dedication.

Rinpoche (Tibetan) (The precious one) An honorific address for reincarnated lamas or eminent Buddhist teachers.

Refuge Vows To become a Buddhist, one takes the preliminary vows of refuge in the Triple Gem, viz. the Buddha, Dharma, and Sangha.

Sadhu(s) (Sanskrit) A sadhu or yogi is a Tantric practitioner who has achieved some level of realization of the nature of mind.

Sakya(pa) (Tibetan) One of four major sects of Tibetan Buddhism.

Samadhi (Sanskrit) A state of concentration or meditative absorption.

Samadhiraja Sutra (Sanskrit) (*The King of Contemplation Sutra*) A Buddhist sutra on the nature of emptiness.

Samaya (Sanskrit) Samaya are religious vows or precepts that practitioners of Vajrayana or the Mantrayana must keep.

Sangtonpa (Tibetan) The interviewer who privately asks the vow-recipient a list of questions. This is a prerequisite for a monk's vow ceremony.

Saraha (Sanskrit) An Indian *mahasiddha* known for his *dohas* of realization: *the King, Queen, and People Dohas.*

Saraswati (Sanskrit) The goddess of knowledge, music, and the arts.

Samadhi (Sanskrit) A state of meditation.

Seven Jewels of Royal Power The seven precious aids to the universal monarch which together represent secular power – the queen, general, horse, jewel, minister, elephant, and wheel of truth.

Shamarpa (Tibetan) Literally, "he who is of (or wears) the Red Hat." The Shamarpa is a spiritual head of the Karma Kagyu sect and is also known as Karmapa Red-Hat. The Shamarpa lineage is the second oldest reincarnate lineage in Tibet, Kamarpa being the first and oldest.

Shinjong (Tibetan) Dharma-protector.

Siddha (Sanskrit) One who has "accomplished" a spiritual practice is said to have attained *siddhi*, and therefore is considered a *siddha* or an accomplished master.

Sithang (Tibetan) A style of thangka painting created by the Tenth Karmapa. *Sithang* is an elision of two words: *si-u* that means brocade fabric, and *thang* from thangka that means painting. The image of a *sithang* thangka is formed by a patchwork of brocade pieces sewn onto a pre-drawn outline.

Si-u (Tibetan) Brocade.

Six Yogas of Naropa A main system of practice of the Kagyu sect. "The Six Yogas of Naropa" are six inner yoga practices taught by the Indian *mahasiddha* Naropa.

Sojong (Tibetan) A purification ritual over the course of one day observing the monastic precepts.

Stupa (Sanskrit) A mound-like structure that contains funeral relics and precious remains.

Sutra (Sanskrit) A discourse of Buddha Shakyamuni.

Ten non-virtues They are: killing, stealing, sexual misconduct, lying, divisive speech, abusive speech, idle speech, covetousness, evil intent, and holding wrong views.

Ten virtues The converse of the ten non-virtues: do not kill, steal, etc.

Terlung (Tibetan) A section in a *terma* that contains a prediction about a positive or negative event.

Terma (Tibetan) Treasure(s) concealed by past masters like Guru

Rinpoche meant to be discovered for the benefit of future generations. These could be in the form of Dharma texts, relics, or Dharma objects.

Terton (Tibetan) One who discovers and reveals hidden Buddhist teachings and/or treasures called *termas*.

Thangka (Tibetan) A scroll painting that is generally mounted on fabric.

Tilopa (Sanskrit) An Indian *mahasiddha*, principal forefather of the Kagyu sect, and guru of Naropa.

Tsokor (Tibetan) A long puja or prayer.

Tsongkhapa (Tibetan) Founder of the Gelug sect and the Gaden Monastery.

Tulku (Tibetan) A reincarnated lama who carries the same identity in each lifetime. Karmapa Dusum Khyenpa was the first Buddhist master to continuously reincarnate, and thus began the tradition of tulku-reincarnates in Tibet.

Tushita (Sanskrit) A heavenly realm where higher non-human beings reside.

Twelve Deeds of Buddha Shakyamuni Buddha Shakyamuni manifested twelve great deeds as a teaching for beings in our world. They are: 1. descend from Tushita heaven; 2. conception in the womb; 3. birth; 4. learning the arts and sciences; 5. marriage and parenthood; 6. renunciation of princely life; 7. practice then renunciation of asceticism; 8. seated under the Bodhi Tree; 9. victory over the *maras* or disturbing emotions; 10. attainment of enlightenment; 11. propagation of the Dharma; 12. *paranirvana*.

Upasaka (Sanskrit) A lay follower of Buddha Shakyamuni.

Upasaka Vows (Sanskrit) The five *Upasaka* vows are: 1) not to take the life of a sentient being; 2) not to take what is not given; 3) to refrain from sexual misconduct; 4) to refrain from false speech; and 5) to refrain from drunkenness.

Vajra (Sanskrit) (*Dorje* in Tibetan) A handheld metal implement or sceptre used in prayer ceremonies.

Vajrapani (Sanskrit) Name of the bodhisattva of the power of the Buddha's compassion, holding a *vajra* (sceptre) in his right hand.

Vajrayana (Sanskrit) A Mahayana system of enlightenment also known as the Diamond Vehicle or the Mantrayana. Mahayana is one of three paths or "vehicles" to enlightenment. Vajrayana is part of Mahayana.

Vajrayogini (Sanskrit) A Tantric female deity; a *yidam* practice of the Kagyu sect.

Vinaya (Sanskrit) (Discipline) One of three sections of the *Tripitaka* (Buddha's canon) that teaches ethics, and discipline as the foundation for all Dharma practitioners.

Yab Sey (Tibetan) A term of protocol created by the Tsang Desi and applicable in a ceremonial setting. The Karma Kagyu *Yab Sey* consists of six high-ranking figures: Karmapa, Shamarpa, Gyaltsab, Situ, Pawo, and Tehor. When the term is used, it can mean all six rinpoches or just several of them.

Yamantaka (Sanskrit) *Yama* is the name of the god of death, and *antaka* means "terminator of death."

Yidam (Tibetan) A meditation deity; one of three roots of spiritual accomplishment in Vajrayana. Buddhism: guru, *yidam*, and protector.

Zhal Ngo (Tibetan) A Tibetan title for the chief administrator of a monastery.

Zabphu (Tibetan) Valley.

List of Tibetan Words

Abum	a 'bum	ཨ་འབུམ།
Amban	am ban	ཨམ་བན།
Arsalang	ar sa lang	ཨར་ས་ལང་།
Atisha	a ti sha	ཨ་ཏི་ཤ།
Atro Gönpa	a khro dgon pa	ཨ་ཁྲོ་དགོན་པ།
Atro Rinpoché	a khro rin po che	ཨ་ཁྲོ་རིན་པོ་ཆེ།
Atso	a mtsho	ཨ་མཚོ།

B

Baram Kagyü	'ba' ram bka' brgyud	འབའ་རམ་བཀའ་བརྒྱུད།
Baram Drak	'ba' ram brag	འབའ་རམ་བྲག
Belyül	bal yul	བལ་ཡུལ།
Béri	bai ri	བཻ་རི།

Bé Lotsawa	bai lo tsA ba	བཻ་ལོ་ཙཱ་བ།
Bo Gangkar	’bo gangs dkar	འབོ་གངས་དཀར།
Bön	bon	བོན།
Bönpori	bon po ri	བོན་པོ་རི།
Buchur	bu chur	བུ་ཆུར།
Bumnyak	’bum nyags	འབུམ་ཉགས།
Butsa Chato	bu tsha skya tho	བུ་ཚ་སྐྱ་ཐོ།

C

Chagar	cha gar	ཆ་གར།
Chakmo Goshri	lcag mo go shri	ལྕག་མོ་གོ་ཤྲི།
Chakmo Lama	lcag mo bla ma	ལྕག་མོ་བླ་མ།
Chakmo Lhünpotsé	lcag mo lhun po rtse	ལྕག་མོ་ལྷུན་པོ་རྩེ།
Chakri Ngönpo	lcag ri sngon po	ལྕག་རི་སྔོན་པོ།
Chamdo	cha mdo	ཆ་མདོ།
Chatrengpa	phya phreng ba	ཕྱ་ཕྲེང་བ།
Chéchen	che chen	ཆེ་ཆེན།
Chelpo Zhika	chal po gzhis ka	ཆལ་པོ་གཞིས་ཀ།
Chen-nga	sbyan nga	སྦྱན་ང་།
Chim Namkha Drak	chims nam mkha’ brag	ཆིམས་ནམ་མཁའ་བྲག
Chögyal Pakpa	chos rgyal ’phags pa	ཆོས་རྒྱལ་འཕགས་པ།
Chöjung Teng	chos ’byung steng	ཆོས་འབྱུང་སྟེང་།
Choktu	chog thu	ཆོག་ཐུ།
Chösi kar jam yuk chik	chos srid dkar ’jam yug chig	ཆོས་སྲིད་དཀར་འཇམ་ཡུག་ཅིག
Chuda	chu ’da’	ཆུ་འདའ།
Chung Dzong	phyung rdzong	ཕྱུང་རྫོང་།

D

Daklha Gampo	dwags lha sgam po	དྭགས་ལྷ་སྒམ་པོ།
Dalaï Lama (4e) - Yönten Gyatso	ta la'i bla ma yon tan rgya mtsho	ཏ་ལའི་བླ་མ་ཡོན་ཏན་རྒྱ་མཚོ།
Dalaï Lama (5e) - Ngawang Lopzang Gyatso	ta la'i bla ma ngag dbang blo bzang rgya mtsho	ཏ་ལའི་བླ་མ་ངག་དབང་བློ་བཟང་རྒྱ་མཚོ།
Damaru	Da ma ru	ཌ་མ་རུ།
Dampa Künga	dam pa kun dga'	དམ་པ་ཀུན་དགའ།
Dargyé Tashi	dar rgyas bkra shis	དར་རྒྱས་བཀྲ་ཤིས།
Dartsédo	dar rtse mdo	དར་རྩེ་མདོ།
Dawé Chulung	zla ba'i chu klung	ཟླ་བའི་ཆུ་ཀླུང་།
Dengmadreng	deng ma breng	དེང་མ་བྲེང་།
Denpa Tsoché	'den pa 'tsho byed	འདེན་པ་འཚོ་བྱེད།
Densa Til	gdan sa mthil	གདན་ས་མཐིལ།
Dépa Pelmar Nédzangwa	sde pa spel mar ne rdzangs ba	སྡེ་པ་སྤེལ་མར་ནེ་རྫངས་བ།
Dergé	sde dge	སྡེ་དགེ
Dési Puntsok Namgyal	sde srid phun tshogs rnam rgyal	སྡེ་སྲིད་ཕུན་ཚོགས་རྣམ་རྒྱལ།
Dhagpo kagyü	dwags po bka' brgyud	དྭགས་པོ་བཀའ་བརྒྱུད།
Dhagpo Kurabpa	dwags po sku rabs pa	དྭགས་པོ་སྐུ་རབས་པ།
Dhagpo Rinpoché	dwags po rin po che	དྭགས་པོ་རིན་པོ་ཆེ།
Dhagpo Shédrup Ling	dwags po bshad sgrub gling	དྭགས་པོ་བཤད་སྒྲུབ་གླིང་།
Dingri	dengs ri	དེངས་རི།
Dingri Langkor	dengs ri glang 'khor	དེངས་རི་གླང་འཁོར།
Ditsa	d+hi tsha	དྷི་ཚ།
Ditsa Rinpoché	d+hi tsha rin po che	དྷི་ཚ་རིན་པོ་ཆེ།
Diyi Drakar	d+hi yi brag dkar	དྷི་ཡི་བྲག་དཀར།

Doha	do ha	དོ་ཧ།
Dölchö Dzong	dol chos rdzong	དོལ་ཆོས་རྫོང་།
Domé Tak-ku	mdo smad thag ku	མདོ་སྨད་ཐག་ཀུ
Domtsa Yéshé Drak	dom tsha ye shes grags	དོམ་ཚ་ཡེ་ཤེས་གྲགས།
Dong	rdong	རྡོང་།
Dopa Minyakpa	do pa mi nyag pa	དོ་པ་མི་ཉག་པ།
Dorjé Gyalpo	rdo rje rgyal po	རྡོ་རྗེ་རྒྱལ་པོ།
Dorjé Namjom	rdo rje rnam ’joms	རྡོ་རྗེ་རྣམ་འཇོམས།
Dorjé Nampar Jompa	rdo rje rnam par ’joms pa	རྡོ་རྗེ་རྣམ་པར་འཇོམས་པ།
Dorkha Pangshong	rdor kha spang shong	རྡོར་ཁ་སྤང་ཤོང་།
Doshö	mdo shod	མདོ་ཤོད།
Drachi Tarpa Ling	grwa phyi thar pa ling	གྲྭ་ཕྱི་ཐར་པ་ལིང་།
Drak Gyalché Tsal	sgrag rgyal byed tshal	སྒྲག་རྒྱལ་བྱེད་ཚལ།
Drakhawa	gra kha ba	གྲ་ཁ་བ།
Drakpa Pelzang	grags pa dpal bzang	གྲགས་པ་དཔལ་བཟང་།
Drépung	’bras spungs	འབྲས་སྤུངས།
Dréyül Kyétsal	’bras yul skyed tshal	འབྲས་ཡུལ་སྐྱེད་ཚལ།
Drichu	’bri chu	འབྲི་ཆུ།
Drikung	’bri gung	འབྲི་གུང་།
Drin Nyénam	brin snye nam	བྲིན་སྙེ་ནམ།
Drogang	bro sgang	བྲོ་སྒང་།
Dromtönpa	’brom ston pa	འབྲོམ་སྟོན་པ།
Droshong Gönpa	dro shong dgon pa	དྲོ་ཤོང་དགོན་པ།
Drukpa	’brug pa	འབྲུག་པ།
Drungpa	drung pa	དྲུང་པ།

Drungtsé Tsédzin	drung tshe tshe ’dzin	དྲུང་ཚེ་ཚེ་འཛིན།
Druptap Gyatso	sgrub thabs rgya mtsho	སྒྲུབ་ཐབས་རྒྱ་མཚོ།
Düsölma	dud sol ma	དུད་སོལ་མ།
Dzakhok	rdza khog	རྫ་ཁོག
Dzokchen	rdzogs chen	རྫོགས་ཆེན།

G

Gadong	dga’ gdong	དགའ་གདོང་།
Gadong Lhamo	dga’ gdong lha mo	དགའ་གདོང་ལྷ་མོ།
Gampopa	sgam po pa	སྒམ་པོ་པ།
Gandan Tri Rinpoché Könchok Chöpel	dga’ lden khri rin po che dkon mchog chos ’phel	དགའ་ལྡན་ཁྲི་རིན་པོ་ཆེ་དཀོན་མཆོག་ཆོས་འཕེལ།
Ganden	dga’ lden	དགའ་ལྡན།
Gangkar	gangs dkar	གངས་དཀར།
Gangkar Chödé	gangs dkar chos sde	གངས་དཀར་ཆོས་སྡེ།
Garchen	gar chen	གར་ཆེན།
Garpa	gar pa	གར་པ།
Garwang	gar dbang	གར་དབང་།
Gatsel Zhungluk Ling	dga’ tshal gzhung lugs gling	དགའ་ཚལ་གཞུང་ལུགས་གླིང་།
Gélek Lhündrup	dge legs lhun grub	དགེ་ལེགས་ལྷུན་གྲུབ།
Gélong	dge slong	དགེ་སློང་།
Géluk	dge lugs	དགེ་ལུགས།
Gémala	gad ma la	གད་མ་ལ།
Gendün Gang	dge ’dun sgang	དགེ་འདུན་སྒང་།
Gendün Yangri	dge ’dun yang ri	དགེ་འདུན་ཡང་རི།
Gengis Khan	jeng ge si khan	ཇེང་གེ་སི་ཁན།

Gényen	dge bsnyen	དགེ་བསྙེན།
Géshé	dge shes	དགེ་ཤེས།
Go Rapten Ling	sgo rab rten gling	སྒོ་རབ་རྟེན་གླིང་།
Golok	’gu log	འགུ་ལོག
Gomasala	sgo ma sa la	སྒོ་མ་ས་ལ།
Gomtsül	sgom tshul	སྒོམ་ཚུལ།
Gongchik	dgongs gcig	དགོངས་གཅིག
Gongkar	gong dkar	གོང་དཀར།
Gongkarwa	gong dkar ba	གོང་དཀར་བ།
Goshri	go shri	གོ་ཤྲི།
Guru Rinpoché	gu ru rin po che	གུ་རུ་རིན་པོ་ཆེ།
Guru yoga	bla ma’i rnal ’byor	བླ་མའི་རྣལ་འབྱོར།
Gyaja Gönpa	rgya bya dgon pa	རྒྱ་བྱ་དགོན་པ།
Gyaltang	rgyal thang	རྒྱལ་ཐང་།
Gyaltang Rik-nga	rgyal thang rigs lnga	རྒྱལ་ཐང་རིགས་ལྔ།
Gyaltsap	rgyal tshab	རྒྱལ་ཚབ།
Gyaltsap (5e) - Drakpa Chöyang	rgyal tshab sku phreng lnga pa grags pas chos dbyangs	རྒྱལ་ཚབ་སྐུ་ཕྲེང་ལྔ་པ་གྲགས་པས་ཆོས་དབྱངས།
Gyelgyi Shri	rgyal gyi shri	རྒྱལ་གྱི་ཤྲི།
Gyeljé Ling	rgyal byed gling	རྒྱལ་བྱེད་གླིང་།
Gyelmo Ngülchu	rgyal mo dngul chu	རྒྱལ་མོ་དངུལ་ཆུ།

J

Jaba Zhapdrung	bya ba zhabs drung	བྱ་བ་ཞབས་དྲུང་།
Jang Sadam Gyalpo Karma Chimé Lhawang	’jang sa dam rgyal po kar+ma ’chi med lha dbang	འཇང་ས་དམ་རྒྱལ་པོ་ཀརྨ་འཆི་མེད་ལྷ་དབང་།
Jangchup Gyaltsen	byang chub rgyal mtshan	བྱང་ཆུབ་རྒྱལ་མཚན།

Jasa	'ja' sa	འཇའ་ས།
Jatangwa Tenpa Namgyal	bya btang ba bstan pa rnam rgyal	བྱ་བཏང་བ་བསྟན་པ་རྣམ་རྒྱལ།
Jéwön Namkha	rje dbon nam mkha'	རྗེ་དབོན་ནམ་མཁའ།
Jokhang	jo khang	ཇོ་ཁང་།
Jomo	jo mo	ཇོ་མོ།
Jonangpa	jo nang pa	ཇོ་ནང་པ།
Jowo	jo bo	ཇོ་བོ།
Jowo Lokeshvara	jo bo spyan ras gzigs	ཇོ་བོ་སྤྱན་རས་གཟིགས།
Ju Tashi Dargyé Gönpa	ju bkra shis dar rgyas dgon pa	ཇུ་བཀྲ་ཤིས་དར་རྒྱས་དགོན་པ།
Juzhak	ju zhags	ཇུ་ཞགས།

K

Kadampa	bka' gdams pa	བཀའ་གདམས་པ།
Kampo Nénang	kam po gnas nang	ཀམ་པོ་གནས་ནང་།
Kamzi Tang	kam zi thang	ཀམ་ཟི་ཐང་།
Kanam Dépa	ka nam sde pa	ཀ་ནམ་སྡེ་པ།
Kanam Dépa de Powo	spo bo ka nam sde pa	སྤོ་བོ་ཀ་ནམ་སྡེ་པ།
Kanam Séwa Gang	ka nam se ba sgang	ཀ་ནམ་སེ་བ་སྒང་།
Kangyur	bka' 'gyur	བཀའ་འགྱུར།
Karma Chakmé	kar + ma chags med	ཀརྨ་ཆགས་མེད།
Karma Döndrup	kar + ma don grub	ཀརྨ་དོན་གྲུབ།
Karma Gön	kar + ma dgon	ཀརྨ་དགོན།
Karma Gung Gyal Ling	kar + ma gung rgyal gling	ཀརྨ་གུང་རྒྱལ་གླིང་།
Karma Kagyü	kar + ma bka' brgyud	ཀརྨ་བཀའ་བརྒྱུད།
Karma Lhündrup	kar + ma lhun grub	ཀརྨ་ལྷུན་གྲུབ།
Karma Nyinjé	kar + ma nyin byed	ཀརྨ་ཉིན་བྱེད།

Karma Puntsok Wangchuk (Prince)	rgyal sras kar+ma phun tshogs dbang phyug	རྒྱལ་སྲས་ཀརྨ་ཕུན་ཚོགས་དབང་ཕྱུག
Karma Rinchen	kar ma rin chen	ཀརྨ་རིན་ཆེན།
Karma Rinchen Nyingpo	kar ma rin chen snying po	ཀརྨ་རིན་ཆེན་སྙིང་པོ།
Karma Sönam Rabten	kar ma bsod nams rab brten	ཀརྨ་བསོད་ནམས་རབ་བརྟེན།
Karma Tenkyong Wangpo	kar ma bstan skyong dbang po	ཀརྨ་བསྟན་སྐྱོང་དབང་པོ།
Karma Tséring	kar ma tshe ring	ཀརྨ་ཚེ་རིང་།
Karma Zapsel	kar ma zab gsal	ཀརྨ་ཟབ་གསལ།
Karmapa (1er) - Düsum Khyenpa	kar ma pa sku phreng dang po dus gsum mkhyen pa	ཀརྨ་པ་སྐུ་ཕྲེང་དང་པོ་དུས་གསུམ་མཁྱེན་པ།
Karmapa (3e) - Rangjung Dorjé	kar ma pa sku phreng gsum pa rang byung rdo rje	ཀརྨ་པ་སྐུ་ཕྲེང་གསུམ་པ་རང་བྱུང་རྡོ་རྗེ།
Karmapa (4e) - Rölpé Dorjé	kar ma pa sku phreng bzhi pa rol pa'i rdo rje	ཀརྨ་པ་སྐུ་ཕྲེང་བཞི་པ་རོལ་པའི་རྡོ་རྗེ།
Karmapa (5e) - Dézhin Shekpa	kar ma pa sku phreng lnga pa de bzhin gshegs pa	ཀརྨ་པ་སྐུ་ཕྲེང་ལྔ་པ་དེ་བཞིན་གཤེགས་པ།
Karmapa (8e) - Mikyö Dorjé	kar ma pa sku phreng brgyad pa mi bskyod rdo rje	ཀརྨ་པ་སྐུ་ཕྲེང་བརྒྱད་པ་མི་བསྐྱོད་རྡོ་རྗེ།
Karmapa (9e) - Wangchuk Dorjé	kar ma pa sku phreng dgu pa dbang phyug rdo rje	ཀརྨ་པ་སྐུ་ཕྲེང་དགུ་པ་དབང་ཕྱུག་རྡོ་རྗེ།
Karmapa (10e) - Chöying Dorjé	kar ma pa sku phreng bcu pa chos dbyings rdo rje	ཀརྨ་པ་སྐུ་ཕྲེང་བཅུ་པ་ཆོས་དབྱིངས་རྡོ་རྗེ།
Karmapa (10e) - Jikten Wangchuk	kar ma pa sku phreng bcu pa 'jig rten dbang phyug	ཀརྨ་པ་སྐུ་ཕྲེང་བཅུ་པ་འཇིག་རྟེན་དབང་ཕྱུག
Karmapa *yapsé*	kar ma pa yab sras	ཀརྨ་པ་ཡབ་སྲས།
Kétsé Dzong	ke rtse rdzong	ཀེ་རྩེ་རྫོང་།
Kham	khams	ཁམས།

Khandro Lopzang Tenkyong	mkha' 'gro blo bzang bstan skyong	མཁའ་འགྲོ་བློ་བཟང་བསྟན་སྐྱོང་།
Khandro Nyingtik	mkha' 'gro snying thig	མཁའ་འགྲོ་སྙིང་ཐིག
Khangsar	khang gsar	ཁང་གསར།
Kharnak Lotsa	khar nag lo tswa ba	ཁར་ནག་ལོ་ཙྭ་བ།
Khawa Karpo	kha ba dkar po	ཁ་བ་དཀར་པོ།
Khenpa Jong	khan pa ljongs	ཁན་པ་ལྗོངས།
Khenpo	mkhan po	མཁན་པོ།
Kholoji	kho lo ji	ཁོ་ལོ་ཇི།
Khyiku	khyi ku	ཁྱི་ཀུ
Khyikutar	khyi ku thar	ཁྱི་ཀུ་ཐར།
Khyitül	khyi thul	ཁྱི་ཐུལ།
Könchok Chidü	kon mchog gcig 'dus	ཀོན་མཆོག་གཅིག་འདུས།
Könchok Géwé Jungné	kon mchog dge ba'i byung gnas	ཀོན་མཆོག་དགེ་བའི་བྱུང་གནས།
Kongpo	kong po	ཀོང་པོ།
Kubilaï Khan	kub ka khan	ཀུབ་ཀ་ཁན།
Kudung	sku gdungs	སྐུ་གདུངས།
Künga Lekpa	kun dga' legs pa	ཀུན་དགའ་ལེགས་པ།
Küntu Zangpo	kun tu bzang po	ཀུན་ཏུ་བཟང་པོ།
Kurabpa	sku rabs pa	སྐུ་རབས་པ།
Kyergangpa	skyer sgang pa	སྐྱེར་སྒང་པ།
Kyidrong	skyid grong	སྐྱིད་གྲོང་།
Kyishö Dépa	skyid shod sde pa	སྐྱིད་ཤོད་སྡེ་པ།
Kyishö Dépa Sönam Gyaltsen	skyid shod sde pa bsod nams rgyal mtshan	སྐྱིད་ཤོད་སྡེ་པ་བསོད་ནམས་རྒྱལ་མཚན།

Kyishö Dépa Sönam Namgyal	skyid shod sde pa bsod nams rgyal mtshan	སྐྱིད་ཤོད་སྡེ་པ་བསོད་ནམས་རྒྱལ་མཚན།
Kyishö Dépa Yülgyal	skyid shod sde pa g.yul rgyal	སྐྱིད་ཤོད་སྡེ་པ་གཡུལ་རྒྱལ།

L

Lac Madrö	ma dros mtsho	མ་དྲོས་མཚོ།
Lac Mapam	mtsho ma pham	མཚོ་མ་ཕམ།
Lachen Jampa Puntsok	bla chen byams pa phun tshogs	བླ་ཆེན་བྱམས་པ་ཕུན་ཚོགས།
Lama Dzokchenpa	bla ma rdzogs chen pa	བླ་མ་རྫོགས་ཆེན་པ།
Lama Nyingpowa	bla ma snying po ba	བླ་མ་སྙིང་པོ་བ།
Lama Zhang	bla ma zhang	བླ་མ་ཞང་།
Lamrim	lam rim	ལམ་རིམ།
Lapchi Chubar	lab phyi chu bar	ལབ་ཕྱི་ཆུ་བར།
Lé kyi lopön	las kyi slob dpon	ལས་ཀྱི་སློབ་དཔོན།
Lekshé Ling	legs bshad gling	ལེགས་བཤད་གླིང་།
Lha Totori	lha mtho tho ri	ལྷ་མཐོ་ཐོ་རི།
Lhakhang	lha khang	ལྷ་ཁང་།
Lhassa	lha sa	ལྷ་ས།
Lho Drowo Lung	lho bro bo lung	ལྷོ་བྲོ་བོ་ལུང་།
Lhodrak Sékhar	lho brag sras mkhar	ལྷོ་བྲག་སྲས་མཁར།
Lhünpo Gang	lhun po sgang	ལྷུན་པོ་སྒང་།
Lignée Namchö	gnam chos rgyud pa	གནམ་ཆོས་རྒྱུད་པ།
Lijiang	li 'jang	ལི་འཇང་།
Lojong	blo sbyong	བློ་སྦྱོང་།
Lopön	slob dpon	སློབ་དཔོན།
Lopzang Tendzin	blo bzang bstan 'dzin	བློ་བཟང་བསྟན་འཛིན།

Lung	lung	ལུང་།

M

Ma Yül	rma yul	རྨ་ཡུལ།
Machu	rma chu	རྨ་ཆུ།
Mahasiddha Saraha	grub chen sa ra ha	གྲུབ་ཆེན་ས་ར་ཧ།
Mandeltang	man Dala thang	མན་ཌལ་ཐང་།
Mangyül	mang yul	མང་ཡུལ།
Mapam	ma pham	མ་ཕམ།
Mar Röl	smar rol	སྨར་རོལ།
Marmépuk	mar me phug	མར་མེ་ཕུག
Marpa	mar pa	མར་པ།
Mélong	me long	མེ་ལོང་།
Milarépa	mi la ras pa	མི་ལ་རས་པ།
Mipam Chökyi Wangchuk	mi pham chos kyi dbang phyug	མི་ཕམ་ཆོས་ཀྱི་དབང་ཕྱུག
Mipam Tenpé Nyima	mi pham bstan pa'i nyi ma	མི་ཕམ་བསྟན་པའི་ཉི་མ།
Mön Dzumlang	mon dzum lang	མོན་ཛུམ་ལང་།
Monastère de Chakra	lcag rwa dgon	ལྕག་རྭ་དགོན།
Monastère de Lha Lung	lha lung dgon	ལྷ་ལུང་དགོན།
Monastère de Lhodrak	lho brag dgon	ལྷོ་བྲག་དགོན།
Monastère de Riwoché	ri bo che dgon	རི་བོ་ཆེ་དགོན།
Monastère de Zurmang	zur mang dgon	ཟུར་མང་དགོན།
Mönlam	smon lam	སྨོན་ལམ།

N

Nakartsé	rna dkar rtse	རྣ་དཀར་རྩེ།
Namkha	nam mkha'	ནམ་མཁའ།

Namling Luding	rnam gling klu lding	རྣམ་གླིང་ཀླུ་ལྡིང་།
Namsé Ling	rnam sras gling	རྣམ་སྲས་གླིང་།
Nangchen	nang chen	ནང་ཆེན།
Nangso	nang so	ནང་སོ།
Nangso Rinpoché	nang so rin po che	ནང་སོ་རིན་པོ་ཆེ།
Naropa	na ro pa	ན་རོ་པ།
Nartang	snar thang	སྣར་ཐང་།
Nénang	gnas nang	གནས་ནང་།
Nénang Gyalwé Ri	gnas nang rgyal ba'i ri	གནས་ནང་རྒྱལ་བའི་རི།
Néudong	sne'u gdong	སྣེའུ་གདོང་།
Ngawang Tashi Drakpa	ngag dbang bkris grags pa	ངག་དབང་བཀྲིས་གྲགས་པ།
Ngönshé	sngon shes	སྔོན་ཤེས།
Nordzinma	nor 'dzin ma	ནོར་འཛིན་མ།
Nyangpo Gyeldo	nyang po rgyal do	ཉང་པོ་རྒྱལ་དོ།
Nyarong	nyag rong	ཉག་རོང་།
Nyémo	snye mo	སྙེ་མོ།
Nyenchen Tanglha	gnyen chen thang lha	གཉེན་ཆེན་ཐང་ལྷ།
Nyingmapa	snying ma pa	སྙིང་མ་པ།
Nyingtik	snying thig	སྙིང་ཐིག
Nyinjé Ling	nyin byed gling kam tshang bshad grwa	ཉིན་བྱེད་གླིང་ཀམ་ཚང་བཤད་གྲྭ།
Nyung-né	snyung gnas	སྙུང་གནས།
Nyung-né Réchen	snyung gnas ras chen	སྙུང་གནས་རས་ཆེན།

O

Orgyen	o rgyan	ཨོ་རྒྱན།
Orgyen Kyap	o rgyan skyabs	ཨོ་རྒྱན་སྐྱབས།

Özer Chenma	'od zer can ma	འོད་ཟེར་ཅན་མ།
Özer Ling	'od zer gling	འོད་ཟེར་གླིང་།

P

Padma Sengé	pad+ma seng+ge	པདྨ་སེངྒེ
Pakdru	phag gru	ཕག་གྲུ
Pakdru *chen-nga*	phag gru spyan nga	ཕག་གྲུ་སྤྱན་ང་།
Pakdru kagyü	phag gru bka' brgyud	ཕག་གྲུ་བཀའ་བརྒྱུད།
Pakmo *zhelngo*	phag mo zhal ngo	ཕག་མོ་ཞལ་ངོ་།
Pakmodru	phag mo gru	ཕག་མོ་གྲུ
Pakpa	'phags pa	འཕགས་པ།
Pakpa Lha	'phags pa lha	འཕགས་པ་ལྷ།
Pakpa Rinpoché	'phags pa rin po che	འཕགས་པ་རིན་པོ་ཆེ།
Paksam Wangpo	dpag bsam dbang po	དཔག་བསམ་དབང་པོ།
Palais Lekdo	legs mdo pho brang	ལེགས་མདོ་ཕོ་བྲང་།
Palais Taï Tu	tA'i tu pho brang	ཏཱའི་ཏུ་ཕོ་བྲང་།
Palmopatang	dpal mo dpa' thang	དཔལ་མོ་དཔའ་ཐང་།
Pam Zhung	spam gzhung	སྤམ་གཞུང་།
Panam	pa nam	པ་ནམ།
Panchen Lama (6e) - Palden Yéshé	pan chen sku phreng drug pa dpal ldan ye shes	པན་ཆེན་སྐུ་ཕྲེང་དྲུག་པ་དཔལ་ལྡན་ཡེ་ཤེས།
Panchen Shakya Shri	pan chen shAkya shri	པན་ཆེན་ཤཱཀྱ་ཤྲཱི།
Pawo (3e) - Bodhisattva Gawé Yang	byang chub sems dpa' dga' ba'i dbyangs	བྱང་ཆུབ་སེམས་དཔའ་དགའ་བའི་དབྱངས།
Pawo (4e) - Trinlé Gyatso	dpa' bo sku phreng bzhi pa phrin las rgya mtsho	དཔའ་བོ་སྐུ་ཕྲེང་བཞི་པ་ཕྲིན་ལས་རྒྱ་མཚོ།
Pawo Tsuklak Gyatso	dpa' bo tsug lag rgya mtsho	དཔའ་བོ་གཙུག་ལག་རྒྱ་མཚོ།

Pel Lhakhang	dpal lha khang	དཔལ་ལྷ་ཁང་།
Pelgyé Ling	’phel rgyas gling	འཕེལ་རྒྱས་གླིང་།
Pongdzira	spong dzi ra	སྤོང་ཛི་ར།
Potala	po ta la	པོ་ཏ་ལ།
Pulungpa	phu lung pa	ཕུ་ལུང་པ།
Pungri Nangso	spung ri nang so	སྤུང་རི་ནང་སོ།
Puntsok Namgyal	phun tshogs rnam rgyal	ཕུན་ཚོགས་རྣམ་རྒྱལ།
Purang	pu rang	པུ་རང་།

R

Radreng	re sgreng	རེ་སྒྲེང་།
Ralung Tuchen Chögyal	rwa lung mthu chen chos rgyal	རྭ་ལུང་མཐུ་ཆེན་ཆོས་རྒྱལ།
Rangjung Garap Dorjé	rang byung dga’ rab rdo rje	རང་བྱུང་དགའ་རབ་རྡོ་རྗེ།
Rapgang	rab sgang	རབ་སྒང་།
Réchung Rinpoché	ras chung rin po che	རས་ཆུང་རིན་པོ་ཆེ།
Rikden yölwa	rigs ldan yol ba	རིགས་ལྡན་ཡོལ་བ།
Rikdzin Jatsön Nyingpo	rig ’dzin ’ja’ tshon snying po	རིག་འཛིན་འཇའ་ཚོན་སྙིང་པོ།
Rikdzin Zhikpo Lingpa	rig ’dzin zhig po gling pa	རིག་འཛིན་ཞིག་པོ་གླིང་པ།
Rimdrowa	rim gro ba	རིམ་གྲོ་བ།
Rinpung	rin spung	རིན་སྤུང་།
Rinpung Tsokyé Dorjé	rin spung mtsho skyes rdo rje	རིན་སྤུང་མཚོ་སྐྱེས་རྡོ་རྗེ།
Riwoché	ri bo che	རི་བོ་ཆེ།
Ruzhima	ru bzhi ma	རུ་བཞི་མ།

S

Sakya	sa skya	ས་སྐྱ།
Sakya Dakchen	sa skya bdag chen	ས་སྐྱ་བདག་ཆེན།
Salané	sa la nas	ས་ལ་ནས།
Samdé	bsam sde	བསམ་སྡེ།
Samdrup Tsé	bsam 'grub rtse	བསམ་འགྲུབ་རྩེ།
Samten Ling	bsam gtan gling	བསམ་གཏན་གླིང་།
Samyé	bsam yas	བསམ་ཡས།
Sangtönpa	gsang ston pa	གསང་སྟོན་པ།
Sangyé Lingpa	sangs rgyas gling pa	སངས་རྒྱས་གླིང་པ།
Satsojin	sa 'tsho sbyin	ས་འཚོ་སྦྱིན།
Sékhar	sras mkhar	སྲས་མཁར།
Sengé Gönpa	seng ge dgon pa	སེང་གེ་དགོན་པ།
Séra	se ra	སེ་ར།
Shakabpa	zhwa gab pa	ཞྭ་གབ་པ།
Shamarpa (1er) - Drakpa Sengé	zhwa dmar pa sku phreng dang po grags pa seng ge	ཞྭ་དམར་པ་སྐུ་ཕྲེང་དང་པོ་གྲགས་པ་སེང་གེ
Shamarpa (2e) - Khachö Wangpo	zhwa dmar pa sku phreng gnyis pa mkha' spyod dbang po	ཞྭ་དམར་པ་སྐུ་ཕྲེང་གཉིས་པ་མཁའ་སྤྱོད་དབང་པོ།
Shamarpa (3e) - Chöpel Yéshé	zhwa dmar pa sku phreng gsum pa chos dpal ye shes	ཞྭ་དམར་པ་སྐུ་ཕྲེང་གསུམ་པ་ཆོས་དཔལ་ཡེ་ཤེས།
Shamarpa (4e) - Chökyi Drakpa	zhwa dmar pa sku phreng bzhi pa chos kyi grags pa	ཞྭ་དམར་པ་སྐུ་ཕྲེང་བཞི་པ་ཆོས་ཀྱི་གྲགས་པ།
Shamarpa (5e) - Könchok Bang	zhwa dmar pa sku phreng lnga pa dkon mchog 'bangs	ཞྭ་དམར་པ་སྐུ་ཕྲེང་ལྔ་པ་དཀོན་མཆོག་འབངས།
Shamarpa (5e) - Könchok Yenlak	zhwa dmar pa sku phreng lnga pa dkon mchog yan lag	ཞྭ་དམར་པ་སྐུ་ཕྲེང་ལྔ་པ་དཀོན་མཆོག་ཡན་ལག
Shamarpa (6e) - Bodhisattva Chökyi Wangchuk	zhwa dmar pa sku phreng drug pa byang chub sems dpa' chos kyi dbang phyug	ཞྭ་དམར་པ་སྐུ་ཕྲེང་དྲུག་པ་བྱང་ཆུབ་སེམས་དཔའ་ཆོས་ཀྱི་དབང་ཕྱུག

Shamarpa (6e) - Garwang Trülpéku	zhwa dmar pa sku phreng drug pa gar dbang sprul pa’i sku	ཞྭ་དམར་པ་སྐུ་ཕྲེང་དྲུག་པ་གར་དབང་སྤྲུལ་པའི་སྐུ
Shamarpa (7e) - Bodhisattva Zhiwa Drayang Kyi Gyalpo	zhwa dmar pa sku phreng bdun pa byang chub sems dpa’ zhi ba sgra dbyangs kyi rgyal po	ཞྭ་དམར་པ་སྐུ་ཕྲེང་བདུན་པ་བྱང་ཆུབ་སེམས་དཔའ་ཞི་བ་སྒྲ་དབྱངས་ཀྱི་རྒྱལ་པོ།
Shelkhok	shel khog	ཤེལ་ཁོག
Shukdé Gönpa	shug sde dgon pa	ཤུག་སྡེ་དགོན་པ།
Siddha Mitra	grub chen mi tra	གྲུབ་ཆེན་མི་ཏྲ།
Sitang	si thang	སི་ཐང་།
Situ (5e) - Chökyi Gyaltsen	si tu sprul sku chos kyi rgyal mtshan	སི་ཏུ་སྤྲུལ་སྐུ་ཆོས་ཀྱི་རྒྱལ་མཚན།
Si-u	si’u	སིའུ།
Sojong	gso sbyong	གསོ་སྦྱོང་།
Sönam Rapten	bsod nams rab brtan	བསོད་ནམས་རབ་བརྟན།
Sungrap Gyatso Ling	gsung rab rgya mtsho gling	གསུང་རབ་རྒྱ་མཚོ་གླིང་།
Sungrap Ling	gsung rab gling	གསུང་རབ་གླིང་།

T

Tachok Khabap	rta mchog kha ’bab	རྟ་མཆོག་ཁ་འབབ།
Takar	tha dkar	ཐ་དཀར།
Taklung	sta lung	སྟ་ལུང་།
Taklung Kagyü	sta lung bka’ brgyud	སྟ་ལུང་བཀའ་བརྒྱུད།
Taktsé Namgyal Gang	stag rtse rnam rgyal sgang	སྟག་རྩེ་རྣམ་རྒྱལ་སྒང་།
Takzhi	rtag zhi	རྟག་ཞི།
Tanglha	thang lha	ཐང་ལྷ།
Tarlam	thar lam	ཐར་ལམ།
Tashi Dowori	bkra shis do bo ri	བཀྲ་ཤིས་དོ་བོ་རི།
Tashi Drakpa	bkra shis grags pa	བཀྲ་ཤིས་གྲགས་པ།

Tashi Lhünpo	bkra shis lhun po	བཀྲ་ཤིས་ལྷུན་པོ།
Tashi Paldrup	bkra shis dpal grub	བཀྲ་ཤིས་དཔལ་གྲུབ།
Tashi Zilnön	bkra shis gzil gnon	བཀྲ་ཤིས་གཟིལ་གནོན།
Temple de Réchungpuk	ras chung phug lha khang	རས་ཆུང་ཕུག་ལྷ་ཁང་།
Tendzin Chökyi Gyalpo	bstan ’dzin chos kyi rgyal po	བསྟན་འཛིན་ཆོས་ཀྱི་རྒྱལ་པོ།
Terlung	gter lung	གཏེར་ལུང་།
Terma	gter ma	གཏེར་མ།
Tertön	gter ston	གཏེར་སྟོན།
Tisé	ti se	ཏི་སེ།
Tokmé	thog med	ཐོག་མེད།
Tokmé Zangpo	thog med bzang po	ཐོག་མེད་བཟང་པོ།
Trayül	bkra yul	བཀྲ་ཡུལ།
Tréhor Rinpoché Tendzin Dargyé	tre hor rin po che bstan ’dzin dar rgyas	ཏྲེ་ཧོར་རིན་པོ་ཆེ་བསྟན་འཛིན་དར་རྒྱས།
Trétapuri	tre ta pu ri	ཏྲེ་ཏ་པུ་རི།
Trodé Tashi Gang	kro sde bkra shis sgang / spro bde bkra shis sgang	ཀྲོ་སྡེ་བཀྲ་ཤིས་སྒང་། སྤྲོ་བདེ་བཀྲ་ཤིས་སྒང་།
Tromsa	khrom sa	ཁྲོམ་ས།
Tromsa Karma Lhakhang	krom sa kar+ma lha khang	ཀྲོམ་ས་ཀརྨ་ལྷ་ཁང་།
Trülku Yölmo	yol mo sprul sku	ཡོལ་མོ་སྤྲུལ་སྐུ།
Trülku Chökyong Zangpo	sprul sku chos skyong bzang po	སྤྲུལ་སྐུ་ཆོས་སྐྱོང་བཟང་པོ།
Trülku Kalzang Nyingpo	sprul sku bskal bzang snying po	སྤྲུལ་སྐུ་བསྐལ་བཟང་སྙིང་པོ།
Trülku Mingyur Dorjé	sprul sku mi ’gyur rdo rje	སྤྲུལ་སྐུ་མི་འགྱུར་རྡོ་རྗེ།
Trülku Palmo	dpal mo sprul sku	དཔལ་མོ་སྤྲུལ་སྐུ།
Trülku Pendé	sprul sku phan bde	སྤྲུལ་སྐུ་ཕན་བདེ།
Trülku Tserlha	rtser lha sprul sku	རྩེར་ལྷ་སྤྲུལ་སྐུ།

Trülku Zhagom	zhwa sgom sprul sku	ཞྭ་སྒོམ་སྤྲུལ་སྐུ།
Tsari Tsokor	tsa ri mtsho skor	ཙ་རི་མཚོ་སྐོར།
Tsaritra	tsa ri tra	ཙ་རི་ཏྲ།
Tsatri Gang	rtsa khri sgang	རྩ་ཁྲི་སྒང་།
Tsé Lha Gang	rtshe lha sgang	རྩེ་ལྷ་སྒང་།
Tségané Chöjé	rtse ga nas chos rje	རྩེ་ག་ནས་ཆོས་རྗེ།
Tséring Ché-nga	tshe ring mched lnga	ཚེ་རིང་མཆེད་ལྔ།
Tsétang	rtse thang	རྩེ་ཐང་།
Tsokar	mtsho dkar	མཚོ་དཀར།
Tsokor	mtsho skor	མཚོ་སྐོར།
Tsongkhapa	tsong kha pa	ཙོང་ཁ་པ།
Tsurpu	mtshur phu	མཚུར་ཕུ།
Voeux de *gélong*	dge slong sdom pa	དགེ་སློང་སྡོམ་པ།

W

Wartu	war tu	ཝར་ཏུ།
Washül inférieur	wa shus smad	ཝ་ཤུས་སྨད།
Washül supérieur	wa shus stod	ཝ་ཤུས་སྟོད།
Worpa Chödzé	’or pa chos mdzad	འོར་པ་ཆོས་མཛད།

Y

Yang Gönpa	yang dgon pa	ཡང་དགོན་པ།
Yangpachen	yangs pa can	ཡངས་པ་ཅན།
Yangri Drungpa Shakrokpa	yangs ri drung pa shag rogs pa	ཡངས་རི་དྲུང་པ་ཤག་རོགས་པ།
Yangtang	g.yang thang	གཡང་ཐང་།
Yapsé	yab sras	ཡབ་སྲས།
Yardrok	yar ’brog	ཡར་འབྲོག

Yargyabpa	yar rgyab pa	ཡར་རྒྱབ་པ།
Yartö	yar stod	ཡར་སྟོད།
Yartö Lhünpo Gang	yar stod lhun po sgang	ཡར་སྟོད་ལྷུན་པོ་སྒང་།
Yayang	g.ya' yang	གཡའ་ཡང་།
Yerpa	yer pa	ཡེར་པ།
Yidam	yid dam	ཡིད་དམ།
Yongshöl Pu	yong shol phu	ཡོང་ཤོལ་ཕུ།
Yugur	yu gur	ཡུ་གུར།
Yung Rapjampa	g.yung rab 'byams pa	གཡུང་རབ་འབྱམས་པ།

Z

Zadam	za dam	ཟ་དམ།
Zang Puk	zang phug	ཟང་ཕུག
Zapu Lung	za phu lung	ཟ་ཕུ་ལུང་།
Zawok	za 'og	ཟ་འོག
Zhagom	zhwa sgom	ཞྭ་སྒོམ།
Zhagom Rinpoché	zhwa sgom rin po che	ཞྭ་སྒོམ་རིན་པོ་ཆེ།
Zhak-kha	zhags kha	ཞགས་ཁ།
Zhang Tri Drak	zhang khri grags	ཞང་ཁྲི་གྲགས།
Zhapdrung Yugyal Norbu	zhabs drung g.yu rgyal nor bu	ཞབས་དྲུང་གཡུ་རྒྱལ་ནོར་བུ།
Zhelngo	zhal ngo	ཞལ་ངོ་།
Zhelpön Dropen	zhal dpon 'gro phan	ཞལ་དཔོན་འགྲོ་ཕན།
Zhikatsé	gzhes ka rtse	གཞེས་ཀ་རྩེ།
Zhinkyong	zhing skyong	ཞིང་སྐྱོང་།
Zhukhang Rapjampa	zhu khang rab 'byams pa	ཞུ་ཁང་རབ་འབྱམས་པ།
Zimpön Ngönga	gzim dpon mngon dga'	གཟིམ་དཔོན་མངོན་དགའ།

Zirka Lhamo Dartang	zir ka lha mo dar thang	ཟིར་ཀ་ལྷ་མོ་དར་ཐང་།
Zurchok	zur lcog	ཟུར་ལྕོག
Zurudong	zur ru gdong	ཟུར་རུ་གདོང་།

List of Chinese terms

Dabao Si 大宝寺
daoshi 道士
fengshui 风水
Fuguoshi 福国寺
guoshi 国师
Lijiang 丽江
Ming (dynasty) 明
qi 气
Qing (dynasty) 清
shifu 师父
Shunzhi (Qing emperor) 顺治
Wenfeng Si 文峰寺
Wanli (Ming emperor) 万历
Wenzong (Yuan emperor) 文宗
Yongle (Ming emperor) 永乐
Zhongdian 中甸

Bibliography

(DL) Ngawang Losang Gyatso, The Fifth Dalai Lama (ngag dbang blo bzang rgya mtsho 1617–1682). *za hor gyi ban de ngag dbang blo bzang rgya mtsho'i 'di snang 'khrul ba'i rol rtsed rtogs brjod kyi tshul du bkod pa du ku la'i gos bzang las glegs bam gnyis pa bzhugs (ngag dbang blo bzang rgya mtsho'i rnam thar*) [Autobiography of the Fifth Dalai Lama]. 3 vols. Lhasa: bod ljongs mi dmangs dpe skrun khang, 1989.

(KAC) Choying Dorje, The Tenth Karmapa (chos dbyings rdo rje 1604–1674). *"byang chub sems dpa'i rtogs brjod 'dod 'jo'i ba mo"* [The Bountiful Cow: Biography of a Bodhisattva]. from *rgyal ba'i dbang po skyabs rje karma pa sku phreng bcu ba chos dbyings rdo rje mchog gi gsung 'bum legs bshad nor bu'i gtsug rgyan bzhugs* [Collected Writings of the Tenth Karmapa]. Chengdu: si khron mi rigs dpe skrun khang, 2004 [17th century]. vol. 1. pp. 1–334.

(KAB) Choying Dorje, The Tenth Karmapa (chos dbyings rdo rje 1604–1674*). "byang chub sems dpa'i rtogs brjod ka la ping ka'i lam glu"* [The Story of My Trip, Song of a Bird of Paradise Along Its Journey]. from *rgyal ba'i dbang po skyabs rje karma pa sku phreng bcu ba chos dbyings rdo rje mchog gi gsung 'bum legs bshad nor bu'i* *gtsug rgyan bzhugs* [Collected Writings of the Tenth Karmapa]. Chengdu: si khron mi rigs dpe skrun khang, 2004 [17th century]. vol. 2. pp. 1–118.

(KAD) Choying Dorje, The Tenth Karmapa (chos dbyings rdo rje 1604–1674). *"byang chub sems dpa'i rtogs brjod chos kyi rnga bo che"* [The Drum of Dharma: Autobiography of a Bodhisattva]. from *rgyal ba'i dbang po skyabs rje karma pa sku phreng bcu ba chos dbyings rdo rje mchog gi gsung 'bum legs bshad nor bu'i gtsug rgyan bzhugs* [Collected Writings of the Tenth Karmapa]. Chengdu: si khron mi rigs dpe skrun khang, 2004 [17th century]. vol. 2. pp. 119–368.

Mendong Tsampa Karma Ngedon Tengye (sman sdong mtshams pa kar ma nges don bstan rgyas b. 1867). *chos rje karma pa sku 'phreng rim byon gyi rnam thar mdor bdus bdag bsam khri shing zhes bya ba bzhugs so (dpal karma pa'i rnam thar dpag bsam khri shing bzhugs so*). [The Wishfulfilling Tree: Brief Biographies of the Spiritual Leaders, the Successive Karmapas]. Manuscript, no publication data available.

(SH) Shakabpa, W.D. Tsepon (zhva skab pa dbang phyug bde ldan 1907–1989). *Bod Kyi Srid Don Rgyal Rabs* [An Advanced Political History of Tibet]. 2 vols. Dharamsala: Shirig Parkhang, 1997 5th edition (1976).

(BL) Situ Panchen Chokyi Jungne and Belo Tsewang Kunkhyap (situ pan chen chos kyi 'byung gnas 1699–1774; 'be lo tshe dbang kun khyab) *sgrub brgyud karma kam tshang brgyud pa rin po che'i rnam par thar pa rab 'byams nor bu zla ba chu shel gyi phreng ba* [The Garland of Omnipresent Wishfulfilling Crystal Gems], 18th-century Palpung Monastery woodblock edition. This is the original edition used in this book.

Situ Panchen Chokyi Jungne and Belo Tsewang Kunkhyap (situ pan chen chos kyi 'byung gnas 1699–1774; 'be lo tshe dbang kun khyab) *sgrub brgyud karma kam tshang brgyud pa rin po che'i rnam par thar pa rab 'byams nor bu zla ba chu shel gyi phreng ba* [The Garland of Omnipresent Wishfulfilling Crystal Gems], vol. 2. New Delhi, 1972. This photo facsimile of a 17th-century woodblock edition contains the variant version of the Tenth Karmapa's biography, as explained in the note at the conclusion of chapter 35.

Ahmad, Zahiruddin

1970 *Sino Tibetan Relations in the Seventeenth Century*, Rome: Istituto Italiano per il Medio ed Extremo Oriente.

Debreczeny, Karl

2009 "*Dabaojigong* and the Regional Tradition of Ming Sino-Tibetan Painting in the Kingdom of Lijiang," in Kapstein M. (ed.), *Buddhism Between Tibet and China*, Boston: Wisdom Publications, 97–152.

2011 "Tibetan Interest in Chinese Visual Modes: The Foundation of the Tenth Karmapa's 'Chinese-style *Thang Ka* Painting," in Jackson R. and Kapstein M. (eds.), *Mahāmudrā and the Bka'-Brgyud Tradition*, Andiast, Switzerland: International Institute for Tibetan and Buddhist Studies GmbH, 387–421.

2012 *The Black Hat Eccentric: Artistic Visions of the Tenth Karmapa*, with contributions by David Jackson, Ian Alsop, and Irmgard Mengele, New York: Rubin Museum of Art.

Douglas, Nik & Meryl White

1976 *The Black Hat Lama of Tibet*, London: Luzac and Company, Ltd.

Kamay, Samten G.

2003 "The Fifth Dalai Lama and the Reunification of Tibet," in Françoise Pommaret (ed.), Harold Solverson (translator), *Lhasa in the 17th Century: The Capital of the Dalai Lamas*, Leiden: Brill, 65–80.

Mengele, Irmgard

2005 The Life and Art of the Tenth Karma-pa *Chos-dbyings-rdo-rje* (1604–1674): A Biography of a Great Tibetan Lama and Artist of the Turbulent Seventeenth Century. Ph.D. thesis, University of Hamburg.

Richardson, Hugh E.
1998 "*Chos-dbyings rdo-rje*, the Tenth Black Hat Karma-pa," in H. E. Richardson, *High Peaks, Pure Earth*, ed. by M. Aris, London: Serindia Publications, 499–515.

Rockhill, William F.
1910 "The Dalai Lamas of Lhasa and Their Relations with the Manchu Emperors of China, 1644–1908," *T'oung Pao, Second Series* 11(1): 1–104.

Sperling, Elliot
2003 "Tibet's Foreign Relations during the Epoch of the Fifth Dalai Lama," in Françoise Pommaret (ed.), Howard Soverson (translator), *Lhasa in the 17th Century: The Capital of the Dalai Lamas*, Leiden: Brill, 119–132.

(SH(ENG)) Shakabpa, Tsepon W.D.
1988 *Tibet: A Political History*, New York: Potala Publications (Fourth Edition).

2010 *One Hundred Thousand Moons: An Advanced Political History of Tibet*, translated by Derek F. Maher, Leiden: Brill (3 volumes).

Snellgrove, David L. & Hugh Richardson
2003 *A Cultural History of Tibet*, Bangkok: Orchid Press.

Thinley, Karma
1980 *The History of the Sixteen Karmapas of Tibet*, Boulder: Prajna Press.

Tuttle, Gray
2006 "A Tibetan Mission to the East: The Fifth Dalai Lama's Journey to Beijing, 1652–1653," in Bryan J. Cuevas and Kurtis R. Shaeffer (eds.) *Power, Politics, and the Reinvention of Tradition: Tibet in the Seventeenth and Eighteenth Centuries (Proceedings of the Tenth Semimar of the IATS, 2003, 3)*, Leiden: Brill, 65–83.

van Schaik, Sam
2011 *Tibet, A History*, New Haven and London: Yale University Press.

Publishing finished
in March 2021 by Pulsio
Publisher Number: 4012
Legal Deposit: March 2021
Printed in Bulgaria